T0354954

Also by Adrian Harrison Arvin

LifeConscious – an Alternative Theory to Evolution and Creationism

The Linear Heritage of Women

Heidi Louise Arvin
and
Adrian Harrison Arvin

iUniverse, Inc.
Bloomington

The Linear Heritage of Women

iUniverse books may be ordered through booksellers or by contacting:

iUniverse
1663 Liberty Drive
Bloomington, IN 47403
www.iuniverse.com
1-800-Authors (1-800-288-4677)

ISBN: 978-1-4502-6297-2 (pbk)
ISBN: 978-1-4502-6299-6 (cloth)
ISBN: 978-1-4502-6298-9 (ebk)

Library of Congress Control Number: 2010914982

Printed in the United States of America

iUniverse rev. date: 12/21/10

This Book is dedicated to both of our Mothers and all of their mothers before them – without whom life itself would have been impossible.

Jeanne Hemphill Lesser
and
Antonina Pino Arvin

Thank You

for purchasing our book and we both hope that you thoroughly enjoy it.

Heidi and Adrian Arvin

Preface

We have undertaken the work necessary for this book as a guide for women, as well as men, in order to understand our symbiotic connection with nature and ultimately the universe. Women especially need to know what is really going on in their bodies and their minds when they are confronted by the procreative forces of PMS, ovulation and pregnancy, which are all tenaciously controlled by nature. It is our way of sharing what we have learned in our search for what we feel is the truth, that we are part and parcel creatures of our earth and are bound by its living consciousness. This living consciousness has been there from the meager beginnings of life eons ago, whether you believe it was initiated from a deity or some primordial pool.

Whichever way your beliefs lie, there is no denying the fact that you are the current result of a long line of living creatures who stretch back to life's beginnings. You can also not deny the fact that all living creatures, because they are alive and procreate, are capable of interacting with other sentient beings because of this consciousness. What we have strived to accomplish in this book is to enlighten our readers to the existence and source of this very special consciousness that we call LifeConscious.

Contents

List of Illustrations

All by Adrian Arvin

Introduction

Women have experienced a chauvinistic bottleneck that began a couple of thousands years ago. A bottleneck brought on by a special gift that has confounded and frightened men so much so that they felt the need to alienate, chastise, degrade, enslave, and even hang, stone or burn women at the stake. It is a gift known to have many mystifying rituals and prohibited treatments that have gone by many names such as, midwifery, PMS, witches, hags, and mothers.

What is this gift that frightens men so much that they would go so far as to change passages in religious writings thereby preventing women from holding high secular offices such as priests, rabbis or imams, and prevent them from voting or driving a car? The answer is surprisingly very simple and it all has to do with procreation.

Women have the distinct honor of being the procreative force for the human race. However, this honor has its disadvantages such as enduring the mental and physical stresses of menstruation that happens to you once a month. These menstruation periods are as a consequence of women being inexorably closer to nature and its effects and can cause you to sometimes feel out of control with yourself as far as your body and sanity are concerned. What you don't realize is that this "out of control" feeling is caused by the conflict of two consciousnesses that we are all endowed with at birth – one of which is your very own personal consciousness. This is the consciousness that your parents gave a name to and is made up off all the stored memories of what you experienced during your lifetime, good or bad. It is the consciousness that everyone communicates with and the face that you put forward in public. The second consciousness is what this book is all about, and we call it LifeConscious.

This book will focus on these two consciousnesses, their effects on women and how they can come to grips of this age old problem of PMS along with the hormonal influences induced by the natural procreative process.

We will introduce you to the duality of consciousness (personal and LifeConscious) and its impact on your body, psyche and mental well being; as well as an attempt to explain not only what is going on biologically in your bodies, but psychologically because of the conflicting influences of the two consciousnesses.

Chapter 1 We introduce you to the concept of the psyche and how it is interrelated to the breath, spirit, soul, and water, along with a brief introduction to the loss of women's status in religious and secular societies.

Chapter 2 is devoted to explaining the matrilineal heritage and the predominant positions that women held in ancient times. We introduce you to the many goddesses in the past, go into more detail of how women lost their leadership roles, and how they are just now regaining these roles.

Chapter 3 Is a reintroduction to the concept of LifeConscious, where it resides, what it controls, how it controls, and how it is transferred. We introduce you to the importance of women in maintaining the linear organism that we call life.

Chapter 4 We'll begin to look internally at ourselves to reveal the many faces of your linear heritage which you still carry with you – why some of you may think that you have multiple personalities and why you are *not* crazy.

Chapter 5 LifeConscious begins to explain the many faces in the mirror, who these faces are and how this is possible. Why is LifeConsciousness strongest in women?

Chapter 6 Heidi takes us through her early life along with her experiences, good and bad. Then, she enlightens us about the people whom she saw that frightened her as a child, how she could retain her "gift," and how she can control the people in the mirror.

Chapter 7 What you can learn from Heidi's experiences and how you can take control of your people in the mirror. Then, how you may be able to find them in your linear ancestry and how you cannot only communicate with them, but possibly control them.

Chapter 8 The Conclusion chapter where we will show you where to get more information along with support groups and web sites, along with a few words on PMS pregnancy, and alternative medicine.

Addendum is an explanation of our own personal thoughts on physics, the afterlife, and memories.

Throughout this book, we will be writing from both of our perspectives. When Heidi is writing about her experiences, we will put her name in parentheses before she speaks. The rest of the time will be both of our thoughts.

The Authors

We are a recently married couple that maybe 30 years apart in age but rarely apart in heart and in like minds – thus the creation of this book.

Heidi Louise Arvin is a graduate of the University of West Georgia in Physics and is now employed as a central control room supervisor at the Spallation Neutron Source (SNS) at the Oak Ridge National Laboratory in Tennessee. The SNS is the most powerful neutron production accelerator in the world and is in the Guinness book of records.

I also work at the SNS project and my name is Adrian Arvin. I'm a control room shift supervisor at this site. I've worked at three different National Labs for 29 years, and we've both been associated and worked with some of the brightest and most gifted minds in the world. I'm also the author of the book *LifeConscious* that was published in 2004. Because of this book and because of our experiences and knowledge about the subjects involved, we were compelled to write *The Linear Heritage of Women* to help ladies understand and cope with the conflict of their dual consciousnesses.

We hope you enjoy our book, and that it clears up a lot of misunderstandings between men and women, and we also hope to have eased the troubled minds of a lot of ladies.

This book is not intended to be religious in nature, but we've found it difficult not to include passages from doctrinal text since the subject matter is so entwined with ancient religions and these texts are usually the only historical references when dealing with ancient topics. Since a majority of our readers are religious, we felt that it was important for you to find solace in these familiar passages in the hope that you may better understand their connotation from a different perspective. We trust that those of you who don't have a church going background will also find the evidence that we've provided here is compelling and beneficial information.

We've tried our best not to promote one religion over another, since we feel that it is inappropriate to do so in this book. We've also tried to make all theological viewpoints equal in nature and are only using selected religious passages to back up our theories. If we offend your beliefs in any way then we would like to apologize to you right now since this certainly is not our intent.

We firmly believe that if you have any kind of faith in a positive religion then you are an exemplary person to us because you have chosen a path that is acceptable and cherished by you. We know that a person's faith is more than their corner stone; it is your foundation, your legs, your heart, and your soul. It would trouble us greatly if we were to harm, in any way, your foundation in your chosen faith.

More information and help are available on our website: http://www.lifeconscious.com.

Thank you for purchasing our book, and we hope that you can find understanding, encouragement and harmony within it.

Heidi and Adrian Arvin

Both of our thoughts and ideas will be presented in regular text, Heidi's personal thoughts will be presented in ***bold text and begin with (Heidi).***

Chapter 1

The Psyche of Procreation

It's all interrelated

What is Psyche – the breath, spirit, soul?

The importance of water within the breath

The hint of memory

The downfall of the Goddess

The body of B. Franklin, Printer, Like the Cover of an Old Book,
It's Contents Torn Out and stripped of its Lettering and Gilding, Lies Here,
Food for Worms
But the Work shall not be Lost, For it Will as He Believed
Appear Once More in a New and more Elegant Edition
Revised and Corrected
By the Author

Ben Franklin's epitaph that was never used on his grave possibly alluding to reincarnation.

It's all interrelated

Women were inexplicably relegated to second class citizenship as effective leaders in both secular and spiritual positions of authority 2000 years ago.

A young girl has trouble sleeping because of a reoccurring nightmare of an old lady who relentlessly tries to possess her body.

It's "that time" again for an employed mother who has excruciating cramps that keep her out of work for yet another day. She knows that this is jeopardizing her position with her company and places her under an enormous amount of mental and physical stress.

A teenager looks at her face in a mirror, and in the dim light, she stares at what appears to be innumerable faces peering back at her; faces who are strange and different but somehow familiar.

All of these experiences, at first glance, appear to be completely unrelated, but are, in fact, *interrelated,* because they all have to do with women and how they have coped with a very precious gift, a gift that men have envied since the dawn of time, a gift that is simultaneously a curse and a boon to mankind. That gift is the power of procreation.

Birthing children are indeed a gift and a curse that has brought with it tremendous responsibilities to women along with taxing their psyches and bodies. How women have had to deal with this gift since ancient times and how knowledge is passed down from mothers to their young is the concept of this book and the very reason that all the above incidents are interrelated.

This interrelationship will become more evident as you journey through this book. We begin the journey by concentrating on the precious *gift* of procreation itself.

Like it or not, giving birth to a new human being is the primary function of women's bodies. Yes, you read that correctly. Go ahead and read it a second time just to make sure. I know that we will take a lot of heat for this statement, but it is the natural truth. As most of you well know by now, this gift comes with a lot of physical and emotional baggage which includes monthly menstruation and mood swings, headaches, nausea, and sensitivity – and that doesn't include being pregnant.

With the advent of pregnancy a woman's body is burdened with swollen or tender breasts, fatigue, nausea, backaches, headaches, a bladder that is constantly working overtime, and cravings for the most unusual combinations of foods, which in turn, leads to the constipation and nausea. Emotionally, this is supposed to be one of the happiest experiences of a soon-to-be mother's life. However, mentally, she may find herself filled with undue anxiety and worry, as she tries to cope with the numerous emotional and physical changes that her mind and body are going through.

Many women develop depression during their pregnancies. This is mainly due to the elevated increase in hormone levels that their bodies produce as the result of the pregnancy. During pregnancy, the rapid adjustment in hormones can trigger a change in the levels of chemicals in the brain. These chemicals govern moods, and when the chemicals become disrupted, depression can set in. At least 20% of expectant women experience some depressive symptoms during their pregnancies, while 10% of expectant women develop full-blown clinical depression (http://www.momknowsbestonline.com/Depression_And_Pregnancy.html).

What can be more perplexing to women all over the world, is that they don't seem to have any control over these physical processes that are going on within their bodies during pregnancy, or even when it's "*that time*" of the month again. It's as if someone or something else is running the show. And not just running the show – someone else wrote the script…the scene…the scenario…the dialogue…and the body that was once so familiar now feels as if puppet strings are attached to it. Worst of all, the woman is *aware* that she is mentally and physically out of control and with that awareness comes anxiety and/or depression.

Ladies you are definitely not alone in your experiences of anxious feelings, self-doubt, and sense of being controlled. These feelings are alive and well in all women…and yes, even young girls. The reason that you feel as if someone or something else is in control of your body is because that is *exactly* what is happening. You feel happy one minute, angry the next, or some strange combination of giddiness and grief at the same time, which causes you to feel as though you are mentally out of sorts. The problem is that you are experiencing a duality of mind, or two consciousnesses if you will.

First of all, what is "consciousness"? Here are a few definitions that any search of the web will show:

*An alert cognitive state in which you are aware of yourself and your situation, the state of being conscious or aware; awareness (*http://wordnet.princeton.edu/perl/webwn?s=consciousness*).*

*loosely as a constellation of attributes of mind such as subjectivity, self-awareness, sentience, and the ability to perceive a relationship between oneself and one's environment (*en.wikipedia.org/wiki/Consciousness*).*

*In Sanskrit Devangari is translated as "consciousness" or "life force" or simply "mind"(*en.wikipedia.org/wiki/Consciousness_ (Buddhism)).

So, according to these searches, "consciousness" just means to simply *be aware* of one's surroundings or the environment. We believe it is so much more than this. Scientists, physicists, philosophers, religious leaders, doctors, teachers, and laymen have written countless books and articles on just this subject alone. There are as many opinions about it as there are people because it is such a subjective and abstract topic. There is one theorist, however, who stands out among the throngs of researchers and writers as the premier expert in this field and has become a standard in the field of consciousness study.

(Heidi) Dr. Sigmund Freud was a pioneer in his study of human consciousness. He believed that human beings had two types of consciousness (or mind). Firstly, there is the *conscious* mind – the part of the brain that allows humans to talk and think rationally. It is the

awareness of being awake and the act of processing thoughts from memory. Secondly, there is the *unconscious* mind – the part of the brain that is responsible for all involuntary functions; including sleep, pain, emotions, urges, and memory storage. He believed that it was the unconscious part of the brain that constantly *influences* thoughts and behavior, even though we may never be aware of it.

Freud also came up with theories on how the personality of the mind functioned. He divided the personality into three main components – the id, ego, and superego. Without getting too in depth of Freudian psychology, I will briefly define each of these components. The id was what Freud referred to as the entire unconscious mind that is present with a person from birth. It is responsible for instinctual behaviors and (strangely enough) psychic energy. The ego is what Freud called the part of the personality that is reality. It deals with the present moment in all functions and behaviors. Freud believed that the ego was present in both types of consciousness. Finally, the superego is the part of personality that is responsible for all our principles and morals that we believe in. It is what makes us individuals and acts upon ideals instead of instincts (www.allpsych.com)

While Freud is considered by some to be the forerunner of modern psychological theory and is thought to have paved a tremendous road for the science of psychiatrics as well as philosophy, I have to be frank and say that I do not care for Dr. Freud as a person. I know that some of the readers may highly regard Sigmund Freud, but in reviewing some of his beliefs (especially about women) I am inclined to say that his other ideas regarding specific philosophical and societal theories are incorrect, in my opinion.

In 1925, Freud wrote a paper entitled *The Psychical Consequences of the Anatomic Distinction Between the Sexes*. In it, he writes:

> ***"Women oppose change, receive passively, and add nothing of their own."***

I find this statement frightfully chauvinistic and crude. Unfortunately, his opinions were well accepted facts at a time when women still did not have the right to vote or own their own property.

In 1933, he introduced the concepts of "penis envy" and "Oedipus complex." He theorized that by the time girls reach the age of five years, they begin to realize that they do not have a penis and blame their mother for being different – thus attaching themselves to their father. He also suggested that young boys at around this same age become psychosexually attached to their mothers and become jealous of their fathers because of the attention the father receives from the mother. Therefore, the boy sees his father as a rival. Needless to say, these methods of psychoanalysis seem primitive and crude. Thankfully, most of today's psychologists have taken away the beneficial aspects to Freud's research and have rejected the negative chauvinism.

Today's research on consciousness is ongoing. It is our hope that perhaps some of our ideas of LifeConscious can shed some light on this highly debatable and studied topic.

Today's scientific community will say that consciousness is just the collection of memories that one attains through experiencing life and that the synapses and other networking parts of the brain somehow account for an acquired sudden awareness. Philosophy and Religion say that it is a gift from a deity which makes us superior to animals, or that there are different levels of consciousness one can attain through meditations or reciting mantras (prayers). The difference between the scientific and the philosophical/religious points of view simply amounts to education and experiences. It takes many devoted years to be competent in either area of study. And scientists will fervently defend their point of view with "scientific evidence" collected during their years of research and study, while philosophers and religious experts do the same quoting verses and passages. Few scientists have the time to devote to being pious enough to meditate and pray, and in turn, very few philosophers have the time to devote to scientific inquiry. So naturally they will both defend their points of views that they have devoted their entire lives to and to change their opinions would mean to scrap their life's work.

Consciousness is an abstract subject since it is something that can't be seen, touched, tasted, heard or smelled. None of our five senses can be used to detect its existence, and yet we know that it is real and does exist. We can sense consciousness in living humans, animals, plants or insects but what is it exactly that we sense and what sense are we using? When we view a newly dead human body, that hasn't died from a horrible accident, you can immediately recognize that something is missing but what is that something? The freshly dead organs, heart and brain are still capable of functioning but have stopped for some unknown reason. Many patients who are clinically dead are kept "alive" artificially every day in today's modern hospitals in hopes of some miraculous recovery but conscious-wise they are dead, and if they are organ donors the parts that are harvested continue to live without them.

There is no denying that consciousness exists since we can observe proof of it every day. When we communicate with one another aren't we are using a consciousness that is unique to each person? When we play with a pet aren't we both using our singular consciousnesses that are interacting with one another? So to deny the existence of consciousness is to deny the existence of life itself. This tells you that life and consciousness go hand in hand, thus the term *LifeConscious.* We propose that life itself has a consciousness; therefore, the something that is missing in a dead body is its LifeConscious.

That we are dealing with a duality of mind or consciousness is obvious when faced with this question:

When you ask yourself a question in your own mind, who is answering?

Well obviously your personal consciousness is asking the question while a second consciousness is answering (two minds).

You've never realized it before now, but you are actually feeling the struggle between two consciousnesses trying to gain control of the same mind and body. The first of these two consciousnesses is your own unique personal consciousness, and the second is life's own consciousness and what we now call LifeConscious. Both can at times conflict with one another for control of your body. More detail on the differences of these consciousnesses is discussed in Chapter 3, but here is a brief introduction.

Your personal consciousness is the *real* you that communicates to the world. It contains all of your experiences, educations, likes and dislikes. Your other consciousness (LifeConscious) controls all the living functions of your body, but works primarily in the background of your personal consciousness. Before your tiny infant body could develop a personal consciousness, your LifeConscious controlled all of your life sustaining functions and instincts. As you grew older, your personal consciousness took over the day to day planning of your activities while your LifeConscious still maintained your living bodily activities.

As the personal consciousness grows stronger and more dominant, it wants to stay in control at all times–even during those "Ladies Days" or pregnancy–when it is clearly incapable of doing so. This is because the personal consciousness is not intended to control bodily functions. LifeConscious controls all life sustaining functions, including menstrual cycles, PMS, sex drive and pregnancy. Therefore, your personal consciousness conflicts with your very own LifeConscious hence the duality or conflict of minds.

How can this be proven? Try to purposefully control your own heart rate, or digest a meal, or your liver functions by using your personal consciousness. You will find that it's impossible to try to keep up with all the body's functions while trying to participate in everyday life – much less control them while sleeping. It's been said that it is easier to control a jumbo jet airplane with your personal consciousness then it is to maintain your own liver functions.

Here is a rather hectic modern medical explanation of breathing that is obviously written in a manner that promotes the purely physiological viewpoint of breathing control from Wikipedia.

> *"Unconsciously, breathing is controlled by specialized centers in the brainstem, which automatically regulate the rate and depth of breathing depending on the body's needs at any time. When carbon dioxide levels increase in the blood, it reacts with the water in blood, producing carbonic acid. Lactic acid produced by anaerobic exercise also lowers pH. The drop in the blood's pH stimulates chemoreceptors in the carotid and aortic bodies in the blood system to send nerve impulses to the respiration centre in the medulla oblongata and pons in the brain. These, in turn send nerve impulses through the phrenic and thoracic nerves to the diaphragm and the intercostal muscles, increasing the rate of breathing. Even a slight difference in the bloods normal pH, could cause death, so this is an important process"* (http://en.wikipedia.org/wiki/Breathing).

Holy Cow! Could we be more clinical in this explanation? Can this process of simply breathing be this complicated? It doesn't seem like it should be considering the fact that we've been breathing every moment of every day, since we were spanked on the bottom at birth. Breathing is obviously an automatic function, a function that we don't have to *think* about doing; just one of a myriad of functions that LifeConscious is controlling in the background of your own personal consciousness.

To recap, this consciousness that we call LifeConscious, again handles all the bodily functions in the background. There is no need to ever have to think about keeping tabs with the heart rate, breathing, locomotion, digestion, etc. Also, without LifeConscious, there is no life, thus the "Linear" part of the title to this book. Life is a linear organism, not a haphazard or magical thing. Life and LifeConsciousness go hand in hand and have both been transferred from mothers to their young in a seemingly unending fashion since the beginnings of life on our earth. Both are caught in a symbiotic embrace that has spanned a countless number of generations.

This duality of consciousnesses has a natural adaptive defensive purpose too. It wasn't that long ago that man could sense when a woman was receptive to mating by the scent that she gave off when she was ready. This is similar to what occurs in the animal world when males try to tell if a female is receptive to mate, or is in heat. If the male was immature or sick and didn't have the experience to recognize when the female was accommodating then the female would fight or fend him off. It is this fighting instinct that also causes irritability and anxiety during a human female's menstruation, since this is obviously not the right time to mate. In the animal world, it is the female's only recourse that she has to defend herself from the overpowering strength of males when she isn't ready. This irritability and anxiety are caused by the hormones controlled by her own LifeConscious, which in turn is empowering her to defend herself.

Mammalian females advertise their fertility to males with visual behavior and/or the giving off of pheromones during their receptive stage. This is known as estrus or heat. When a female doesn't become pregnant, the uterus reabsorbs the endometrium without a vaginal discharge known as covert menstruation. This is a natural adaptation to prevent predators from being aware of the female's condition and especially her location. Only human females and other primates have menstruation, in which blood flows from the vagina. This is probably due to the protection that was provided by the clan, family or group against predators.

The animal world is loaded with different procreative techniques that allow the males to force their control over the process of creating offspring. African male lions that take over a pride of females will immediately kill all the cubs sired by the previous males and drive off or kill any immature males still in the pride. These murderous technique forces the females to become more sexually receptive, creating another brood of cubs with the new male's genes coursing through their veins.

American elk will nearly kill themselves fending off rival arduous males from his harem of receptive cows. Some will fight to the death in an entangled mortal embrace as their massive antlers lock up with one another. Some males will starve themselves living off of the testosterone that its body is providing while driving his maniacal urge to mate with as many cows as possible.

Salmon will also die in their final attempt to procreate by facing tremendous odds in returning to the very streams of their birth. Their bodies will change drastically from the graceful, slippery oceanic figures to aggressive fresh water fiends bent on reaching their goals. Once they find their birthed stream beds they are totally spent with just enough energy to release their eggs and milt. They will then die leaving their bodies to rot in the stream beds. Insects, plants and the rushing water help to disintegrate their bodies, which initiate another concept of LifeConscious that we will cover later in this book. This decomposition causes their eggs to receive their parents LifeConscious instinctual memories as they develop and grow using water as the carrier from the dead bodies of their parents to the eggs. Once the fry hatch, they will eat the insects and plants who consumed their parent's bodies while drinking and breathing the water that is now pregnant with their parent's DNA fragments in yet another way of receiving their parents LifeConscious instinctual memories.

This book will provide evidence of the existence of LifeConscious and go over its importance to women and to nature. More evidence of the existence of LifeConscious and the transference of memories using water as the carrier is covered in Chapters 3 and 5. It will also show that this anxiety women feel is due to this struggle with two consciousnesses and that the female psyche is actually fine. The real challenge is dealing with the duality of consciousnesses that you never knew existed before – until now.

What is Psyche – the breath, spirit, soul?

Water is so important to LifeConscious and our psyches that they are seemingly locked in a symbiotic relationship that benefits both. To understand this, let's tackle our connotation for the word Psyche. The word psyche means "breath", "spirit" or "the soul" and refers to the forces in an individual that influence thought, behavior and personality, or what we now call our personal consciousness. This book focuses on the association of this breath, spirit or soul as these are some of the elements that help make up LifeConscious. By showing how influential these elements were to ancient man, we can show how it was forgotten as we grew into our modern age, only to be revealed once again by my wife and I. It is relevant to understand at this point that the word "Psyche" is synonymous with the mind, breath, spirit or soul.

The breath is made up of both air and water vapors, but in ancient religions was also the expelled exhaust (spirit) of a living, air breathing entity or god/goddess. We find it very significant that this image of breath, spirit, or soul has been used by religions since the dawn of time. So when thinking of "breath," remember that it is the breathing of air and water vapors, and is synonymous with the Judeo/Christian meaning of "Spirit" – a life initiating "Spirit" that is prevalent in so many scriptural passages that we could write another entire book on the subject. Suffice it to say, here are other religious examples of just a few of these passages involving the breath, spirit or water used to connote the beginnings of life.

In the King James English copies of the Bible, the word "spirit" occurs about 823 times. "Spirit" occurs most often in the Old Testament book

Isaiah and the New Testament book Acts. Its first occurrence is in Genesis 1:2.

> *"And the earth was without form, and void; and darkness was upon the face of the deep. And the* ***Spirit*** *of God moved upon the face of the* ***waters****."*

The Hebrew word translated "spirit" or "breath" is *ruach*. Breath first appears in Genesis 2:7

> *"And the lord God formed man of the dust of the ground, and* ***breathed*** *into his nostrils the* ***breath*** *of life; and man became a living soul."*

The Greek word "pneuma", Latin "spirare", means to breathe. Thus it equals both the Hebrew (RUACH) and Greek (PNEUMA) for "breath." The phrase "spirit of God" is reasonably rendered "Breath of God" or "Wind of God." The word "spirit" has since taken on the unfortunate corporeal tone for *ghost.*

Another religious example from India comes from Shri Mataji Nirmala Devi, a renowned revered mother. Her parents played a key role in India's Liberation Movement from under British rule. Her father, a close associate of Mahatma Gandhi, was a member of the Constituent Assembly of India and helped write free India's first constitution. He was a renowned scholar, master of 14 languages, and translated the Koran in Marathi. Her mother was the first woman in India to receive an Honors Degree in Mathematics.

Devi's definition of spirit is remarkably the same as the Judeo/Christian.

> *"The Self is the Spirit. This Spirit resides in the heart of every human being and is in a witness-like state. The Spirit is the projection of God Almighty, while the Kundalini (coiled, corporeal energy) is the projection of the power of God, of His desire, which is the Primordial Mother, or you can call it Adi Shakti, Holy Ghost (breath, spirit) or Athena.*
>
> *So the Kundalini is the projection of the Holy Ghost (breath, spirit), while the Spirit is the projection of God Almighty. The All-pervading Power of love is the power of the*

> *Primordial Mother, which creates and evolves, and does all the living work."*

Also in the Hindu scripture of the Upanishads comes the concept of *Prana* which is Sanskrit for "breath". It is one of the five organs of vitality or senses: *prana* "breath", *vac* "speech", *caksus* "sight", *shrotra* "hearing", and manas "thought" (nose, mouth, eyes, ears and mind). In Vedantic philosophy, it is the notion of a vital, life-sustaining force of living beings and vital energy, comparable to the Chinese notion of Qi and/or Japanese Ki.

The Islamic Koran is loaded with such passages containing the breath, spirit and water:

> ***21:30*** *ARE, THEN, they who are bent on denying the truth not aware that the heavens and the earth were [once] one single entity, which We then parted asunder? And [that] We made out of* ***water*** *every living thing? Will they not, then, [begin to] believe?*

> ***24:45*** *And it is God who has created all animals out of* ***water****; and [He has willed that] among them are such as crawl on their bellies, and such as walk on two legs, and such as walk on four. God creates what He will: for, verily, God has the power to will anything.*

> ***25:54*** *And He it is who out of this [very]* ***water*** *has created man, and has endowed him with [the consciousness of] descent and marriage-tie: for thy Sustainer is ever infinite in His power.*

> ***32.9*** *Then He made him complete and* ***breathed*** *into him of His* ***spirit****, and made for you the ears and the eyes and the hearts; little is it that you give thanks.*

> ***32:9*** *and then He forms him in accordance with what he is meant to be, and* ***breathes*** *into him of His spirit: and [thus, O men,] He endows you with hearing, and sight, and feelings as well as minds: [yet] how seldom are you grateful!*

> ***66:12*** *And [We have propounded yet another parable of God-consciousness in the story of] Mary, the daughter of*

> *Imran, who guarded her chastity, whereupon We **breathed** of Our spirit into that [which was in her womb], and who accepted the truth of her Sustainer's words – and [thus,] of His revelations – and was one of the truly devout.*

So the *Psyche of Procreation* means that as women you have the procreative clout of continuing the human race. You are encouraging the linear living entity of your own family line that began either from the *spirit breath* (psyche) of a deity or miraculously from a tepid pool of water billions of years ago. Either way you are the end result of that linear heritage and your job within your lifetime is to help continue life itself. So Psyche not only is a reference to your personal consciousness but to the breath/spirit/water that is within each of us. It is through the carriers of breath and water that your life controlling LifeConscious memories can be passed on to your children.

Historically, water, spirit, breath and soul were important to our ancestors and all the major religions. This was because they were much closer and in tune with nature than modern man is today. We have lost that connection in our urban sprawling, technology enriched environments. However, some of us still feel the need to be next to nature in some form or other as confirmed by the vast numbers of visitors to our national parks each year. It becomes an outlet for us to get away from it all and rejuvenate ourselves somehow. It is this much needed closeness to nature, water, air and spirit that this book is all about.

So the *Psyche of Procreation* also means that all women are much closer to nature than men and for this reason you are endowed with very special gifts and traits, most of which have to do with continuing your line of the human race. It was just a few hundred years ago that women were still intimately close to their family/clan/tribes and their environment. An environment that they protected, hunted, farmed, fought and died for, an environment pregnant with their family/clan/tribes ancient memories.

As an example let's just go back a thousand years to the four corners area of the United States where Utah, Colorado, New Mexico and Arizona meet. Here at Mesa Verde lived a tribe of ancient pueblo Indians surviving on maze and their hunting abilities living in the cliff faces of the mesas. I've been to Mesa Verde many times and took Heidi there for her first visit last fall. She was amazed how they could clamber down into the cliff faces and thought about the children playing and working so near to these deadly abysses. She also thought of how close these families had to be to survive in such a meager setting. Such a place as Mesa Verde is a microcosm of what LifeConscious is all about.

It is the tenacity of these ancient pueblo Indian families and their unique LifeConsciousness that has enabled them to thrive for nearly 700 years in this region. Generations eating the same foods, drinking the same waters, breathing the same air, worshiping the same gods, buried in the same grounds and giving birth to continue their family's lineage.

It all comes down to what you eat, drink, breath and touch. It can be something contagious like a cold or flu, or it can just as easily be something passed on from your mother to you – something very special called LifeConscious.

The importance of water within the breath

In the book *LifeConscious,* there is a tremendous importance placed on water as a carrier of memories. Water is such an amazing compound that its importance is explained here very briefly along with the transference of memories.

Water constitutes about 90% of blood and 75% of the brain. Brains are literally swimming in H2O. This is due to all living creatures on this planet earth having initially spawned from the ocean eons ago. Eggs and wombs are the portable containers of procreation and are reminders of our oceanic past. Humans, in essence, are made of water, and because we are water creatures, water has no taste or smell to us. Water is so important to our bodies that if we stopped drinking it, we would die in a matter of days, suffering terribly. This is ample evidence that the mind or body cannot sustain its existence without consuming water.

We consume vast amounts of water during our lifetime through breathing, drinking and bathing. It is so important to us that people in ancient times worshiped it as a life sustaining deity. The Egyptians worshiped the Nile River; the Sumerians did the same with the Tigris and Euphrates, the Indians with the Ganges, the Chinese with the Yangtze, the Mississippian tribes with the Mississippi as well as the Amazonian tribes with the Amazon River. Not only do we cleanse our bodies with water, but our souls as well through baptisms, casting out demons through anointing, and burying our dead in the seas, rivers and lakes.

Water also contains some unique properties in it that makes it one of the most important compounds in the universe. The importance of water in LifeConscious is explained in Chapter 3. It is enough to realize right now that water is the key to LifeConscious because LifeConscious isn't just another consciousness, but a repository of memories that is transferred from one generation to the next, using water as the carrier of these memories. Therefore, water and consciousness go hand in hand when it comes to life and memories.

The hint of memory

What exactly are memories anyway? Memories appear to be transitory or brief periods of reoccurring accumulated knowledge. Is this true or is memory just simply a way to store information? Whatever it is we see evidence of memory everywhere in our everyday lives.

In computer jargon memory must be encoded into packets to be stored in chips or buffer areas on a hard disk setup to hold a certain amount of binary arrangements. These packets are then retrieved when asked by the computer and synced by the computer's clock – since work in a computer has to be timed perfectly with its peripherals in order to function properly. As an example, if I were to ask this computer to print this page that you are now reading it would need to first store this page in a temporary memory repository called a buffer, sync up with the printer by initializing the timing between it and the printer, and then send the buffered information to the printer in the proper digital format. This, of course, is a simplified explanation of this highly complex and technical process. It wouldn't surprise you then to know that computers were built to emulate the way humans deal with memory.

So how does memory retention work in humans? Instead of memory chips or a hard disk, people use the cerebral cortex of the brain. Instead of a clock, the body uses the heart and breathing rhythms. If I wanted to hand write this page, I would have to first visually recognize the first word, place my hand and pen correctly on a blank sheet of paper, and write the word down one letter at a time. The buffering (temporary storage to short term memory) is done when I read and recognize the word or group of words and then transfer that information to my eyes and hand.

How long are memories retained in my brain? This depends on how often a particular bit of knowledge is updated. For instance, when you interact with your family daily you are continually updating this information in your brain to keep up with your family's current events, voices and appearances. What's funny is that you don't realize that you are perpetually updating information. To your vantage point your family hardly changes. Nevertheless, let's say that you bumped into a childhood friend at a store, and he yells out your name, but you are at a loss to retrieve the necessary information in order for your brain to give you the name of this friend. You frantically search in all the nooks and crannies of your brain for any reference to this person standing in front of you because the face, features, and voice are not recognizable. He sticks his hand out and tells you his name because he can tell from the perplexing look on your face that you don't have a clue as to who he is. Even so, the mere sound of the name triggers a recognition response as that part of your brain retrieves its last known reference of your friend when you were both 15 years old. Your brain instantly updates not only the new graphical features of your friend but his height, weight, hairstyle, voice, gait, smell and clothes to make it easier in the near future to recognize him again. In effect, your memory has been modified but have you ever noticed that this was done in the background. In other words, while you were talking and catching up with your old friend using your personal consciousness these corrections to your memory were being done automatically. You didn't have to think about saving or storing this new knowledge because your own LifeConscious was handling this renewing process but in the background of your personal consciousness.

More importantly–your LifeConscious is also responsible for the transference of so called "instinctual" memories. These ancient instinctual memories are passed down from mother to her young during gestation in her womb. These memories are comprised of instinctual automatic responses that are triggered when needed, such as fight or flight, the fear of falling, fire, fear of large cats or snakes, and "simple" tasks such as finding your mother's nipple and knowing how to suck for sustenance. This includes other automatic responses such as grabbing your mother's hair to hold on to, holding your breath under water and standing still when you were being hunted. These are memories of a thriving and surviving line of living human beings that held on to their mother's hair when running from predators or fording rivers and streams, and hid successfully while eluding their enemies and carnivorous animals. These are ancient memories that are ingrained and have survived the test of time and survivability in helping your family's line of life to be successful.

The animal world is loaded with such ingrained memory examples such as salmon returning to their exact same spawning pool to breed and die after spending many years in the ocean. A sheep dog puppy fearlessly herding sheep it had never seen before, blind termites rebuilding a demolished section of their nest, and a cuckoo bird chick shoving the eggs of its host birds own young out of the nest so that it will be the sole feeder in the nest – its survival being assured. Today's scientist will tell you that these examples are obviously instinctual; but what exactly is instinct if it isn't a latent ancient memory?

Nature is teeming with such deep-rooted "instinctual" knowledge that has to be stored somewhere, and transferred somehow. We will show how both processes are performed and controlled through females of all of living species and their LifeConscious.

We will also explain why women have been relegated to a second class citizenship over the past 2000 years or so. This is due to the advent of philosophical changes of the three burgeoning major religions along with empire building.

The downfall of the Goddess

Prior to the dawning of the big three religions in the Middle East, women were looked upon as the magical purveyors of procreation and healing. They were erudite scholars of the future (oracles), healers that were knowledgeable with herbs and chemicals, and influential priestesses of some of the earliest religions. As a matter of fact, the very first sculptures ever made by man's hands are figurines of the female figure, enhancing the mysterious procreative qualities of women.

One of the oldest of these figurines found is the so called Venus of Willendorf which stands 4 3/8 inches high and graced the front of the book *Life Conscious.* It is estimated to have been carved between 24,000 BCE – 22,000 BCE and was discovered in 1908 at a Paleolithic site near the Austrian village of Willendorf. It is carved from a Neolithic limestone that is not local to the area, which could mean that this rock held special powers or meaning to the people. The statue was also tinted with red ochre. This was used in place of blood to redden, or tint, the statuette thereby instilling the spirit of life into it – enabling it to be used for magical or religious purposes. At over 20,000 years old it predates the Egyptian, Indian, Chinese, and even the Sumerian civilizations by over 10,000 years.

An illustration of the Venus of Willendorf.

Since the Venus of Willendorf's discovery, several similar statuettes and other forms of art have been discovered. They are collectively referred to as Venus figurines – even though they are older than the mythological figure of Venus by over 10 millennia, and are not thought to be representations of any specific goddess. The figurines were made during a time when women were lauded as unique procreative life forces, were leaders of their communities and, quite possibly, considered the more important of the two sexes.

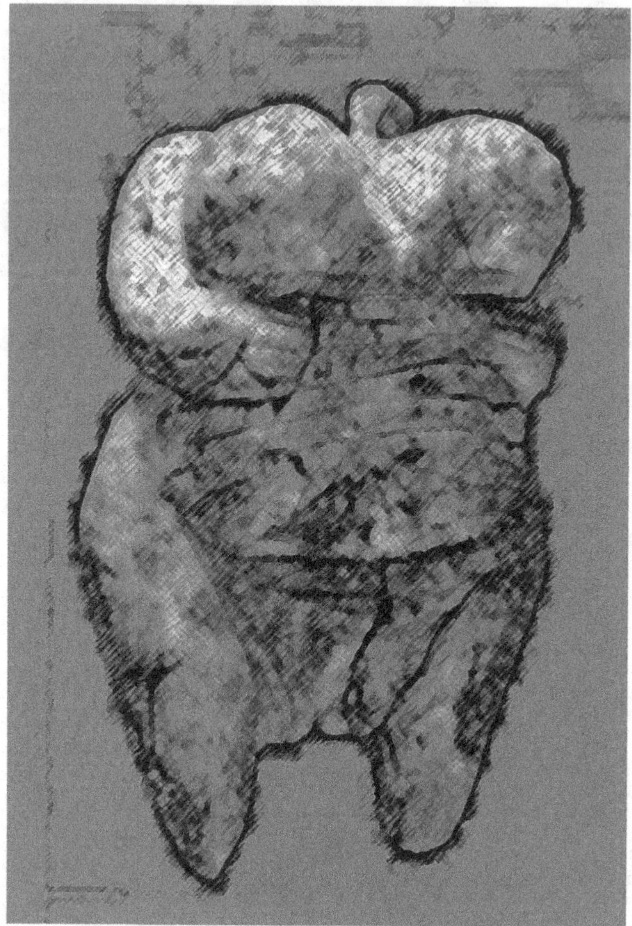

An illustration of the Venus of Hohle Fels.

The newly discovered Venus of Hohle Fels is a recent find in Germany that predates the Venus of Willendorf by some 15,000 years. It is the oldest know manmade carving in the world today and is estimated to have been produced some 35,000 years ago.

What then has changed since the advent of these statuettes when it comes to the importance of women in our modern societies? When were women placed in the back of the bus, so to speak? This change certainly hadn't occurred prior to the Greco/Roman period because women were still looked upon as purveyors of future knowledge and healing. However, something disturbing took place a little over 2,000 years ago that caused this backward thinking toward women and this is discussed in Chapter 2.

Chapter 2

Goddesses in Man's History

The Matrilineal Heritage

The time when women were sought after for answers and foretelling the future.

The current negativity towards women especially amongst the major religions.

Your special gift of procreation

The new Goddess arises

Each month when her period arrives she bears an influence with which she must be careful, for the presence of a woman in this condition may take away the power of a holy man. It was customary that during each menstrual period the woman or young girl should go to a small tipi apart from the camping circle; food was brought to her, and no one else could go near the tipi.

The power of woman grows with the moon and comes and goes with it.
Black Elk – a holy man of the Oglala Sioux

The Matrilineal Heritage

Is it a miracle that mitochondrion DNA is inherited exclusively from mothers? It is a fact that mitochondrial DNA is maternally inherited, which enables matrilineal lines of individuals to be traced by genetic analysis. In other words, the best way to trace the linear heritage of mankind is through our mother's side and not our father's.

In 1987, scientists publicized in the journal *Nature* that they had discovered what could be a common ancestor to all of mankind to a woman who lived in Africa some 200,000 years ago. The scientist had given her the biblical name "Eve." The name "Eve" gave the mistaken notion that this ancestor was the very first of our species, when, in fact, she would have been the original common ancestor through matrilineal descent of all humans living today. That is, all people alive this day can trace some of their genetic heritages through all mothers back to this one single woman. The scientists hypothesized this woman's existence by looking within the cells of living people and analyzing short loops of the genetic code known as mitochondrial DNA (mtDNA). In recent years, scientists have used mtDNA to trace the evolution and migration of human species. This is also useful for tracing Neanderthals – the ancient cousin of the modern human. Entire new industries of ancestral databases such as the DNA Ancestry Project and genetic labs are devoted to using the information from the mtDNA.

Although this technology of using online databases for ancestry research is new, the tracing of our ancestors has been going on for hundreds of generations. The Egyptians and ancient Greeks are perfect examples of ancestry tracing in a pre-modern culture. Many of their family records keeping skills are still in wide use by many societies today.

In pre-historic times, the method for how a child's sex is determined was assumed to be the mother's charge – or matrilineal heritage. The complex reproductive system of males and females still held many mysteries that ancient science could not explain. It was, nonetheless, a very mysterious, magical, or even religious event. The mother of a certain child could seldom be disputed, but the real father of the child could always be questioned, thus commencing the logical beginnings of matrilineal societies.

Women were looked upon as the leaders of their communities while the men would be away most of the time hunting, raiding, or trading – leaving the women to mind the day to day activities in their villages and care for the children. These activities meant making decisions and judgment calls on all sorts of problems – including punishments for crimes. This led to women guarding the secular and spiritual laws of the community. The abundance of female statuettes at this time is evidence of the power of matriarchal society. It is no wonder then that many of the first religions had to do with goddess worship.

Matrilineal culture has been long believed as a mother and child relationship. This is the centerpiece of all communal life. Motherhood itself was a source of great celebration, honor, and authority – as well as the core of societal, political and spiritual organization. It was women who were responsible for transmitting local government rights, surnames, and social positions.

The emergence of male dominated, patriarchal societies came with violent pillaging invaders. These militia groups forced not only new religions but societies based on the physical strength of men. Enslavement, forced marriages, a caste system, and new warlike gods overcame the matrilineal cultures, which had lasted for the past 25,000 years – maybe longer. Many of these matriarchal cultures are still thriving in Africa, India and Asia today.

Matriarchal evidence still exists even in religious texts if you look closely enough. In Orthodox Judaism it states that, to be a Jew, one must be either a proselyte (gentile student) *or the child of a Jewish mother*. This ruling is based on the fact that sexual intercourse between Jews and non-Jews is forbidden. Any offspring resulting from such an act is considered to have no paternity. This fundamental belief is not mentioned directly in the Bible, but is derived from Oral law (Mishnah tractate Kiddushin 3:12). The Talmudic commentary finds scriptural backing from various verses in the Torah and the rest of Tanakh (the Jewish Bible).

Many religions want you to become "reborn" into their faith thereby relegating your natural birth to something totally unimportant or meaningless. Some even go so far as to renouncing their own family and to submit unconditionally to the faith. These new dogmatic teachings seemed to relegate child birth into something insignificant and certainly not as important as a spiritual rebirth or being born again. Obviously, the early religious male dominated teachings proposed that since only women had the ability to give birth than by promoting spiritual rebirth they now had control over the faith and their followers.

It is women's procreative power that religious men feared and misunderstood over 2000 years ago. Many mythologies that were the foundations of indigenous cultures' beliefs were rewritten to accommodate the new religious beliefs of the time. Women in these stories that had perhaps been portrayed as goddesses were now made into saints or even demonic figures by these newborn religions. Men began to replace women as the "god figure" in monotheistic religions. It seems to us that when these indigenous beliefs were replaced by the new religions that the importance of natural birth and women's power in society began to wane tremendously. This advocated a novel way of looking at spiritual rebirth as the path to attain a pleasant afterlife. This nearly replaced the idea of a woman giving birth as a sacred act. Even today, many people would probably not consider giving birth to be holy or sacred – just a part of everyday life. This is disheartening considering that at one time women were not just looked upon as the holy harbingers of life, but were deified as well in ancient cultures.

Some of the First Deities were Women

The ancient history of man is loaded with goddesses that helped control man's destinies and fortunes. Goddesses were totally involved not only in man's everyday lives but in their futures as well. Their beauty, voluptuousness, or wisdom was sought out not only by gods but men as well. Women were so highly regarded over two thousand years ago. What has changed in the minds of men since then? There were so many examples of women deities and leaders prior to 2000 years ago that it would take a rack of encyclopedias to present them to you, here are just a few of them presented as evidence:

The earliest of civilizations known is the Sumerian, who began somewhere around 5000 BCE. Their culture was a bastion of goddesses with over 10 in their lower pantheon and one that was included with the four major deities: **Ninhursag** Mother Goddess, Goddess of childbirth, Queen of the mountains. Ninhursag means "lady of the mountain". She had many names including Ninmah ("Great Queen"); Nintu ("Lady of Birth"); Mama or Mami (mother); the source for the word "mammal" and "mama".

Other notable goddesses were **Inanna** goddess of love, fertility, procreation, war, Queen of the beasts, protector of the city of Uruk, and perhaps the original Dianna and Athena. Also – **Ninisinna,** Goddess of healing and medicine was a sister of Inanna and was the originator of midwifery and nursing.

In ancient Egypt one of the major deities was **Isis.** She started the institution of marriage and taught women the domestic arts. She is also said to have introduced the practice of agriculture. As the Great Enchantress, she had magical powers and knowledge of the arts of medicine and healing. Isis was often portrayed in Egyptian art as a Madonna suckling the infant **Horus,** the son of Isis and Osiris, who was believed to be the god of the pharaohs. With the advent of Christianity, many of the chapels of Isis were converted to churches and images of her with the infant Horus were adapted into the Virgin Mary caressing and nursing the baby Jesus.

Hathor was the Egyptian mother goddess and the protector of women which is why all Egyptian women worshiped her. She was also the goddess of music and dancing.

Bastet was the cat goddess who protected humans against contagious diseases and evil spirits. She was the very popular protector of women, children, and domestic cats. Cats were very important in ancient Egypt controlling the troublesome vermin from devouring their stores of grain. Her cult can be traced all the way back to about 3200 BCE. She was perhaps the originator behind the later stories of witches having cats as familiars.

One of the notable of Greek goddesses was **Psyche**. In psychoanalysis, the **psyche** refers to the forces in an individual that influence thought, behavior and personality. The word is borrowed from ancient Greek, and refers to the concept of the self – encompassing the modern ideas of soul, self, and mind. The Greeks believed that the soul or "psyche" was responsible for all types of human behavior.

Psyche appears in Greco/Roman mythology, as a personification of the human soul or spirit. Greek author Apuleius wrote a segment about Psyche in "The Golden Ass," which relates her beautiful, allegoric story.

Psyche was the youngest of the three daughters of a king, who were all beautiful ladies. Even so, Psyche was exceptionally lovely and her loveliness brought about an extreme jealousy and envy of the goddess Venus (Aphrodite). So envious was the goddess that she ordered her son Amor (Eros) to smite Psyche with a love for the most contemptible of all men with one of his darts. However, Amor's trick backfired when he accidentally pricked himself with his own dart. He was so stricken with Psyche's beauty that he fell in love with her. He accordingly brought her to some charming place, where he, unseen and unknown, visited her every night and left her as soon as the day began to dawn. Psyche might have continued to have enjoyed Amor's visits without interrupting this state of happiness if she had attended to the advice of her beloved – under no circumstances to give way to her curiosity. Amor had strongly insisted that she never inquire who he was. However, her jealous sisters made her believe that in the darkness of night she was embracing some hideous monster. So, one night, Psyche approached Amor while he was asleep, she carefully lifted a lamp over his head to gaze at his face in the darkness. To her amazement, she beheld the most handsome and lovely face of all the gods on Mount Olympus. In her excitement of joy and fear, a drop of hot oil fell from her lamp upon his shoulder. This awoke Amor, who censured her for her mistrust, and escaped. Psyche's peace was now gone all at once, and after having attempted in vain to throw herself into a river, she wandered about from temple to temple, inquiring after her beloved. At length, she came to the palace of Venus. There, her real sufferings began. Venus retained her, treated her as a slave, and imposed upon her the hardest and most humiliating tasks. Psyche would have perished under the weight of her sufferings, had not Amor, who still loved her in secret, invisibly comforted and assisted her in her labors. With his aid, Psyche at last succeeded in overcoming the jealousy and hatred of Venus. She became an immortal and was united with him forever.

The myths of the Greek goddess Psyche exemplify a woman's search for authentic personal growth. She reminds us all that the integration of our experiences, however sad or frightening they may be, matures and transforms us. Perhaps this is why her symbol was of a butterfly emerging into the light from a dark cocoon.

Gaia was the first of the ancient Greek goddesses. The word "Gaia" meant "land" or "earth. "Gaia is a primordial and underworld deity in the ancient Greek pantheon and considered a Mother Goddess or *Great Goddess.* Her equivalent in the Roman pantheon was Terra.

Terra Mater or **Tellus** was a goddess personifying the earth in Roman mythology. The names *Terra Mater* and *Tellus Mater* both mean *"Mother Earth"* in Latin. *Mater* was considered a lauding title also bestowed on other goddesses. Romans prayed to her during earthquakes. She was responsible for the productivity of farmland along with the grain goddess Ceres. She was also associated with marriage, motherhood, pregnant women, and animals.

There were other pre-Judeo/Christian goddesses in India, Sumeria, and Egypt. The pre-historic world was filled with great goddesses such as Kali, Hariti, Isis, Ma'at, An, and Mami. It is evident from the artifacts and archeological findings from these areas of the world that these goddesses were definitely front stage center in their societies and cultures. They were certainly not thought of as witches, demons, or even unclean.

Egyptians and Babylonians had many goddesses and temples designated to female deities. Women, including royalty, served and participated actively in running these temples and ritual ceremonies. Ample evidence suggests that these powerful women held important positions in their communities as well as the temples. Here is an Egyptian list of possible female Pharaohs or at least regents or mothers of Pharaohs. The Pharaohs at the peak of Egyptian ancient civilization were thought of as gods in the human form.

Merneith – around 3000 BCE
Her tomb showed that she was buried with honors fit for a male king that included a boat to travel to the next world.

Nimaethap from the third Dynasty
May have served as a regent for Djoser the second king of the third dynasty and builder of the famous step pyramid at Saqqara.

Khentkaus–Fourth Dynasty
Held the distinguished titles of "King's Mother" and "God's Daughter" and may have served as regent as her sons inherited and started the fifth dynasty.

Only known as the Wife of Djedkare-Izezi–Fifth Dynasty
She may have ruled as king as royal insignia was found at her site.

Ankhnesmeryre II–Sixth Dynasty
Could have served as regent for her son, Pepi II, who was about six when he assumed the throne after his father, Pepi I died.

Neithhikret–Sixth Dynasty
She is mentioned by Herodotus and on one of the kings lists in Turin.

Sobeknefru -Twelfth Dynasty
Ruled Egypt for a few years possibly as co-regent with her father and was the daughter of Amenemhet III and half-sister of Amenemhet IV

Ashotep–Eighteenth Dynasty

Was regent for her young son Ahmose I, the pharaoh who defeated the Hyksos

Ahmose-Nefertari -Eighteenth Dynasty
Served as regent for her son Amenhotep I and was the wife and sister of the dynasty's founder, Ahmose I.

Hatshepsut-Eighteenth Dynasty
One of the more famous of the regents who ruled after the death of her husband Thutmosis II, for her minor son and heir, and then as Pharaoh. She was often depicted in a fake beard and men's attire.

Nefertiti-Eighteenth Dynasty
There are claims that Nefertiti ruled after the death of her husband, Akhenaton and was given more honor than usual for a Great Wife. She is sometimes portrayed as a co-equal with the king officiating at ceremonies.

Tausret-Nineteenth Dynasty
The head wife of Seti II and served as regent for his son, Siptah who may have had some physical disability and died about six years into his reign. Tausret seems to have served as Pharaoh after his death for a few years using kingly titles for herself.

Cleopatra VII-Ptolemy
Was the last but most famous of the female Pharaohs of Egypt. She was a daughter of Ptolemy XII in a long succession of Ptolemy descendents that initially came from one of Alexander's bodyguards and general. She tried desperately to keep Egypt out of the clutches of Roman rule to no avail.

What is also interesting is that half of the Olympian gods were women whose powers were relegated to things such as love, marriage, motherhood, fertility, nature, virginity, hearth, and home. The only goddess that was different was Athena, who was the goddess of wisdom, crafts, and war strategy. This was probably due to the strength of the Greek city state of Athens – the most powerful of the city states.

The strengthening of women in Greek mythology, however, is amplified in many tales of mythical women. Some examples of these stories are the Amazons; a race of female warriors who were definitely a matriarchal society. Then there were the Keres that were evil female death spirits, the Sirens that were half-female, half-bird beings that lived on an island to which they enticed sailors with their seductive singing. Also, there was Medusa – a female monster whose gaze would turn onlookers to stone.

So, with all these great stories about renowned women, mythical and real, why did this aspect of civilization die out? How did civilization go from being a predominantly matriarchal society into a patriarchal one? How did women go from being goddesses to second-class citizens? We will show that it was the advent of Greek civilization that heralded the downfall of dominant roles of women in societies and religions through the exploits of Alexander the Great. It is quite evident through historical records that prior to Alexander women were still looked upon as deities and leaders in the Middle East. However, before we discuss how Alexander and other military leaders helped reign in the power of women, we want to discuss the roles that peasants or common women held in everyday society.

Oracles, Witches and Midwives

An **oracle** was usually a woman, who would provide wise counsel or opinions to whoever sought out their services. The earliest known oracle was in ancient Egypt at the renowned temple of Per-Wadjet, which was dedicated to a local goddess Wadjet. She was often represented as a cobra and considered the patron deity of Lower Egypt. This oracle site provided thousands of years of service from the Paleolithic era to 3100 BCE and may have been the source for the oracular practice that spread to Ancient Greece from Egypt. The Per-Wadjet tradition continued through the entire history of the Ancient Egyptian culture.

The earliest tradition of oracular practice in Hellenic culture dates from the archaic period – heralding the arrival of the Hellenes in 1300 BCE. Some of the first oracles were initially associated with the cults of deities such as the great goddess of nature and fertility, Gaia. The most famous of these were the Delphic Oracles at the temple of Delphi. The Delphic Oracle exerted considerable influence throughout Hellenic culture. The Greeks consulted her prior to all major undertakings such as wars, voyages, financial undertakings, and even love matters.

The priestess of the oracle at Delphi was known as the Pythia. Apollo spoke through his oracle and as a god, could choose very specific qualities that he wanted in an oracle. For example, oracles that were chosen for Apollo's temples had to be older women of blameless life chosen from among the peasants of the area. The sibyl or prophetess took the name Pythia and sat on a tripod seat over an opening in the earth. The oracle took this name from the story of Apollo and Python. When Apollo slew Python, its body fell into this fissure, according to legend, and fumes arose from its decomposing body. Intoxicated by the vapors, the sibyl fell into a trance, allowing Apollo to possess her spirit. In this state, she prophesied and received visions.

Further investigation of this story revealed that there may have been a strange gas that emanated from this opening in the earth. This gas is known to produce violent trances – similar to using a hallucinogen such as peyote or LSD in an attempt to heighten one's state of awareness. According to legend, the oracle would often speak in riddles, which were interpreted by the priests of the temple. Perhaps these oracles were engaging in the same vision producing techniques that have been practiced by many other cultures such as African medicine men and Native American soothsayers.

The Oracle of Delphi had origins in prehistoric times and the worship of Gaia but later the temple was changed to worship Apollo during the classical period of Greece and male priests were added to the temple organization, although the tradition of using female priestesses continued to provide the oracular ritual. It is from this Greek site that the English word, oracle, was coined.

Other female Oracles were abundant in the ancient world, including the Igbo people of southeastern Nigeria in Africa. These people have a long tradition of using female oracles for a particular deity. These oracles usually dwell in a cave or other secluded location away from urban areas. Just as the oracles of ancient Greece, these oracles would deliver prophecies in a possessed state to visitors and worshippers seeking advice or answers. Though the vast majority of modern Igbos are Christian, many in Nigeria today still use these oracles.

In Tibet, oracles have played, and continue to play, an important part in religion and government. The word "oracle" is used by Tibetans to refer to the spirit that enters those men and women who act as mediums between the natural and the spiritual realms. The mediums are, therefore, known as *kuten*, which literally means, "the physical basis". The Dalai Lama, who lives in exile in northern India, still consults an oracle known as the Nechung Oracle. The Nechung is considered the official state oracle of the government of Tibet. The Dalai Lama has, according to custom, consulted the Nechung kuten during the New Year festivities of Losar. This is a custom that has endured for centuries. Other oracles the Dalai Lama has been known to consult are Dorje Shugden and Tenma kuten. The Dalai Lama gives a complete description of the process of trance and spirit possession in his book *Freedom in Exile*.

Witchcraft / Shamanism

The Chukchees are a unique community of indigenous people from Russia. They survive in the harsh wilderness by herding reindeer and hunting for fish in the seas. They have a unique saying in their culture, which is that **women are by nature shamans.**

Women have held the very important role of spiritual mothers in their communities since ancient times. It is a fact that some prehistoric male diviners, shamans, or dancers would dress as women when they were providing these same services; probably, because of the trust that these communities had with their female shamans. Shamanism was a role so strongly associated with women that men would have to disguise themselves as females to be credible.

It is a fact that women have been the predominant sex for shamans throughout the world in ancient times. From the Asian countries like China, Japan, the Koreas, Okinawa, the Philippines, and Australia all the way to the Americas, Africa, and Europe, it is female shamans that dominate the practice.

Women provided the roles of dancers, diviners, invokers, healers, herbalists and midwives. Some would even enter trance-like states, using drugs or alcohol to become shape shifters, oracles, or receive spirits into their bodies. Shape shifting into their totem animal forms helped the community with an abundant supply of hunted animals for meat and appeased their dead spirits to return once again during the next hunting season.

In some societies, shamans exhibit a two-spirit identity; assuming the dress, attributes, role or function of the opposite sex, gender fluidity and/or same-sex sexual orientation. This practice is common, and found among the Chukchi, Sea Dayak, Patagonian, Araucarias, Arapaho, Cheyenne, Navajo, Pawnee, Lakota, and Ute, as well as many other Native American tribes.

In India the Iron Age "Atharvaveda" is a collection of charms and spells classically associated with witchcraft, with purposes such as harming an enemy or winning a sweetheart. It incorporates much of early traditions of healing and magic that is paralleled in other Indo-European literatures. There are striking parallels with Hittite and Germanic sorcery stanzas. Belief in the supernatural is ever so strong in certain parts of India, and prosecutions for witchcraft are to this day still reported from time to time.

In pre-Columbian Americas shamans were all over the place and a lot of them were women. Among the Mapuche people of South America, the community shaman, usually a woman is known as the Machi. She serves the community by performing ceremonies to cure diseases, ward off evil, influence the weather and harvest, and by practicing other forms of healing such as herbalism.

South American Aztec Codices show women officiating over sweat lodges to heal afflictions by invoking the evil spirits to exit the stricken person's body. Namibian women in Africa used fire to do the same thing by absorbing the bad spirits ailing a patient and then releasing them into the sacred fire of her ancestors.

Female shamans (*miko*) who transmitted the voices of the dead or departed have been active in Japan from ancient times to the present day. These *miko* made important contributions to the popular religious culture during the Edo period (1600–1868). The overwhelmingly female Mikogami of Japan also kept the "sacred mirror" of the sun goddess Amaterasu.

> *"Sangomas are the traditional female shaman healers in the Zulu, Swazi, Xhosa and Ndebele traditions in southern Africa. They perform a holistic and symbolic form of healing, embedded in the beliefs of their culture that ancestors in the afterlife guide and protect the living. Sangomas are called to heal, and through them ancestors from the spirit world can give instruction and advice to heal illness, social disharmony and spiritual difficulties. Sangomas have many different social and*

> *political roles in the community: divination, healing, directing rituals, finding lost cattle, protecting warriors, counteracting witches, and narrating the history, cosmology, and myths of their tradition. They are highly revered and respected in their society, where illness is thought to be caused by witchcraft, pollution (contact with impure objects or occurrences) or by the ancestors themselves, either malevolently, or through neglect if they are not respected, or to show an individual her calling to be a Sangoma. For harmony between the living and the dead, vital for a trouble-free life, the ancestors must be shown respect through ritual and animal sacrifice.*
>
> *Sangomas are steeped in ritual. They work in a sacred healing hut or Ndumba, where their ancestors reside. They have specific coloured cloths to wear to please each ancestor, and often wear the gallbladder of the goat sacrificed at their graduation ceremony in their hair. They summon the ancestors by burning a plant called Imphepho, dancing, chanting, and most importantly playing drums. Sangomas are able to access advice and guidance from the ancestors for their patients in three ways: possession by an ancestor, or channeling; throwing bones; and interpreting dreams. In possession states the Sangoma works herself into a trance, through drumming, dancing and chanting, and allows her ego to step aside so an ancestor possesses her body and communicates directly with the patient" (* Shamanportal.org*).*

To demonstrate, one of these herbs commonly used by the female shamans was the rose. This old tradition is the origin of men giving roses to women as a romantic gesture. Ancient shamans taught that women should eat rose hips (dried or fresh) to help them during their menstrual periods and her mates would collect roses for this use. As a matter of fact, the earliest known gardening was the planting of roses along the most traveled roadways of early nomadic humans. Today, scientists have identified the rose hip as having the single highest concentration of iron in any plant. Iron is a major component of red blood cells. Many women today know the risk of becoming anemic during their periods and often take iron supplements during this time.

So, contrary to Judeo/Christian and Muslim beliefs, these above examples are just a few of the practices of real "witchcraft." There is nothing unnatural or evil about any of these traditions. Shamans and natural healers were not only looked upon as some of the most respected members of society, but considered essential people for the community. That female shamans have been around for thousands of years is quite evident from recent grave excavations by archeologists.

One such example is a 12,000 year old grave site of a female shaman or medicine woman who was found in Israel by scientists from the Institute of Archaeology at the Hebrew University of Jerusalem. She was part of the Natufian culture that thrived in the Levant from 15,000 to 11,500 BCE. Items in her grave included over 50 complete tortoise shells, a leopard's pelvis, the wing of a golden eagle, tail of a cow, some marten skulls, and a human foot. The forearm of a large boar was found alongside her left leg. What's strange is that all of these animals are rarely found in Natufian grave sites, which make this assemblage seem very special indeed. We know that she was considered a shaman because of these totemic animals that graced her grave. Rocks were placed over her head, pelvis, and arms; probably, in an attempt to keep animals from scavenging her or to help keep her spirit in the cave among her clan. She was about 45 years old at death, which was twice the life expectancy of the Natufians. She was very petite and had a spinal disability which would have caused her to limp or drag her foot. Her survival and upkeep meant that she must have been a very important female of the community – enough so that they chose to keep her fed and alive to an old age.

She is evidence of a real, historical, and ancient female shaman – a woman who used her medicinal and spiritual skills to help keep her clan healthy. She was obviously revered, protected, and looked after during her old age – even while suffering afflictions. Much care was taken to place sacred and hard to find objects in her grave; reverently burying her in this fashion. She must have been sorely missed by her family and clan.

Another archaeological example, found by a team of Russian archaeologists led by Natalia Polosmak, was of a female shaman known as the Ice Maiden of Siberia. She is one of the most famous of the undisturbed burial sites in Pazyryk, Russia. She was buried in the 5th century BCE and accompanied by six horses. She was obviously a woman of great importance as a leader or shaman because of her dress and the opulence of her coffin, which was a hollowed-out tree trunk covered with images of deer and snow leopards carved in leather. The six horses that were sacrificed wore elaborate harnesses and were laid over her coffin forming a roof with their bodies. The Ice Maiden stood 5 feet 6 inches, which was fairly tall for a woman of that era and was blonde. She died when she was young and was embalmed with peat and bark. Her pale skin was covered with tattoos of animals with horns that turned into flowers. She wore a silk blouse, a long crimson wool skirt, and felt stockings. The final touch that truly set her off as a shaman was the tall felt headdress that she was wearing.

The words from a shaman were powerful indeed. Their followers, whether the shaman was a man or a woman, would never want to see the wrong side of her gift of seeing. Some examples in early historic writings tell about how some shamans were feared – either through personal experience with them or by reputation. Here is an example from the Code of Hammurabi (about 2000 BCE) pertaining to magical spells.

> *If a man has put a spell upon another man and it is not justified, he upon whom the spell is laid shall go to the holy river; into the holy river shall he plunge. If the holy river overcome him and he is drowned, the man who put the spell upon him shall take possession of his house. If the holy river declares him innocent and he remains unharmed the man who laid the spell shall be put to death. He that plunged into the river shall take possession of the house of him who laid the spell upon him.*

Here in this example, we see again the use of water as a powerful tool to be used to cleanse a sinner. Does any part of this passage above seem familiar? How many times have we heard of the story of a witch being thrown into the water to judge his or her innocence from the sin of witchcraft? It may seem like a comical joke today, but in many of the 13th century witch trials in Europe, this method was actually used to judge whether or not a person was guilty of witchcraft. However, now we know that the European judges of the witch trials were not the first ones to come up with this type of inhumane judgment.

Some of the main female deities in the ancient Middle East and Mediterranean empires were worshiped by shamans and witches. One of the most important of the pre-Roman female deities was Dianna, goddess of the forest and childbirth. In Roman mythology, Dianna was the goddess of the hunt, associated with wild animals, the woodland, and also of the moon. In literature, she was the equivalent of the Greek goddess Artemis; although in cult beliefs she was Italian, not Greek in origin. Dianna was worshiped in ancient Roman religion and is currently revered in the religions of Religio Romana Neopaganism, and Stregheria. In Italy, this old religion of Stregheria embraced the goddess Dianna as Queen of the Witches; witches being the wise women healers and shamans of the time. Along with her main attributes, Dianna was an emblem of chastity. Oak groves were especially sacred to her, and she was regarded with great reverence by lower-class citizens and slaves who could receive asylum in her temples. Dianna remains an important figure in some modern mythologies. Those who believe that prehistoric people lived in matriarchal societies consider Dianna to have originated from a mother goddess worshiped at that time.

Dianna's counterpart, Artemis, first originated as a goddess of the Anatolian people (Troy). Artemis entered the Greek religion (Hellenism) when the Greeks conquered Anatolia. Creating stories made famous in Homer's "Iliad," the Epic of Helen of Troy and the Trojan War. The Greeks already associated Artemis with the ancient Egyptian Goddess, Bast (the cat goddess) before the Greeks were conquered by the Romans. Later Neo-pagan sects such as Diannic Witchcraft, in turn, associated Bast with Dianna.

The Greeks, unlike many indigenous cultures at the height of Greek popularity, were a highly militaristic, patriarchal culture. They denied women any civil rights and considered women to be property, like chattel. Hellenism started out with only male deities, usually tempestuous sky or war gods. However, because of the dim view of women, Hellenism had no goddesses. These Hellenistic ideas combined with newborn philosophies from the Greek schools in Athens were quickly spreading all over the Greek peninsula and surrounding areas. Alexander the Great, Aristotle's pupil, carried over these new beliefs to other regions as he fought his way east toward Persia. This is why you will see no female deities in the patriarchal religions of Zoroastrianism, Judaism, Christianity, and Islam. The only possible exception is the Catholic Church regarding the Virgin Mary as a near equal to Jesus Christ. There is even a methodical study under Catholicism called Mariology that is totally devoted to Mary, the Mother of Jesus.

In the Roman Empire, the two most popular deities among women were Isis and Bast. The city of Paris, France was named for a large temple to Isis or *Per Isis* (Temple of Isis). On orders from the Christian Roman Emperor, Christian soldiers raided the Temple of Isis, killed all the priestesses, stole all the temple treasures, and used the building as a Christian Church. In the 10th century, the Roman Catholic Church built the Notre Dame Cathedral on the same spot. The Roman Catholic Church even kept the original carved wood statue of Isis from the original Temple of Isis. However, in the 1500s, a woman stormed into the cathedral one day and claimed to be a priestess of Isis. She went to the priests and demanded the return of the property. She pointed out to the priests that the myth of Isis and Osiris was carved into the altar. The Roman Catholic priests immediately declared the altar "Satanic" and had it smashed into little pieces and then burned. The priests also ordered that the woman priestess of Isis be tortured and burned alive as a witch.

The cathedral of Notre Dame brings up another topic of sacred site rebuilding or recycling. Building modern churches or mosques over ancient religious sites was a tradition of Judeo/Christian religions as well as Islam. This act of tearing down the old and building the new on top of the debris was believed to nullify the old religion. The hope was that the place would remain holy, but now retain only the spiritual energy of the newest religion that was being practiced on the site. However, is this entirely true? Does the old spiritual energy of the dead religion just evaporate, or does it remain retaining even more powerful energy on its holy grounds and felt by the subjects that worship there? The builders are kind of a LifeConscious metaphor of building a new temple or church with new materials upon the old dead ground while at the same time using the old spiritual energy.

(Heidi) When my husband and I visited Paris during our honeymoon, we went to Notre Dame three times in one week. We were both very drawn to the place in the deepest spiritual sense. Many people might think that Notre Dame is another "tourist trap" of Europe. Nothing could be further from the truth. We saw many French people go into the cathedral several times a week for worship, meditation, and prayer. There were people who would travel in and out of the sanctuary constantly during the day. Some would stay to pray for a long time – kneeling on the floor, sobbing. Some people would stand in the middle of the aisle and stare at the altar with a blank stare. Folks of all ages and races would sometimes just sit in the sanctuary and be quiet.

One night, we attended a Catholic mass there. All kinds of people were in Notre Dame. At this particular service, the ambassador of Croatia was attending with his guests. Almost half of the seating was roped off for the ambassador and his distinguished companions. Then, on the other side of the aisle where we were sitting, there was a mentally disabled French man sitting next to us. He was dirty and wearing raggedy clothes.

When the mass began, the disabled man began to sing the hymns in a tone-deaf voice while the ambassador and his group were singing the hymns beautifully. Although his singing was terrible, I was deeply touched by this man's faith and his dedication to worship. It made his singing the most beautiful out of anyone else's. It was amazing to me that everyone was comfortable with each other and no one was judging this man or giving him dirty looks – not even the children. Many tourists, like us were there. I saw people from Japan, India, and Germany sitting together singing the hymns.

It made me think about how many centuries this place of worship has been there – how many different religions have been established on this very spot? Pagans, Romans, Christians, and Muslims all worshiped there at one time or another. Even though Notre Dame is Catholic, and only Catholic masses are held, there is a sense that anyone is welcome to worship there – no matter what deity you believe in or what religious sect you belong to.

I am so glad that my French was good enough when we went to Paris that I could understand the mass and what the priest was saying. I was so touched at the end of the service when he said that everyone was welcome at Notre Dame and he hoped that God would go with us when we left that place – no matter what life path we had come from that day.

It is a shame that many places, like Notre Dame, are historically tainted with the memories of witchcraft accusations and trials. Here in this book, we will look more closely at the witch-craze phenomenon of the middle ages, how it got started, and what implications they had on modern views of women in Western society.

Witchcraft is oldest of all women skills with the exception of childbirth. Although it may not have always been known by this name, witchcraft originated as a practical method for dealing with women's health issues – especially fertility, pregnancy, and childbirth. Over thousands of years, witchcraft expanded to include but not limited to treating men and children's health needs, nutrition, planting and harvesting of crops, astrology, and mineralogy. The passing down of herbal treatments was done through oral tradition from one generation to the next and continued this way for thousands of years. However, it was only until fairly recently that this special knowledge was looked upon by other members of society – especially the wealthy and male members of a community, as something evil.

In Brian P. Levak's excellent work *The Witchcraft Sourcebook* he states that the word "witchcraft" can have many meanings but is generally used to denote a person who possesses some type of supernatural, occult, or mysterious powers that may be used to injure others or cause some type of misfortune. He also states that a witch is a term that can be used for both men and women but is predominately identified with women.

In modern Western society, a witch is an enchanter, sorcerer, or magician. The word comes from the German *wicken*, which means to bewitch, *wīh* meaning holy, or from the Old English word, *wigle* meaning divination. In ancient times, it was probably very easy to be considered a magician with a little sleight of hand and a few fiery flashes as spectacles for a believing audience. However, witches were known for their natural medicinal treatments from herbs and minerals as well as having some so-called "magical" abilities.

Since older, hard working women seldom held on to their good looks hundreds of years ago it wasn't uncommon for them to have a haggard, unkempt, and even frightening appearance as they aged. This disheveled look along with the unknown uses for the herbs, chemicals, and medicines that they prescribed to the common folks only added revulsion and mistrust towards these poor women.

Written examples of witchcraft in historical religious texts are unmistakable. In the only example in the Bible, a clear description of the practice of witchcraft is that of the divining woman in The Book of Samuel 28. Here, we are told how Saul went to fight the Philistines, but, before doing so he went to visit a woman in Endor. Saul was looking for a way to speak with Samuel again, who was recently deceased, to get his guidance prior to battling the Philistines.

[3]Now Samuel was dead, and all Israel had lamented him, and buried him in Ramah, even in his own city. And Saul had put away those that had familiar spirits, and the wizards, out of the land.

[4]And the Philistines gathered themselves together, and came and pitched in Shunem: and Saul gathered all Israel together, and they pitched in Gilboa.

[5]And when Saul saw the host of the Philistines, he was afraid, and his heart greatly trembled.

[6]And when Saul enquired of the LORD, the LORD answered him, neither by dreams, nor by Urim, nor by prophets.

[7]Then said Saul unto his servants, ***Seek me a woman that hath a familiar spirit, that I may go to her, and enquire of her. And his servants said to him, Behold, there is a woman that hath a familiar spirit at Endor.***

[8]And Saul disguised himself, and put on other raiment, and he went, and two men with him, and they came to the woman by night: and he said, I pray thee, divine unto me by the familiar spirit, and bring me him up, whom I shall name unto thee.

[9]And the woman said unto him, Behold, thou knowest what Saul hath done, how he hath cut off those that have familiar spirits, and the wizards, out of the land: wherefore then layest thou a snare for my life, to cause me to die?

[10]And Saul sware to her by the Lord, saying, as the Lord liveth, there shall no punishment happen to thee for this thing.

[11]Then said the woman, whom shall I bring up unto thee? And he said, bring me up Samuel.

[12]And when the woman saw Samuel, she cried with a loud voice: and the woman spake to Saul, saying, why hast thou deceived me? For thou art Saul.

13And the king said unto her, Be not afraid: for what sawest thou? And the woman said unto Saul, I saw gods ascending out of the earth.

14And he said unto her, what form is he of? And she said, an old man cometh up; and he is covered with a mantle. And Saul perceived that it was Samuel, and he stooped with his face to the ground, and bowed himself.

15And Samuel said to Saul, Why hast thou disquieted me, to bring me up? And Saul answered, I am sore distressed; for the Philistines make war against me, and God is departed from me, and answereth me no more, neither by prophets, nor by dreams: therefore I have called thee, that thou mayest make known unto me what I shall do.

16Then said Samuel, Wherefore then dost thou ask of me, seeing the LORD is departed from thee, and is become thine enemy?

17And the LORD hath done to him, as he spake by me: for the LORD hath rent the kingdom out of thine hand, and given it to thy neighbour, even to David:

18Because thou obeyedst not the voice of the LORD, nor executedst his fierce wrath upon Amalek, therefore hath the LORD done this thing unto thee this day.

19Moreover the LORD will also deliver Israel with thee into the hand of the Philistines: and tomorrow shalt thou and thy sons be with me: the LORD also shall deliver the host of Israel into the hand of the Philistines.

20Then Saul fell straightway all along on the earth, and was sore afraid, because of the words of Samuel: and there was no strength in him; for he had eaten no bread all the day, nor all the night.

21And the woman came unto Saul, and saw that he was sore troubled, and said unto him, Behold, thine handmaid hath obeyed thy voice, and I have put my life in my hand, and have hearkened unto thy words which thou spakest unto me.

[22]Now therefore, I pray thee, hearken thou also unto the voice of thine handmaid, and let me set a morsel of bread before thee; and eat, that thou mayest have strength, when thou goest on thy way.

[23]But he refused, and said, I will not eat. But his servants, together with the woman, compelled him; and he hearkened unto their voice. So he arose from the earth, and sat upon the bed.

[24]And the woman had a fat calf in the house; and she hasted, and killed it, and took flour, and kneaded it, and did bake unleavened bread thereof:

[25]And she brought it before Saul, and before his servants; and they did eat. Then they rose up, and went away that night.

So, this divining woman brought up Samuel's spirit for King Saul so that he could make inquiries of him about the impending conflict. She did this similarly to what an oracle would have done. She did this even though she knew that Saul had persecuted her kind for years. If this wasn't enough, she also showed kindness and mercy toward Saul by feeding him and his men when she realized how weak Saul was. What a woman!

Here are other examples of women to whom the Bible accuses of witchcraft such as Jezebel, the daughter of the king of Sidon. Regarding Jezebel, we are told in II Kings 9:22 that:

"And it came to pass, when Joram saw Jehu, that he said, is it peace, Jehu? And he answered, What peace, so long as the whoredoms of thy mother Jezebel and her witchcrafts are so many"?

And the degrading words of the prophet Nahum (3:4), who compares Nineveh to a harlot:

" Because of the multitude of the whoredoms of the wellfavoured harlot, the mistress of witchcrafts, that selleth nations through her whoredoms, and families through her witchcraft".

The Bible clearly is opposed to women who were prostitutes for their profession. In their defense, perhaps many of these women did not feel that they had a choice. They had to find enough money to support themselves and any children they may have had. Prostitution was the most reliable profession that a woman could do at that time because of men's carnal needs. The prophet Ezekiel (13:17-23) says:

> *"Likewise, thou son of man, set thy face against the daughters of thy people, which prophesy out of their own heart; and prophesy thou against them,*
>
> *18 And say, Thus saith the Lord GOD; Woe to the women that sew pillows to all armholes, and make kerchiefs upon the head of every stature to hunt souls! Will ye hunt the souls of my people, and will ye save the souls alive that come unto you?*
>
> *19 And will ye pollute me among my people for handfuls of barley and for pieces of bread, to slay the souls that should not die, and to save the souls alive that should not live, by your lying to my people that hear your lies?*
>
> *20 Wherefore thus saith the Lord GOD; Behold, I am against your pillows, wherewith ye there hunt the souls to make them fly, and I will tear them from your arms, and will let the souls go, even the souls that ye hunt to make them fly.*
>
> *21 Your kerchiefs also will I tear, and deliver my people out of your hand, and they shall be no more in your hand to be hunted; and ye shall know that I am the LORD.*
>
> *22 Because with lies ye have made the heart of the righteous sad, whom I have not made sad; and strengthened the hands of the wicked, that he should not return from his wicked way, by promising him life:*
>
> *23 Therefore ye shall see no more vanity, nor divine divinations: for I will deliver my people out of your hand: and ye shall know that I am the LORD".*

One can see from these examples from religious texts that females, with the exception gifted women, are not looked highly upon but chastised. We can now see how this animosity towards female shamans, oracles, and witches began with expansion of Greek ideals. From the Greek philosophies, the religions of the Fertile Crescent embraced these Greek beliefs and incorporated them into their religious texts. This is how Christians, Muslims, and Jews began to see women in a subservient light in these now male-dominated societies and religions.

So what exactly initiated this male-dominated negative change in attitude toward female shamans, midwives, oracles, and witches? Was there a specific time in history in which women and their esteemed roles were suddenly admonished? There were many such events during empire building in the East.

The first of these events occurred during the Macedonian invasion of the Middle East by Alexander the Great. Prior to Alexander, Egypt and the Middle East were considered the homeland of healers and magicians. The gods and goddesses in Egypt were not mortal, peaceful beings as we imagine gods should be. They were simply sources of knowledge and power, the ultimate source of magic. These crafts were respected because it was limited to the priests and scribes who were, unlike peasants, literate. One of the most worshiped goddesses, Isis, was thought to have gained her divine powers through magic. Gods in Egypt were neutral (either good or bad) and thus magic could be used for good or bad purposes.

Although Alexander the Great lived a short life, he literally changed the face of the world when he set out for the Hellespont (modern Dardanelles) in the spring of 334 BCE until his death in 323 BCE. His armies conquered Egypt, Persia, Asia Minor, Palestine, Babylon, and all the way into the Indus Valley in India where he suffered a wound and had to retreat back to Persia. Along the way, he left commanders to build cities with Greek thinking and influences. Unfortunately, these influences also included the debasing of women in those regions that lasted to this day. With these conquests came Greek philosophy and the relegation of women to second-class citizenship. To the Greeks, women had no vote and little role in politics. Women could not own property, could not sue, could not file for divorce, and were entirely dependent on men to perform these roles. Wives and courtesans were known to influence the course of men's political lives; where wives were carefully sequestered in the homes of the men for purposes of bearing children. The courtesans were allowed to move more freely about in public life, but their vocation was limited to entertaining men.

This Greek change in philosophy towards women was certainly different than the philosophies of the countries that were conquered. For instance, in the Persian Empire, aristocratic women enjoyed economic independence, were involved in the administration of economic affairs, traveled, and controlled their wealth and position by being active, resolute, and enterprising. The common women could be supervisors within certain work groups and would receive more rations than the men who were working under their supervision. They could be professional career women as well as own and rent out property.

The conquered Persian King Darius III married off his daughters to military leaders throughout the empire. He reciprocated by marrying the daughters of nobles Gorbryas, Otanes, his own niece and daughters of the Cyrus II, Cambyses II and Bardiya. Darius's marriages indicated an ancient importance through matrilineal descent for marrying all the royal women of the previous kings. This might have been an attempt to eliminate any contestants to his throne.

Other documents found in Babylonia, Elam, and Egypt showed that women owned properties, which they could sell or lease. After the death of her husband, the widowed wife inherited from the deceased – even if she did not have any children. A woman could not act as a witness in the drawing up of contracts, but she could act as a contracting party and have her own seal.

The change in attitude towards women continued to grow when Greek, and later, Roman cultures became dominant. The educated societies turned away from female- influenced healing toward a more, so called, logical, scientific approach to problems. Women's intuition and oral traditions were no longer looked upon as respectful because they were not scientific. The feelings of a woman were now seen as base, animalistic, and even ridiculous. Philosophy, mathematics, and science occupied the minds of the literate elite. There was still belief in witchcraft and shamanism, but mainly in the lower classes. The practice was generally approached with caution – especially after the new religions began forcing their dogma on the people.

Midwives and Healers

Midwifery began in ancient times because of the obvious need for knowledgeable women who had experience with childbirth. It is strange that humans are the only mammals that need some sort of assistance during labor and delivery. Observing animals in the wild, all of them give birth alone. Usually, females do not need help birthing their young out of their bodies. However, complications do sometimes occur and the newborn is left to die or the mother dies in the attempt at giving birth. The main hindrance is the size of human females' pelvis. A baby's head coming out of a woman's body has the potential to be quite hazardous to the child's health – thus the reason for midwives to help the mother pass the baby and the placenta safely. Nevertheless, there is a movement that has gained ground in recent years of women who choose to give birth at home with no assistance whatsoever. Although many of these women understand the risks, they still choose to birth their baby alone with no midwife, nurse, or doctor present.

(Heidi) To add a note to the above statement, many women do not need much intervention. Depending on the health of the mother, many women (contradictory to modern belief) are capable of giving birth at home with minimal intervention from a midwife. While many ladies scoff at the idea of giving birth with no pain medication and without a doctor present, they also forget that births were done in this way for ages – much longer than the current standard birth in a hospital room surrounded by monitoring devices, IVs, and medical practitioners.

The word "mid-wife" derives from the Anglo-Saxon "med-wyf," meaning wise-woman. An ancient "wise-woman" garnered her knowledge from experience, oral traditions, and teachings from older and wiser midwives. Most of these women were their very own mothers. For this reason, midwifery had its uses and was present throughout all the ancient cultures. Without it, the mortality rate of babies would have been disastrous. Therefore, as modern humans we owe our very existence to the dedication and bravery of many midwives in our families' past.

In ancient Egypt, midwives and female healers were common at every level of society – from peasants who were nothing more than experienced friends or neighbors, to learned and accomplished practitioners. These women plied their skills on the social elites and became midwives, nurses and healers to affluent households and even royalty. In all cases, these women became skilled through apprenticeships from knowledgeable, wise, older, and experienced women. These healers filled an important, specialized niche by providing emotional support, medical care, and treatments for child labor, pregnancy, fertility, and contraception – all the while invoking the prayerful help of a familiar deity such as Isis or the Virgin Mary.

Egyptian female practitioners of midwifery and healing were very active and were aided by their faith in their goddess Isis. We've already mentioned she was the goddess of medicine. Her learned priestesses were sought after as physicians and healers throughout the Mediterranean. Women's schools for specializing in childbirth and childbearing were found at the city of Sais at the mouth of the Nile. Women were both students and teachers at the school. Ancient records show that some women studied at a royal medical school in Heliopolis and female healers were common subjects painted on the walls of tombs and temples. This shows that women were very well accepted as doctors in their communities.

Painted vessels and pottery found in tombs provide a glimpse of the life of an ancient midwife through drawings that show depictions of women giving birth while kneeling or on an assistant's lap. These techniques were used for thousands of years along with birthing stools. These stools were also discovered during excavations in Asia, Africa, Middle East, South Pacific and the Americas.

An illustration of an Aztec midwife applying herbs to a woman who has just given birth.

An example of midwives in ancient text includes its first reference in the Bible in Genesis 35:16:

> *"And they moved on from Bethel, and there was still a distance of land before they came to Ephrathah. And Rachel began to give birth, and had it hard in her childbearing. And so it was, as she had a very hard time in her childbearing that the **midwife** was saying to her, "Don't be afraid, because this one also is a son for you." As her soul departed – for she died – she named her son Ben-Oni. But his father named him Benjamin."*

This passage shows that midwifery was an accepted practice in biblical history and was in existence in the Jewish tribes approximately 4000 years ago.

In Rome, wealthy families had their own trusted midwives and healers that came from humble beginnings, probably as Greek or Egyptian slaves. Often these wise women would either be given their freedom or pay for it outright as they seemed to be well paid for their services.

We've already read about the Greek goddess Athena who cured the blind and Hera who was the principal deity of healing and also Leto as a surgeon. They were all venerated for their skills as goddess healers. Succeeding Greek female healers were teachers of medicine, cared for patients, and cared especially for birthing women's needs. Their skills brought a heavy price in the Roman slave markets when these Greek women were captured after the defeat of the city-state Corinth. Meanwhile, their Roman counterparts were busy practicing medicine and healing as male colleagues of their female contemporaries.

Eventually, Rome fell to the northern barbarian tribes. Female healers found that they were alienated by the early Christian churches. There were a few areas where nuns were being honored as saints such as St Bridget in Ireland, who in some respects can be compared to the Greek goddess Artemis. Like Artemis, she refused to marry, choosing instead to exercise her own authority in a community of women. These female followers were themselves forbidden to marry while in her service. Furthermore, like Artemis, Bridget was a goddess of childbirth, a protector of children, and a fierce advocate of women's rights.

Another of the early woman saints was St Scholastica the sister of St Benedict. She eased the plight of those unfortunate individuals that suffered during a devastating plague in Italy and was the patron saint of convulsive children.

Female education came to a standstill during the Dark Ages in Europe as wave after wave of plagues ravaged the populations. Midwifery suffered a tremendous setback as the onset of religious, authoritarian persecutions commenced. Trying to find blames for the raging plagues was probably one of the causes of these persecutions, tortures, and executions.

At last, during the European Renaissance midwives served on all social levels. Paris became the center of childbirth training. However, in Briton a conflict developed between British physicians and midwives over professional territory. Wise women in Britain began to write about their techniques in an effort to educate practitioners and protect their profession from regulation. In 1671, Jane Sharp wrote the first known text written by a midwife, *The Midwives Book*. The text included anatomy, diagnostic tests, and herbal treatments for pregnant women. She argued for women's expertise in birth and advised against intervention except in extreme cases.

(Heidi) Jane Sharp was revolutionary for her time. She wrote ***The Midwives Book*** in 1671 – a time when not many women were known for writing reference books. In fact, all the references that Sharp cites in her work are all male authors – mostly from the Greek and Italian anatomists.

Surprisingly, licensed midwives, such as Jane Sharp, were well respected by the church as well as the community. Midwives' services usually weren't cheap and most were considered respectable in their own right – independent of their husband's reputation. The Church even used midwives as witnesses in witchcraft trials. They were considered experts on woman anatomy and were used to examine the accused person's genitals (Elaine Hobby, ed. ***The Midwives Book, Introduction,*** xiii).

The Church was the authority on who could practice midwifery and actually licensed women based on their prior experience and how many years they had apprenticed with a licensed midwife. In addition to being witnesses for "witches' marks," midwives also aided the Church in baptisms and mothers' Blessings. A Blessing is a religious ceremony in which the new mother is cleansed by the church after giving birth to symbolize her acceptance back into the Church. The priest would deem her clean again and worthy to worship in the house of God (Elaine Hobby, ed. ***The Midwives Book, Introduction,*** xii).

However, the midwives that were persecuted for witchcraft were most likely the "unofficial" midwives – ones that did not have a license from the church to practice. These women would have been poorer, perhaps widowed, and older. These characteristics would have all been suspicious in the eyes of the community and the Church for accusations of witchcraft.

A Woman Giving Birth on a Birth Chair – an illustration of a painting by Eucarius Rößlin.

It is strange how Medieval Europe accepted midwifery as a woman's profession when it strangled women in so many other socio-political settings. Elaine Hobby, the main editor for Jane Sharp's book explains how the male-dominated world of medicine and literature accepted midwifery as nearly strictly female.

> *"In male-authored books, 'most midwives are ignorant' (Compleat Midwives Practice, sig. A3); although Sharp briefly laments that too many lack anatomical knowledge, it is surgeons and physicians, not midwives, who are repeatedly*

said by her to be 'at a stand' (perplexed), or in disagreement with one another. Sharps's 'sisters' are women with considerable anatomical knowledge, whose work in the birthing chamber includes the manipulation of surgeons' tools to deliver dead babies. By contrast, bother Sermon (Ladies Companion, 141) and Wolveridge (Speculum, 94) assume that such matters are the prerogative of men, and Chamberlen's express purpose in translating Mauriceau is to teach women the limits of their permitted competence....Such skepticism about women's abilities grows to a vehement attack in the unpublished work of a man midwife, Percival Willughby. On almost every page of his unfinished books, his female counterparts are castigated as 'ignorant,' most especially for their purported tendency to be overly interventionalist in birth. Willughby presents as his own invention the advice that is generally best to let nature take its course and male historians of midwifery have taken at face value his insistence that his patience in the birth chamber was unusual.

'In my first days of ignorance, I thought that it was the best way to suffmidwives to stretch the labia vulvae with their hands and fingers, when the throwes approached. But friendly nature in time shewed mee my mistaken errour. Through the remoteness and large distance of severall places unto

I was called, the women, in the meantime, keeping the labouring woman warm and quiet, and the midwife desisting from using violence by such usage I found the woman oft happily delivered before my coming (Observations, 6).'

*Whilst Willughby attributes this lesson to 'friendly nature,' his acknowledgement that the same thing happened in 'severall places' suggests, rather, that the unnecessary and painful stretching of the labia he had indulged in was his error, not the women's" (*Elaine Hobby, ed. *The Midwives Book Introduction,* xxiii – xxiv).

The reason I include all of this is to prove the point about how women's gifts of midwifery are nothing to snuff at – even for the misogynistic writings of Jane Sharp's period. What then, does this say

about midwifery and childbirth in general? Naturally, women are much better equipped to handle birthing women because they are women! Jane Sharp and her contemporaries understood the pains of childbirth and how to aid women in making their labor process easier. Many midwives were mothers themselves and could directly relate to what their patients were feeling. This makes women even more special – not only because we are able to bear and give birth to children, but also because we can help each other through the whole process.

On the other side of the globe Chinese queens were treated by female physicians some of whom garnered titles of honor such as a Madam Feng in the Song dynasty. She was known as the lady who brought relief to the nation after curing the dowager Empress of a devastating disease. Another female practitioner during the Ming dynasty cured cases of dysphasia (trouble swallowing or speaking) and yet another female doctor, Li developed theories based on several cases on the healing of gynecological disorders.

Condemned because of Knowledge and Ignorance

While the Egyptians regarded magic as neutral, Romans drew a distinction between good and bad magic. Constructive magic in both healing and divination was not only tolerated but officially endorsed. Black magic or bad witchcraft became a crime. Though they still consulted with oracles and divinatory, it was through stories like those about Medea and Circe that the image of a witch began to mean something evil. Medea is known in most stories as an enchantress. She is often depicted as being a priestess of the goddess Hecate – a Greek Goddess that represents elderly or post-menopausal women. Circe's story involves transforming her enemies, for those who offended her, into animals through the use of magical potions. She was renowned for her knowledge of drugs.

Although Alexander the Great can be blamed for transposing the influence of the sexes in the West, another incredible feat of military conquest invasion had the same influence in the East. A thousand years later and on the other side of the globe in Asia, grew the most influential martial empire that the world had ever seen in the 13th century. The Mongols from Siberia and Mongolia came to be known as fierce warriors and their reputation spread all over the world. However, these harsh warriors had religion, too. Shamanism was the Mongols central religion at that time and had been for thousands of years prior to the rise of Kublai Khan and his sons. The most famous of these, Genghis Khan, would form the largest conquered kingdom in the history of the world. The force behind this amazing family was Kublai's mother Chinggis Khan who set the stage for all of her sons to become great kings (khans). The European missionaries who visited Asia at this time were so impressed with her that one physician wrote that "(I doubt) if I were to see among the race of women another who is so remarkable a woman as this."

Chinggis Khan was a Nestorian Christian but she saw that religious tolerance was needed if her sons were to be successful as leaders of such a vast and diversified empire as this was. She had pushed her sons to protect the religious organizations within the Mongol empire. She also drummed into her son Kublai the idea that the "race of women is superior to the race of men".

Kublai however, found himself more inclined with the Chinese way of thinking. He knew that he would need the people's expertise in ruling over 100 million Chinese with so correspondingly few Mongols. The Chinese had the knowledge of collecting taxes, making silk and ruling vast territories, and he needed this information. He moved the capital of Mongolia to modern day Beijing and became a great patron of Chinese art, theatre and culture.

Unfortunately, he also changed the ancient doctrines of the Mongol religion. Where Shamanism used to be its predominant faith, it now began spreading the beliefs of Confucianism, Buddhism, Hinduism and later Islam. These faiths flourished and were protected throughout the Mongol empire up until 1300 AD. Many years after the reign of Kublai Khan, women were no longer the prominent sex as leaders or shamans. They now had to endure the same restraints imposed on Chinese women. This would lead to the persecutions of female shamans, healers and witches imposed by the newly influential religious teachings of Buddhism, Hinduism and Islam.

Ancient Chinese women lived by the dictates spelled out by Confucius's teachings. Women were not considered equal to men and were not educated or even literate. Growing up a young woman had to obey and listen to her father and other male members of her family. Women were not given names in ancient China but were designated as "daughter number 1 or 2, etc."

Even after marriage she was nothing more than a slave to her husband and couldn't even raise her voice without physical retribution. If her husband were to die, she would not be allowed to remarry, if she did so it meant the death penalty. Her primary job was to bear sons for her husband, since she was nothing more than part of his property.

However, as we shall see, the Mongol religions were not the only ones to change the world with the spread of their beliefs. While the Far East was changing into martial-law states, the West was beginning to become more war-like as well. The largest civilizations known at the time were struggling to conquer the smaller groups of people around them while at the same time trying to eliminate each other in the endless race of domination. The Persians, Greeks, Romans, Egyptians, and Babylonians were establishing their laws, customs, and religious beliefs to their corners of the world that they conquered. As their realm of influence expanded, they began to use their religious teachings to influence their newly conquered subjects with their new spiritual views.

As Christianity and Islam spread, so did the fear of witchcraft. These faiths were slowly engulfing and changing the pagan ways. Christian saints were replacing the established personas of the pagan deities. This made conversion much easier, as this transition was more palatable to their new subjects. For example, the earth mother goddess Isis of Egypt was replaced by the Virgin Mary. The Madonna theme (i.e. the relationship between the goddess and her son, the god of men) was kept in line with the Egyptian beliefs. The Egyptian sign of life, the ankh, was replaced by the Christian cross. The Coptic Church still adapts this shape of the cross as their unique symbolic form of Christianity.

An Ankh, the key of life.

In early biblical history the powers of witchcraft were deemed as gifts from God since even Moses was looked upon as some sort of wizard or magician, as exemplified in Acts 7:22: "*Moses 'was learned in all the wisdom of the Egyptians, and he was mighty in words and deeds.*"

This passage demonstrates how the early Jews viewed the prowess of Moses as a great magician. In the Book of Exodus, he confronts the Pharaoh and performs several magical feats that overcome the magicians of Egypt and convince Pharaoh to free the Israelites. Here, Moses' magic is greater and defeats the Egyptian magic, but it is considered "good" because Moses performs his magic to serve God. It could also have been viewed as "good magic" because he was a man performing magical feats and not a woman.

On a decidedly gloomier note are these very unfortunate passages from the Bible. Some of these verses have been horribly misunderstood during the witchcraft trials in Europe. Those Biblical interpreters ruined thousands of innocent female lives. One such passage is from Deuteronomy 18:9-14.

> 9*When thou art come into the land which the LORD thy God giveth thee, thou shalt not learn to do after the abominations of those nations.*
>
> 10*There shall not be found among you any one that maketh his son or his daughter to pass through the fire, or that* ***useth divination, or an observer of times, or an enchanter, or a witch.***
>
> 11*Or* ***a charmer, or a consulter with familiar spirits, or a wizard, or a necromancer****.*
>
> 12*For all that do these things are an abomination unto the LORD: and because of these abominations the LORD thy God doth drive them out from before thee.*
>
> 13*Thou shalt be perfect with the LORD thy God.*
>
> 14*For these nations, which thou shalt possess, hearkened unto* ***observers of times, and unto diviners****: but as for thee, the LORD thy God hath not suffered thee so to do.*

Then, there is Exodus 22:18: ***"Thou shalt not suffer a witch to live."*** This provided scriptural justification for some Christians to place many unfortunate women on trial in Europe and America. In the Bible, the word "witch" is a translation of the Hebrew *kashaph*, which means "sorcerer". As such, a more familiar translation would be "one who uses magic to harm others".

As Christianity took the lead and flourished throughout much of Europe and the Middle East, the church flexed its new muscles and proclaimed that all pre-Christian goddesses and gods were false. This new ideology led to the destruction of pagan shrines and temples along with their priests and priestesses. These acts took their toll of innocent lives through condemnation, trials, tortures, and executions.

A few hundred years later we see the same rhetoric coming from Islam's Mohammed when he condemned and then destroyed the 360 idols that were placed around the Ka'ba in Mecca saying *"Truth has arrived and falsehood has perished for falsehood is by its nature bound to perish" (Koran 17:81)*. This ended a very close relationship with the local deities that had lasted for thousands of years.

Muslims still believe in the existence of *Sihr* or black magic. There is a reference of a prayer (Surah Al-Falaq) to ward off evil spirits or intensions:

> *Say: I seek refuge with the Lord of the Dawn From the mischief of created things; From the mischief of Darkness as it overspreads; From the mischief of those who practise secret arts; And from the mischief of the envious one as he practises envy. (Quran 113:1-5,)*

This quote in the Quran mentions what happens to anyone who practices sorcery.

> *And they follow that which the devils falsely related against the kingdom of Solomon. Solomon disbelieved not; but the devils disbelieved, teaching mankind sorcery and that which was revealed to the two angels in Babel, Harut and Marut.... And surely they do know that he who trafficketh therein will have no (happy) portion in the Hereafter; and surely evil is the price for which they sell their souls, if they but knew. (Quran 2:102)*

In much the same way, the Christian Spanish colonial empire had persecuted women shamans in the Philippines. They would call them "devil-ridden old women" and "witches" while destroying their shrines and sacred objects. In addition, in South America, Mayan oracles and shamans faced the same treatment. A young Tzoltzil priestess named María Candelaria raised an insurrection in Chiapas in 1712 by claiming to have seen a vision of the Virgin Mary. She did this to resist the repression of her indigenous religion from the Spaniards.

A Jesuit priest, Acosta, wrote and accused Peruvian witches of being shape shifters that could journey through the skies and foretell the future "by means of certain stones or other things they highly venerate." He and other Spanish sources agreed that the witches were mostly old women. The colonials imposed their own preconceptions on Peruvian shamans as well and persecuted the Quechua and Aymara tribal women shamans as witches.

The Peruvian Inquisition forbade seeking knowledge through dreams or signs in the sky or through vision quests: *"the said women other times go out to the country by day and at night, and take certain brews of herbs and roots, called achuma and chamico and coca, with which they deceive themselves and numb their senses, and the illusions and fantastic scenes which they experience there, they think and claim afterwards as revelations, or certain news of what will happen."*

Inquisitors tried the curandera Juana Icha for healing with the power of the old Quechua gods. She had offered corn meal, coca and chicha to the mountain spirit *Apo Parato*. An Indian informer told the monks that she "worships the earth and the stars and cries to the water."

Meanwhile in Europe, Witch-hunting spread like wildfire as the Middle Ages ended and the plagues that ravaged her cities subsided. The Christian sport of the inquisition reared its ugly head and spread like a plague itself to the Americas. The Inquisitors' reasoning was that the women obtained their skills in healing from the devil. Spinsters, widows, and other women who refused to conform to the expectations of their low social status, including female healers and midwives, were frequent targets of witch-hunts. Little evidence was needed to convict these unfortunate ladies. One accusation from a so-called tormented village member was enough for a conviction.

During the witch-hunts that occurred amid the 13th to 18th centuries, women had been driven out of medicine and were not allowed formal education. In England and France, the passing of licensure laws and the formation of guilds in the 13th century prohibited women from the practice of medicine. Even midwifery, previously a woman's field, was dominated by men by the 19th century. Women were excluded from practicing in a professional capacity, though they continued to practice medicine in the domestic setting as nurses and midwives, positions considered subordinate to male physicians. What is truly disturbing is the total lack of Christian compassion or practicality from any of the decisions by the judges in any of these witch hunt cases. The judges looked upon these accused as inhumane demons to be destroyed.

In 1595 Nicholas Remy a French magistrate who became famous as a witch hunter and prosecutor wrote a book on his exploits called "Demonolatry" which became the common handbook on the subject for many years. He clearly states that women are the main sources for witches as this examination of Barbeline Rayel in 1587 states.

> *"Barbeline Rayel (Blainville, Jan. 1587) said that the women exceeded the men in number, since it was much easier for the Demon to impose his deceits upon that sex and observation that Torquemada also made in his "Hexamaron". Certainly I remember to have heard of far more cases of women than men; and it is not unreasonable that this scum of humanity should be drawn chiefly from the feminine sex, and that we should hear mostly of women simplists, wise women, sorceresses, enchantresses, and masked Lombard women. For in estimating numbers and frequency it is enough to reckon those who form the majority. Fabius (In declamationibus) says that women are more prone to believe in witchcraft; and Pliny (XXV, 11) that women excel in their knowledge of witchcraft.*

In the *Malleus Maleficarum* (a famous discourse on witches, written in 1486 by Heinrich Kramer, an Inquisitor of the Catholic Church) has yet more evidence of this biasness towards women as witches.

> *"Now the wickedness of women is spoken of in Ecclesiasticus xxv: There is no head above the head of a serpent, and there is no wrath above the wrath of a woman. I had rather dwell*

> *with a lion and a dragon than to keep house with a wicked woman. And among which in that place precedes and follows about a wicked woman, he concludes: All wickedness is but little to the wickedness of a woman*
>
> *Others again have propounded other reasons why there are more superstitious women found than men. And the first is, that they are more credulous; and since the chief aim of the devil is to corrupt faith, therefore he rather attacks them. See Ecclesiasticus xix: He that is quick to believe is light-minded and shall be diminished. The second reason is, that women an naturally more impressionable, and more ready to receive the influence of disembodied spirit; and that when they use this quality well they are very good, but when they use it ill they are very evil.*
>
> *The second reason is that women are naturally more impressionable and more ready to receive the influence of a disembodied spirit; and that when they use this quality well they are very good but when they use it ill they are very evil.*
>
> *The third reason is that they have slippery tongues and are unable to conceal from their fellow-women those things which by evil arts they know; and, since they are weak they find an easy and secret manner of vindicating themselves by witchcraft. . . .*
>
> *For as regards intellect, or the understanding of spiritual things, they seem to be of a different nature from men, a fact which is vouched for by the logic of authorities, backed by various examples from Scripture. Terrence says; Women are intellectually like children. And Lactantius: "No woman under- stood philosophy except Temeste. And Proverbs xi, as it were describing a woman says: As a jewel of gold in a swine's snout, so is a fair woman which is without discretion.*

It is a wonder that the majority of the cases (if not all) were judged and prosecuted by men. Only men were considered to be mentally capable of performing the duties of judge, jury and prosecutors all within the male dominated confines of the church. These men believed in their hearts that what they were doing was a religious duty in trying to control what they deemed was evil. This zeal drove them to persecute and execute these poor women.

The numbers of victims by these so called courts of law is staggering, and it was an even greater wonder that wisdom, providence or compassion never once made these men come to their senses. It is estimated between the years of 1400 to 1750 that there may have been up to 100,000 individuals tried as witches in Europe and the Americas, half of which may have been executed.

In some Central African areas, malicious magic users are believed by locals to be the source of terminal illnesses such as AIDS and cancer. In some cases, children may be accused of being witches. For example, a young niece may be blamed for the illness of a relative. Her aunt has the right to accuse her of witchcraft and likely the niece will be severely punished or killed for her "crime." Most of these cases of abuse go unreported since the members of their communities that witness such abuse are too afraid of being ostracized or accused of being accomplices.

In the most modern of Arabian countries we still see signs of persecution of witches. One example is of a poor woman named Fawza Falih Muhammad Ali, a Saudi woman. She made international headlines after she was condemned to death for practicing witchcraft in 2006. As of August 2008, she was still facing execution. The illiterate, poor woman was detained by religious police in 2005 and allegedly beaten and forced to fingerprint a confession that she could not read. Among her accusers was a man who she supposedly made impotent.

In March of 2008 another "witch" was killed by villagers in the Indian state of Chhattisgarh. The poor 40 year old woman, Phool Kunwar, was dragged from her house, beaten with sticks and sharp rods, and then burned with a red hot iron and shoved into a large fire.

In another Indian incident, a 55 year old woman was hacked to death. Her hut was set afire allegedly by her relatives, who had branded her as a witch. The event occurred at Raghunathpur under Gajole police station. The officer in charge of the police station, Maskesdur Rehman, said, "*Baha Soren, whose husband Dukhu Soren had died last year, used to stay in a hut next to those of her two sons.*" Her elder son, Sunil Murmu, found her hut going up in flames when he came out, hearing his mother crying for help. The woman was bleeding profusely and trying to drag herself out of the hut. *"Sunil jumped into the burning hut lifted her and brought her out. But she breathed her last soon,"* said the officer. Rehman said there were multiple injuries, suspected to be caused by a sickle, on all parts of her body. *"That her hut was set ablaze even after bludgeoning her with a sharp weapon suggests that the attackers wanted to make sure that she was dead,"* Rehman said. *"It was superstition and ill beliefs still prevailing in the tribal society that have led to the incident,"* he added. According to police, Raju Besra, who is Baha's 25 year old nephew, had been ailing for over one year. His family members and some neighbors used to say the youth was unwell because of the black magic practiced by the woman.

In 1998 in another Indian village, Vansva, a 55 year old woman, Gangaben, suspected to be a witch, was murdered by her nephew in this Gujarat village. Gangaben and her daughter, Liliben, were allegedly assaulted by Mangabhai Chhanabhai Rathod, Gangaben's nephew, who suspected them of being witches and responsible for his wife's ill health. Rathod, who was arrested three nights later by the Ichhapore police, has since confessed to the murder, but maintained that Gangaben and her daughter were responsible for his wife's mental problems. While indicating the grip of superstition and *bhagats* (witch doctors) on rural people, the incident also had other villagers taking up for the women, maintaining that there was nothing "supernatural"' about them.

In Nigeria, a deadly but lucrative trade involving the performance of exorcisms had flourished due to superstition and fear. Thousands of children in the Niger valley have been unjustly accused of being witches. They are commonly blamed for the causes of many calamities or misfortunes in their villages. Some have been forcibly driven from their villages, tortured, and even killed because of the superstitions. The causes of the superstitions are false innuendos that are started by rogue pastors that are literally making a killing by charging huge fees for exorcisms. These unfortunate children bear the scars of a witch branding, burns, machete cuts, as well as starvation. One "Bishop" is purported to have bragged about killing up to 110 people, many of whom were children.

In 2006 over 25,000 children in Kinshasa of the Democratic Republic of the Congo have been accused of witchcraft and tossed out of their villages. In one instance, Kinshasa police arrested 14 suspected victims of "penis snatching." These are people that would say that they were sorcerers using black magic to steal, shrink, or make men's penises disappear. Then, they would extort money for cures. The police arrested them to avoid bloodshed as other unfortunate "penis snatchers." In the past, they have been beaten to death by mob rule.

The Current Negativity toward Women, Especially Amongst the Major Religions

Let us say from the start that we, the authors, are not anti-religious at all. On the contrary, we both have come from strong religious backgrounds and families. For this reason, we believe that most religions are generally good for people as long as the main beliefs of the religion are not forced upon non-believers. Freedom of religion is one of the most important tenets of actually living in a free society. Scientific evidence suggests that individuals that belong to a faith are more likely to live longer, happier, and healthier lives in a society espousing the freedom of religion.

I was brought up as a Roman Catholic and became an altar boy and at one time was seriously considering becoming a Priest. Heidi was brought up as a very devout Episcopalian Church member. We both still believe in God but not the war God of the Judeo/Christian Bible.

(Heidi) The main figures or prophets in the major religions such as Jesus, Siddhartha, and Mohammed are/were admirable leaders. It is not difficult to see why people would want to be like them or follow them. Their teachings are definitely something to be studied and sought after. In fact, about 90% of the entire world's populations admit that they believe in some type of higher power that created human beings – either indirectly through evolution, intelligent design, or directly through Creationism. We are very fortunate in the United States that we have many choices as far as what we want to believe in. You can be anything from an Atheist to an Eclectic Pagan!

While these faith-based systems are generally positive, it is hard to ignore past injurious events that have forever shaped the way certain religious customs are practiced. Although most of the major religions have made some attempts at accepting women in more leadership positions, these efforts hardly eradicate centuries of ridicule and abuse. There are several examples in just about every major religion where women are still not seen as equals with men.

We may ask ourselves, how did women go from being the heads of many societies to being submissive subjects of men? There are many historical experts that have theories about this subject. We have discussed some of these theories above.

Could a woman become a Priest, Rabbi or Imam among the major religions a hundred years ago? The answer would have to be No. If we ask this same question today, the answer is a bit confusing because of all the different moderate movements within each of the religions. Let us look at the religious leaders 1500 to 2000 years ago. There were no female Priests, Imams or Rabbis. Yes, there were nuns but that was as high as women were allowed to go. If not to a nunnery, women were relegated to becoming nurses, cooks, cleaners and concubines – if you did not become a wife and mother. Today, this second class citizenship in religions is just now beginning to break down the male dominated barricade.

The new Goddess arises

It wasn't until quite recently with the dawning of the Women's Rights movement in the 1960's in the United States that women finally got to be heard. They began to be recognized as intelligent, philosophical, political and religious leaders again due to some events that we will discuss.

Title VII of the Civil Rights Act in 1964 barred discrimination in employment on the basis of race and sex. At the same time, it established the Equal Employment Opportunity Commission (EEOC) to investigate complaints and impose penalties on individuals and companies that violated this Act.

In 1966, The National Organization for Women (NOW) was founded by a group of feminists including Betty Friedan. The largest women's rights group in the U.S NOW seeks to end sexual discrimination, especially in the workplace, by means of legislative lobbying, litigation, and public demonstrations.

In 1971 *Ms. Magazine* was first published as a sample insert in *New York* magazine; 300,000 copies were sold out in 8 days. The first regular issue was published in July 1972. The magazine became the major forum for feminist voices. Cofounder and editor, Gloria Steinem, was launched as an icon of the modern feminist movement.

In 1972, women saw the Equal Rights Amendment (ERA) passed by Congress and sent to the states for ratification. Finally, with these actions of the Women's Equal Rights movement, ladies steadily broke ground as leaders. With this new reformation also, the three major religions had to cave in to a modern way of thinking. Progress became excruciatingly slow and exasperating to many religious. Many women faced fierce, bigoted persecution when they tried to make their way back into a spiritual leadership position. Even today, there are many sects of religious institutions that do not allow women in their highest positions.

However, despite these setbacks, there are some religious sects today that are advocating women in these roles. For example, in Judaism, nearly all of its secular branches have found one way or another within the protocol of Jewish law, to ordain women as Rabbis and Cantors since the '70s – even the Orthodox branch.

An article in *The Jerusalem Post* in October of 2008 discussed such an unusual event for Orthodox Jewish women. It stated that the ordination was a major change in gender roles. The Hartman Institute, which was founded by Rabbi David Hartman, would open a 4 year program to prepare women of all denominations for rabbinic ordination. It will prepare the new rabbis to teach at the Jewish high school level in North America.

The feeling was that they had been denying themselves of 50% of their potential rabbis and that the distinctions between men and women were irrelevant in this modern age.

In the 20th and now the 21st century, the largest institutions in North America that continue to deny equal rights to women are conservative Christian denominations. These include Roman Catholicism, Eastern Orthodoxy, as well as many denominations within Protestantism such as the Church of Jesus Christ of Latter-day Saints and the Southern Baptist Convention. These groups interpret Bible passages as requiring women and men to follow defined, sexually determined roles. In marriage, for example, men are to lead and women are expected to be submissive to their husbands and be followers. In religious institutions women are not to be placed in a position of authority over men. A logical result of these beliefs is that women are not to be considered for ordination. There is no wiggle room here, unless their theologians follow more liberal Christian theologians and take a different approach to biblical interpretation. Some denominations, like Episcopalian, have recently accepted women into leadership roles and have ordained several as priests.

Until recently this was also the feeling of most Muslims. However, now they are beginning to see the light as female Imams are beginning to show their graceful faces in mosque pulpits. In New York City in 2005, a Friday prayer of just a hundred mixed gender believers was a ground breaking event. Pictures of Dr. Amina Wadud leading the prayers caused quite a stir in the Middle East. The event was part of a growing movement to counter the segregation of women in US mosques denying them leadership roles.

In October 2008 in Europe, the first female Imam made her dramatic appearance in Belgium when Hawaria Fattah was granted this rank. A mother of three and a professor of Social and Islamic Studies, Fattah supervises the preaching activities for women at their mosque. Still she will not be allowed to deliver sermons of the Friday prayers or even lead prayers. Her role will be focused on supervising the preaching and guidance activities for the women only.

Even in China, Muslim Women are getting into the act as women there have wanted to become Imams for centuries. Women such as Wang Shouying lead other women in prayers and chants at The Little White Mosque in China's western Ningxia region. Wang is the current prayer leader in a long line of female imams chipping away at a largely male dominated faith. She feels that she must train and educate other females to become good Muslims. She feels that female imams are more capable of doing so because they can relate to females in ways that men cannot.

The fact that women are finally making progress into the higher religious ranks is a testament to their fortitude, perseverance, and faith. These positions mark the last bastions of male dominated realms that at one time looked impenetrable.

Your Special Gift of Procreation

(Heidi) Let's face it. Sometimes, it seems so hard to be a woman living in this world. Most of us have full-time jobs or school. Some of us have these things plus a husband or partner, and children. We can top all this off with taking care of a household, paying bills, taking the dog to the vet, and taking care of aging parents' needs. When you add all these things together, it can be very overwhelming. In today's American society, women have hardly any time to themselves. Despite this reality, do you still find yourself criticizing the way you live? Perhaps you think that you are not a good enough mother, you don't please your husband or partner, you don't go to church as often as you would like, you don't have the money to make ends meet, or that there's never enough time in the day to get everything done that needs to get done.

As a woman myself, I completely understand the difficulties of dealing with everyday life. Sometimes I can get caught up in the hectic routine of schedules, appointments, chores, errands, and career. Oh yeah, did I mention that wonderful visitor from down below that makes her appearance every month uninvited? I am one of the lucky ladies who have a very hard time dealing with my monthly cycle. I used to absolutely dread my period knowing that the cramps would be so bad that I was going to have to miss school and work. I knew that I would have to isolate myself from my friends and family because my emotional state was like a ride on the Vomit Comet.

I got better by taking herbal supplements before and during menstruation. However, I also took up yoga, martial arts, and meditation to help me deal with all the stress of dealing with the roller coaster of emotions. I am not suggesting that everyone should be like me and do these specific things, but I do know that these activities helped me to be a happier, less stressed-out woman who appreciated her life to the fullest. During my meditations, I reflected on how lucky I am to be a woman. Despite all the pain and suffering that we as women have to go through, we still have special gifts and abilities that men can never have or achieve. This is something we should be actively thankful for.

As far as childbirth is concerned, I realize that I have limited knowledge in this, as I am not a mother yet, as of writing this sentence. However, I have read many books and articles that lead me to believe that it is best for most mothers to give birth as naturally as possible. The accounts of veteran mothers of their natural childbirth experiences seem to be extremely satisfactory; while the stories from mothers who had cesarean sections or gave birth in a hospital had many more negative accounts.

For example, I spoke to a woman that was a first time mother and gave birth in the hospital and opted for an epidural because she was afraid of the pain. The epidural ended up not working properly and she was pushing for a long time. She still experienced excruciating pain and was totally exhausted.

On the other hand, I spoke to another mother who had given birth at home with a midwife. This mother had a much more pleasant and comfortable experience. She was surrounded by loving members of her family and a midwife whom she trusted. The midwife stayed with her throughout her whole labor and delivery – helping her through each contraction and giving her a lot of encouragement. The woman ended up giving birth to a healthy baby boy and was able to give birth to him in the way that she chose. No one made any demands or pushed her to make any unnecessary decisions.

Although this woman's experience was extremely positive, there are many cases where a home birth would simply not be an option. Unfortunately, many pregnant women experience difficulties during their term and cannot have a baby unsupervised outside a hospital. Even more unfortunate are the women who may have been able to have their

child at home but could not at the last minute due to complications that desperately called for medical intervention – such as a C-section.

However, I do believe that medical practitioners are beginning to see the benefits of fewer interventions. For example, I read a study done by Sutter Health (a hospital network based in Northern California) involving several of their maternal patients regarding the benefits of a more hands-off approach. The results were quite revealing. Sutter Health makes five conclusions based on their data.

1.) Admit women to labor unit when cervical dilation is ≥ 3 cm. Their research shows that women who are confined to the hospital bed in early labor have a more difficult time progressing and becomes more painful. When Sutter Health patients were admitted during their active stages of labor, there were fewer incidents of C-sections, significantly shorter labors, and better APGAR scores for the newborn.

2.) Induce labor only when medically necessary. For first-time mothers, inducing in the 37th – 41st week increases the chances of their labor lasting a long time and becoming more difficult. Also, they are two to three more times likely to receive a C-section, suffer 3rd to 4th degree lacerations, and a lower Apgar score.

3.) Perform episiotomies selectively. Recent studies have shown that episiotomies show no medical benefit – although they used to be performed routinely. In first time mothers, especially, episiotomies were shown to increase the risk for third and fourth degree lacerations, which are more likely to lead to bowel incontinence – temporary or permanent.

4.) Provide continuous labor support. Studies showed that women who received constant support and care throughout their labor experienced shorter labors, less use of anesthesia or pain medication, less C-sections, fewer episiotomies, and a more satisfactory birth experience.

5.) Educate women throughout the prenatal process. Expectant mothers need to be informed on new studies that come out about childbirth and delivery – especially first-time mothers. Also, there is a great need for medical practitioners to be on the same page so that women receive consistent information instead of conflicting views.

In conclusion, Sutter Health had this to say about their goals for their maternal patients.

> *"Over the past few decades, the centuries-old concept of labor support has been downplayed in favor of fetal monitoring and other high tech, medical interventions. The pendulum is swinging back, however, now that scientific evidence has validated the benefits of labor support for mothers and babies. FPAD [First Pregnancy and Delivery Project] combines the best elements of high and low tech and encourages affiliates to integrate labor support into their labor and delivery practices."* (www.sutterhealth.org)

This "new" viewpoint that many hospitals are beginning to adopt have been supported by midwives for generations. Leila McCracken, a writer for *Midwifery Today* magazine wrote an article called "A Declaration of Rights for Childbearing Women." She lists 13 specific rights that ALL women have in the child birthing process. I was so moved by her statements that I felt led to share them all here with you in full.

> *"Birth's integrity diminishes as obstetric interventions multiply. The rights of women and babies must be recognized.*

1. *All women have the right to sacred, fantastic, profound and loving birth experiences. Childbirth must never be viewed by birth attendants as routine, cumbersome or insignificant.*

2. *Childbirth must happen in physical and emotional privacy. Women's vaginas in birth are as sacrosanct as they are at any other time; routinely penetrating them with fingers, forceps, scissors or hooks is a severe violation against the most fundamental rights of women to privacy and protection of the self. Women have the right to vocalize, move about, assume any birthing positions they like, and allow their births to unfold uniquely, without feeling the need to gain the acceptance and approval of their birth attendants. Women have the right to refuse birth attendants altogether. All hospital staff, midwives, family members, and friends of birthing women must have full consent before viewing the childbirth process. Women's bodies are never to be regarded*

as learning aids. No institution has the right to impose spectators on any woman's birth.

3. *Women have the right and power of "No": if they understand interventions and procedures and refuse to allow them to be implemented, their refusals must be respected by all medical personnel. Childbearing women will not be barraged with attempts at mind changing or browbeating.*

4. *All women must be physically safe at birth. Instruments of routine interventions seriously harm the bodies of women: scissors, knives, harmful drugs, forceps, catheters, hooks, needles, fingers, tubes, and razors can be classified as tools of assault. Extreme caution must be used whenever obstruction of the natural birth process is considered.*

5. *All babies, either in the process of being born or after their births, deserve not to be harmed: forceps, scalp hooks, violent extraction, careless handling, suctioning catheters, ventilating equipment, intravenous devices, and an oxygen-deprived birth environment—caused by either pain-relieving or induction drugs—all cause a great deal of distress to new babies and can upset their future well-being.*

6. *All women have the right to complete and immediate access to information regarding all procedures done—either to them or their babies—in pregnancy, birth and the postpartum. Women must be informed of any potential harm of all procedures, regardless of the length of time the explaining takes (except in the most extreme cases). Women or their birth attendants cannot take "informed consent" lightly. Women have the right to be made aware of nonintrusive alternatives to common hospital procedures—such as the superior safety of giving birth at home, water birth as a safe method of pain relief, and the advantages of natural, private methods of induction of labor.*

7. *It must be recognized as a criminal act to mutilate women's bodies in childbirth.*

8. *All women must have easy, free access to information that illuminates the natural childbirth process for them—information*

that helps them prepare for their births and assists them in preparation for care of their newborns. This information must be given in a way that does not view birth as a dangerous, biological anomaly, but as a natural, joyous one.

9. *All women have the right to give birth wherever and with whomever they choose, and to know the safety statistics of any individuals and/or institutions they choose to give birth with/in.*

10. *All women have the right of complete access to all their own recorded medical information, as well as access to knowledgeable people for whom the information poses no personal liability.*

11. *The newborn must be viewed as a natural appendage of its mother. Mother and child must remain together, in quiet dignity, for as long as the mother desires. Handling of the baby by anyone other than its mother for the first hours of life is to be strongly discouraged.*

12. *Ongoing breastfeeding information and support must be available to all women.*

13. *The rights of women are inalienable, and will not be undermined by any government, male partner, professional birth attendant, nor any individual or group of individuals whose interests do not reflect the wishes of parturient women, regarding their own or their babies' safety and well-being."* (McCracken, 1999).

Although I realize that many of you may disagree with some or all of these "rights," I believe that Ms. McCracken does bring up some interesting points about how women should feel about their pregnancies. She states a few times above that it is a woman's right to choose how she wants to give birth and with whom – whether she chooses to give birth in a hospital with pain medication or at home with a midwife and no pain medication. It is strictly the mother's choice and no one else's. I have spoken with some mothers who feel very strongly about this issue. Some say that the only way to give birth is naturally with no drugs. Other women say that "you're crazy" if you don't choose an epidural. Whatever the reasons these women chose to give birth in their way, the point is that no one has the right to enforce their personal beliefs about birth on anyone else. Each birth is unique and special for a particular

mother. That is her sacred right. I know a woman in her mid 40's that has three children. She chose to have a C-section with all three of them because she did not want to go through labor and wanted to choose her babies' birthdays. Although I do not agree with giving birth this way, I respect her decision, and I do not criticize her for it. She had a right to give birth this way and no one has the right to say anything to her about it.

Women are often portrayed by the media as being overly emotional, irrational, and selfish people. Women are thought to be stupid if they are beautiful and intelligent if they are homely. It seems that we are constantly criticized by family members, friends, bosses, co-workers, peers, and even our own children. We're made to feel that we can't do anything right – no matter how hard we try. *Sometimes* we are our own worst critics. Men are always praised for how logical and intelligent they are. They are the ones who have it together and seem to always have the answer for everything, right?

Wrong. What many men *and* women don't understand is that being a woman is a very special privilege that men secretly would love to have. Women have traits that most men only wish they could have, but cannot. The fact that we are so perceptive and can tell how a person is feeling just by listening to the sound of their voice, or that we can express our emotions freely and passionately is something that men are actually jealous of! Expressing emotions is a perfect way to maintain your health. There is nothing wrong with crying at good movie or talking on the phone for hours to a friend about how great it was to see that you finally noticed your weight loss when you stepped on the bathroom scale this morning.

There are many gifts that women are blessed to have. We have already discussed expressing deep emotions and being very perceptive and empathetic towards others. Even so, the most important and special gift of all is, of course, procreation. Although it is true that without male sperm we could not give birth, the fact remains that the majority of procreation relies solely on women. Have you ever wondered why women alone are the ones who give birth? Why is it that the male of our species plays only a very small role in creating a child? There are other species of animals in which the male takes the lead role in the birthing process.

The seahorse is a prime example of a gender role reversal in birthing offspring. The female will lay the eggs and place them in the belly of the father who then donates the sperm to the eggs. He proceeds to carry the eggs until they are ready to hatch. In fact, when the babies are ready to emerge, the male seahorse's abdomen undergoes muscular "contractions" to expel his offspring! Surprisingly, the male seahorses' body produces prolactin after the eggs have been fertilized – the same hormone that is produced by pregnant women! Scientists are still not sure exactly why male seahorses become impregnated instead of the females. However, the whole process could not happen if it were not for the female providing the eggs for the male to fertilize and care for. The male seahorses are also at the mercy of the females' heat cycle. If she is not ready to give her mature eggs to the male, then he cannot provide sperm for her eggs. He is totally reliant on her ability to provide the eggs at the appropriate time.

Is it not similar to humans? Men are totally reliant on women's monthly cycle to reproduce. He has to provide sperm at just the right time in order for our egg to be fertilized. Does this not make women powerful? Sometimes, I think women forget how empowered they really are as far as the abilities of our own bodies go. You will recall earlier in this chapter when we explained how women's menstrual cycles, our highly perceptive abilities, and our ability to procreate played a large role in the oppression of women in modern religions, higher education institutes, and by male leaders.

In Celtic society, women were not only respected as equal citizens to men, but they were also allowed to hold high places in Druid cultures as oracles or even Druid priests. In the book, *The Druids*, by Peter Berressford Ellis, he talks about just how much women were revered in ancient Celtic cultures.

> *"Several Greek and Latin writers speak of Dryades or Druidesses, and the existence of such female Druids is certainly confirmed by Celtic sources. One has to bear in mind the fascinating role of women in Celtic society as opposed to their position in other European cultures. The rights and positions of Celtic women far exceeded those of Greece or Rome. The position of women was vastly different. From history, we find numerous female figures of supreme authority, for example,*

Boudicca (Boadicea), the ruler of Iceni, who was accepted as war leader by southern British tribes in 61 A.D. She is perhaps, the most famous of the female Celtic ruler. According to Dio Cassius, Boudicca appears as a priestess of the goddess 'Andrasta', described as a goddess of victory. This seems to be the same goddess as Andarte, worshipped by the Vocontii of Gaul. An argument could, therefore, be made that Boudicca was a Druidess as well as a queen."(Ellis, 91)

Celtic women were also considered to be powerful warriors – ones which many women and men sought after for training and guidance. Ellis explains here.

*"Female warrior queens appear in many stories, notably Medb of Connacht who commanded her army and personally slew the hero-warrior Cethren in combat. Scáthach, a female champion, was the principal of the martial arts to Cúchulainn. Her sister, Aoife, was another famous female warrior and, as great as the hero Cúchulainn was, he had to resort to trickery to overcome her prowess (*Ellis, 92*)."*

Ellis even writes about how women were leaders of their own tribe, or chieftains.

*"We hear of the earlier Goulash chieftains, Monomers, who commanded the Celtic tribes in their wanderings into Iberia (*Ellis, 92*)."*

I especially found this piece of information astonishing about the rights of women in Celtic society. Almost everywhere else in Europe did not have nearly the respect for women that the Celts had as you see here in Ellis' work:

"The position of women, as it emerges in the Breton Law system of Ireland, at a time when women were treated as mere chattels in most European societies, was amazingly advanced. Women could be found in many professions, even as lawyers and judges, such as Bright, a celebrated woman-Breton. Women had the right to succession and, as we have seen, could emerge as a supreme authority, though kingship, in the historic period, was mainly confined to males. A woman could inherit

> *property and remained the owner of any property she bought into marriage. If the marriage broke up, then she not only took out of it her own property but any property that her husband had given her during the marriage. Divorce, of course, was permitted and a woman could divorce her husband just as a husband could divorce his wife. If a man had 'fallen from his dignity', that is, committed a crime and lost his civil rights or had been outcast from society, it did not affect the position of his wife. A woman was responsible for her own debts and not those of her husband (*Ellis, 94-95*)."*

I tend to focus on Celtic cultures because that is the one I am most familiar with. My ancestry is primarily from these cultures; therefore, they are of great fascination for me. However, as I began to do more research about other cultures, I found some fascinating similarities.

For example, in the pre-Columbian Americas, many Native American cultures both in North and South America have very similar gender roles for women that go back for centuries. There is a book by a group of authors and editors called *Racism in the Lives of Women.* Although the title of this book may be offensive and harsh to some people, I found the book to be rather objective despite its obviously asserting title. The authors explain how women were treated in Native American tribes – specifically, the Lakota.

Apparently, the Lakota people had strong foundations of feminism in their belief system. There is a story about the White Buffalo Calf Woman – a prominent female figure believed to have sprung from the underground. A poignant Lakota member, Luther Standing Bear, was known for saying that women were warriors and that mothers help create the community and guide the children's destiny. He also believed, as many Lakota do, that women and men can share some of the same duties in the household. For example, a man can help a woman in childbirth or in preparing meals, when they are not out hunting. Women, also like the men, had the power to divorce their spouse – essentially tossing them away..

Also, a medicine man of the Sioux people, Crow Dog, has been known to say that a holy woman brought sacred buffalo to the Sioux people. He said that without her, the Sioux would not know how to

live and that the White Buffalo Calf Woman put her mind into their minds.

I know how empowering this information may be to some of you. My purpose in bringing this to you is to make you feel assured and confident in whom you are as a woman. You do not need to be ashamed of your gender, your culture, or where you come from. It does not matter what religion you belong to or what faith you have chosen for yourself. These heartwarming stories and encouraging truths about us are empowering, indeed. I know that finding out about my ancient mothers' pasts was incredible!

Our women ancestors went through a lot of struggles and hardships. They understood the importance of sacrificing for others so that their children could prosper. The burden of reproducing and keeping our species alive has always been our responsibility. In such difficult times as many of our ancestors faced, how did we manage to survive? What would we say to those women who worked very hard so that we could be alive today? I've often thought about my many ancient great-grandmothers and what they must have been like.

How would you like to know what their lives were really like? What would you like to say to your ancient grandmothers if they were right here with you now? Did any of your women ancestors rule over clans and communities? Perhaps they were medicine women or religious leaders. What if we told you that you could speak to these ancestors and find out more about what makes you who you are today? The answer lies within your own body. Those women are still alive in you today. In the next few chapters, we will explain how this is possible and how you can become more aware of a deeper sense of what being a woman really means.

Chapter 3

LifeConscious re-introduced

Definition

How it works in the Background

Our Brain

The Memory of Water

Resonant Frequency

Life is a linear organism

Women's important role

Conclusion

Thousands of candles can be lighted from a single candle,
and the life of the candle will not be shortened.
Happiness never decreases by being shared. ***Buddha***

Definition

The idea of life itself is a mysterious concept, if you stop to think about it, since how is proof of its existence possible in the first place? For instance, we have been searching for this proof of life in our very own solar system during the tenure of my generation with no luck at all. To tell you the truth, I don't think that there are any other forms of life in our solar system. Possibilities of course, are likely on Mars and perhaps Jupiter's ice-encrusted moon, Europe. So far, the robotic rovers on Mars have found nothing that resembles life even though the signs of water at its poles gave us great expectations. So as far as our solar system is concerned earth is the only life bearing hunk of rock that it has.

However, despite this pessimistic outlook, scientists have just recently begun searching for sources of water in space. They postulate that since logically where there is water, there must be life. Water, therefore, is the key to life itself. Much progress searching for water in the universe has been ongoing, and we know that water as ice travels through space all the time on comets and asteroids. We will discuss this subject of water in space later.

We've been hinting so far that water is the key to the success of LifeConscious as well. For those of you who are unfamiliar with LifeConscious, this chapter is for you. To become more intimate about it may I suggest that you find a copy of my first book *LifeConscious – An Alternate Theory to Evolution and Creationism.*

Let's start with my definition of LifeConscious:

LifeConscious:
Pronunciation: līf–kŏn'sheəs

Noun:

It is the linear dissemination of procreative and life sustaining memories from females to their developing young. These memories are distributed by the medium of structured water molecules from the female's ancient brain traveling through her blood and other bodily fluids to her fetus, egg or seed. LifeConscious also works in the background as the controlling consciousness for DNA and all bodily life functions by using water as its carrier for communication.

LifeConscious has been known by many names throughout history such as *Qi* (life-force) in China or its equivalent *Ki* in Japan. In Yogic and Sanskrit traditions it is known as *Prana* (energy flow or breath). In Buddhism, it is the *Eighth consciousness* of *ālāyavijñāna* or the "store-house consciousness" which is the basis of the other 7 earth consciousnesses while it supervises and promotes the concept of rebirth. It's known as the ancient Egyptian *Ka* (life force) and *Ba* (individual personality). In ancient Greek it is *Psyche* (life, spirit, consciousness). In Hebrew, it is known as *Nephesh* (life, vital breath or spirit). These are all different names but the concept is the same in that they are all spiritual connotations. Our definitive difference is that LifeConscious shows its true agenda as our second, life sustaining consciousness. A second consciousness that is most important to all mothers and is real – not spiritual.

Mothers are the key to LifeConscious since they are the ones that transfer their own LifeConscious memories to their young. Let me repeat that. **Mother's are the key to LifeConscious since they are the ones that transfer their own memories to their young.** This is the *Linear* meaning of the *Linear Heritage of Women.*

This linearity means that life comes from life. It is an unbroken, linear progression from one generation to the next through *females.* This transfer is accomplished through the mother's fluids, such as blood, water, milk and body oils to her fetus. We will show later how water is the carrier of this background memory that we now call LifeConscious and how this is accomplished. We will also show you how these transference effects the development of the fetus.

An analogy of LifeConscious is like that of the candles presented in the Buddhist saying at the beginning of this chapter. The initial candle's flame is passed from one candle to the next and so on. The initial candle will eventually run out of wax and wick to the point that it loses its flame. One can think of this candle as now being dead. Nevertheless, the flame itself really isn't dead because its flame was transferred to the succeeding candles, and they continue burning just as brightly as their predecessor did. The body of the original candle is now nothing more than a cold lump of wax as its own flame has extinguished and its heat dissipated. This simulates that the LifeConscious of this dead candle is not dead at all as it continues to burn through its descendants.

This flame correlation is also like the transference of the Olympic torch flame that begins its journey from Athens Greece to wherever the games are to be played. The torches and runners are all different but the flame is initially the same. Hence, mothers and their children are different, but their family LifeConscious is initially the same. Descendants will continue to reproduce and make new individuals, but the same LifeConscious energy is reused in successive generations.

How it works in the Background

Remember back in Chapter 1 how we told you that we are each endowed with two consciousnesses at birth? We said that LifeConscious is a consciousness that works in the background and because of this, we have no control over this part of ourselves. The other of the two consciousnesses is our own personal consciousness – that which makes us individuals. Your own personal consciousness is that individual that you see in the mirror in the morning. It is that personality whom you have continually nurtured from birth.

Your personal consciousness grows along with the size of your brain. Your cerebrum will mature into its adult size within a few years after birth. Remember that due to the limiting size of a mature female's pelvis that we are all born prematurely. A mature human head is much too large for a mother to pass safely and so our bodies cannot develop any further without risking the mother's life. This also limits the size of a newborn's cerebellum or the personal conscious part of the brain. This leaves the only part of the brain that is needed during the gestation and birth and this is what we will now refer to as the *ancient brain.* These parts that make up the ancient brain are most important in maintaining and sustaining the life supporting bodily functions for a baby who totally relies on its mother for feeding, nurturing, and protection as his or her personality gradually develops. Therefore, your LifeConscious is your first consciousness that is already preloaded with the breed/species specific memories needed to maintain life – while your personality and knowledge mature and develop. In other words, you weren't burdened with the task of having to think about maintaining your bodily functions when you were just an infant since that would have been impossible for a baby to do. To us this is proof of the existence of another consciousness or LifeConscious.

Even after you mature into adulthood, your LifeConscious will be there controlling all your bodily tasks. It will continue to control your heart rate, respiration, digestion, blood flow, muscles, glandular secretions, and so on. We would all go crazy if we had to stop and physically think about controlling and keeping tabs with our bodily functions every second of the day and night for our entire lives! This is why LifeConscious should be considered as "running in the background" of your own personal consciousness. It is, in effect, operating your body – keeping you alive while you are free to pursue the joys of life through your personal consciousness.

Your bodily functions won't even listen to your personal consciousness. Try stopping your heart by thinking about it, your liver, or stomach's digestion. You can't! This is further proof that LifeConscious controls these tasks through your ancient brain. They are out of your personal consciousness' control – which is good because how many of us would actually want to die as a consequence of just thinking about committing suicide?

It is our belief that LifeConscious memories are stored and passed from what are the ancient parts of the brain like the Hypothalamus, Pineal Gland, Thalamus, Cerebellum and Cranial Nerves. I call this collection of parts the *ancient brain* because our brain has progressed and grown into its current configuration since the beginnings of life, as the illustration shows below, our species evolved and developed from fishes to amphibians to reptiles to mammals to primates and then finally to Man, our ancient brain has had to change and adapt with each new species. Our brains still hold the remnants of all these steps of transition, and these remnants are what compose the ancient brain. These remnants are the parts of the brain that control your bodily life functions such as respiration, heart rate, digestion, and glandular control. It passes messages between the body and brain. This is where LifeConscious resides as memories are passed down from the females of the species.

You can see by the illustration the dark nodule of the cerebellum along with the spinal column, medulla oblongata, and pons on each of these brains from different creatures. These are the sections of the brain that have been with us for millions of years. Although all of these species are very different from one another, it is easy to see the similarities in the structure of their brains. You can also see the growth of the cerebrum with the monkeys and chimps, which is where the personal consciousness is located.

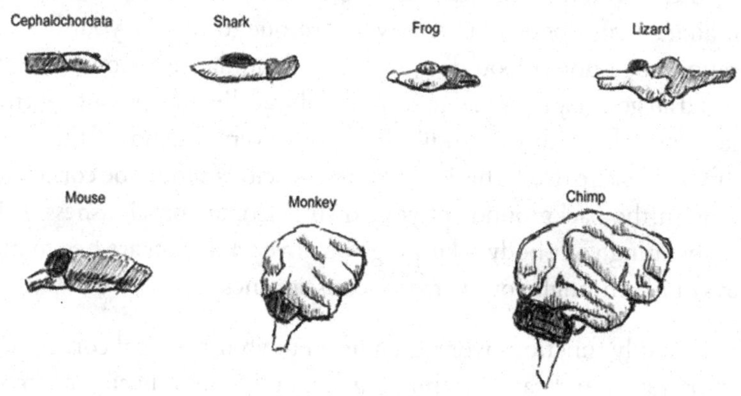

An illustration of the transitional changes of the Ancient Brain.

I propose that LifeConscious memories reside and are stored here in the ancient brain since its progressive beginnings through time are obviously clear. Since the dawn of time when life began LifeConscious was there in the ancient brain struggling to survive. It was finding ways to adapt and grow within the species that it gave life to, into a linear chain of unbroken countless lives. We and the animals, plants, and insects around us are the current end result of these linear chains of unbroken lives.

Your LifeConscious also controls the instinctual, pre-programmed reflexes that are also "downloaded" from your mother, and that we are all endowed with at birth. These automatic reflexes kick in only when they are needed in very stressful or traumatic situations like going into shock or fainting. As an example, when you are completely surprised by a loud noise, your body is preprogrammed to look directly at the noise with all of your focus, and your body will lock itself into a fighting position with your knees bent and hands in front of your body to protect yourself. You can't help but get into this stance when this happens. You can call this instinct if you want, but we must ask ourselves where this instinctual program is stored and how did it get there? Was it through DNA? No, DNA's primary function is to meticulously replicate itself in the cells of your body. Is it in the brain? Yes, but in the ancient part of the brain, not the cerebral cortex (personal conscious part of the brain) and it was deposited there by your mother when you were a fetus. Your mother didn't even know that this was happening because this procreative transference is also controlled by LifeConscious.

In the animal kingdom, LifeConscious memories are what tells a fawn to lie completely still in the tall grass in the presence of a tracking predator – even though its little heart is telling its feet to get up and run away. It's what tells a frightened kitten to raise its back while charging sideways to intimidate an attacker. It also guides a tiny Kangaroo embryo through its perilously journey up its mother's tummy to eventually attach itself to a teat in her pouch with absolutely no help from its mother other then licking a path for it. It's what teaches a baby to smile when seeing a familiar face.

LifeConscious controls the development of all newborn babies as they grow in their mother's womb, which again, is done in the background. The mother does not need to consciously think or control the fetus' process of development. Part of this progression involves the transference of memory from the mother's ancient brain, and we will show you how this is done. LifeConscious, as its background controller, handles the fetus' early growth in life until it leaves its mother's womb and grows to develop a personal consciousness, which will mature and guide this new individual for the rest of its life.

Our Brain

The brain of a modern human is a complex organ that science is still trying to understand. The shaded gray area in the illustration shows were the ancient brain is located.

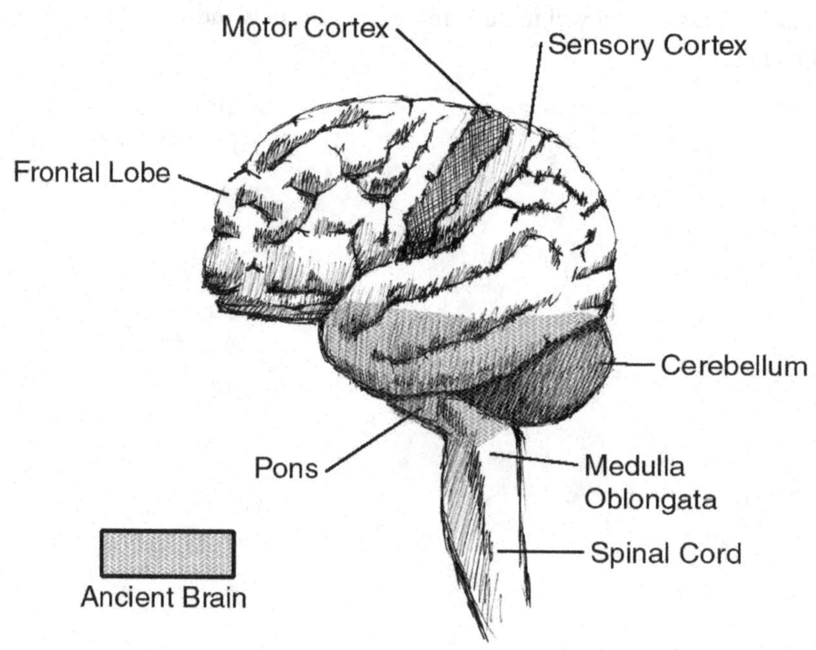

An illustration of the location of the Ancient Brain in humans.

Much about our brains is not yet known, but I suspect that LifeConscious will soon be discovered through future experiments or research. It is an obvious fact that life comes from life and that this background controlling consciousness that we call LifeConscious has to come from somewhere. It can't come from DNA, which are just replicating building blocks for cellular regeneration. For instance, something has to "tell" a neutral stem cell what type of body cell it is to form into and where inside the fetus it is to form. Some type of controller has to tell this stem cell that it will become a heart cell and begin beating or a lung cell, eye cell, blood cell, and so on. DNA can't be the controller, since they have no memory storage capabilities. Only the mother's ancient brain is capable of retaining these memories and this is what is passed on to the fetus by way of the mother's blood and other fluids using water as the carrier. These prehistoric LifeConscious memories are disseminated to the fetus, and LifeConscious controls the entire process. This is the theory of LifeConscious and how it works.

Can the existence of LifeConscious be proven? Only time and research will be able to answer this question. One inevitable fact about LifeConscious is that it is done through transference, and transference happens all the time among humans.

Transference of colds, the flu, mumps, and other diseases could be considered as proof of the existence of LifeConscious. How are diseases spread and accumulated? It is through touching, breathing and eating that these ailments, viruses and germs are transferred from one human to the next. You only have to look at a children's day care center to see how this is accomplished. A single child with a cold can easily infect others by sneezing and coughing while touching furniture, toys, books, door knobs and other children. These cold germs will quickly spread to the other children who come in contact with the infected items along with the air that they breathe.

In the animal world infectious diseases such as rabies and distemper nearly wiped out the wild dog populations in Africa which caused them to be placed in the endangered species list. Rabies decimated packs in the Serengeti, Tanzania, the Masai Mara, and Kenya and was thought to have contributed to the ultimate extinction of wild dogs in these areas. The transference of the disease was naturally done by licking and smelling one another in their greeting and recognition rituals. Licking their diseased infections on one another was their only way of treating their ailments and the disease spread quickly. Their friendly greetings nearly caused their demise.

Another proof the existence of LifeConscious is from allergies. There are news reports of peanut allergies that were transferred through organ donations from hosts who had the allergy to recipients who didn't. This is obviously an example of the transference of the memory of the allergy. The memory of the allergy was still present in the donated organ and this memory became a part of the recipient's own LifeConscious memories that would now trigger an allergic response whenever a peanut product was ingested.

The examples above are just a few of the proofs, and it makes sense that not only does the mother's body help nourish the fetus' body but that her ancient brain nourishes the fetus' blank ancient brain by transferring her LifeConscious memories. The fetuses own developing LifeConscious will gradually enable it to become its own separate living entity by increasingly taking control of its little body. This ancient knowledge that has slowly progressed linearly for thousands of generations has continually been passed down from mother to child and will continue to do so until the extinction of our species.

LifeConscious doesn't just exist in humans but in all living beings – even plants and insects. Scientists may argue that LifeConscious is merely instinct but what exactly is instinct if it is not a retained memory and where did that memory come from? Each species' unique LifeConscious memories are transferred from the females to their young. Even the different breeds of the same species have a singular LifeConscious–for example, a sheep dog's herding nature of LifeConscious in contrast to a wolf's hunting nature.

We will see in the case of LifeConscious that it is indeed a physical level of communication between female and young because it employs a physical connection for transference and this communication is accomplished by use of water as the carrier.

Water and DNA are the two essential ingredients needed for all life-forms to generate new cells for plants, animals, fishes, etc. and to regenerate cells to replace their dead forebears. Water is the medium, DNA is the framework, and LifeConscious is the controller. Together, they are the force that spawns all life on earth. They have been coupled in this labor of life since day one, and their collaboration is what gives LifeConscious and us, life.

To paraphrase author Marshall McLuhan, water is not only the medium, but it contains the message. It is the storage container for memories of the most recent species that just used it. The water in our bodies has lasted millions of years on earth and has passed through countless numbers of other species' bodies both plant and animal. It has sustained many billions of lives on this tiny rock in the universe that we call our home, our earth.

We are all water creatures whose ancestors left the waters of the great oceans millions of years ago. Our eggs, seeds, and wombs are small reminders of those water bound earlier lives. The primordial oceans are carried within the wombs of mammals and the eggs of birds and reptiles for proper procreation to occur because the LifeConscious memories from the mother are carried by the waters of her womb/egg to help in the development of the young. The DNA can't do it alone. They must have a controlling mechanism to go by and LifeConscious, within the mother's ancient brain, is that controller. How else does a stem cell "know" what part of the newborn baby's body it will become without LifeConscious?

DNA is just the blueprint of a human being, but it can't "create" a human being on its own. I like to think of DNA as the blueprint, LifeConscious as the foreman, and the bodily organs as the workers when a fetus is being formed within the body of its living mother. It is a symbiotic relationship that has worked since life first gained a foothold on earth.

LifeConscious doesn't care whether someone believes that the initial spark of life on earth was created by a deity or spontaneously developed in a tepid pool of water. We believe that this theory will stand up to whatever tests, be they scientific, philosophical, or religious that may challenge it.

Now that we have explained LifeConscious and how it functions, there are many things in life that will begin to make sense since we never really had a clue as to how they work? For example, one of the great mysteries in the life of a woman is what happens during the menstrual cycle that makes women suffer so much mentally and physically. Women struggle against the overwhelming forces of their LifeConscious that is controlling the functions of their own bodies. Not realizing that this is happening to can have tremendous repercussions to a woman. Later, we will talk about how women can deal with the stresses of their hormonal cycles and perhaps even overcome the sufferings of PMS!

To recap, your duality of mind is the struggle between two consciousnesses; causing the reaction of losing control or the feeling of split personalities. Your own personal consciousness wants to challenge the control and actions of your body when, in fact, it can't because this falls in the realm of LifeConscious and is a hurdle that your personal consciousness can't seem to overcome. Your body's LifeConscious has full control of your life giving functions and will not relinquish control. This out of control conflict that you feel within yourself is actually the clash of consciousnesses.

The Memory of Water

There is on our earth a very precious molecule without which you and I cannot live without. We breathe it, bath in it, cook with it but more importantly we drink it and so does every other living creature on earth. It is a life-sustaining consumable commodity that, unfortunately, is becoming rarer in its drinkable form. This life-giving compound, this precious commodity is water.

Think for a moment about how important water is to you. Where would you be right now without this compound of hydrogen and oxygen? How long could you survive if you were denied this life-giving liquid? The answer is simple. You would endure a horrible death in a few days. Water is much more important to us than we could ever dream of. Water is not only needed for drinking but is also important to all of life's procreative processes and endurance from conception to birth, all the way to death itself. All life, not just humans but animals, fishes, plants, insects, microorganisms and every other living thing on our planet earth must pass water constantly through their bodies to sustain life.

Today we take water for granted, a simple twist on a faucet handle and like magic, water appears. Water seems to be everywhere and in different states and guises. Shelves of water are showcased at any supermarket in many diverse forms and flavors disguised as cokes, beer, wine, orange juice, and even bottled water. We wash our cars, dogs, dishes, and ourselves with it. It is a compound of many uses and appearances. In winter, it falls as snow and as ice on the lakes and roads. It drops as rain during the rest of the year and emerges as fog or mist on humid mornings. Gaseous mists of water shroud the mountains and billows over them forming into clouds. It encircles the earth as lakes, rivers and oceans. Water towers above us into tremendously high atmospheric oceans of water vapor. When viewed from space, the pulsing, spinning, and churning currents of the earth's atmosphere are the most telling feature visible that would compel any passing alien visitor to exclaim that yes, here there must be life. This fantastic view from space on any part of the globe is evidence of a living breathing giant organism with the rivers for veins, the oceans for a heart and the atmosphere as its lungs.

Water constitutes about 90 percent of your blood; 75 percent of your brain and muscles; 25 percent of body fat, and 22 percent of bone. Since our bodies are composed of mostly water, then it naturally has no taste or smell to us. It covers 70% or our earth's surface as seas, rivers and oceans whose depths average 2 miles, and that's just in its liquid form.

The air that we breathe has water in it along with nitrogen and oxygen. The transition from liquid water to gaseous water vapor is evident on any lake, stream, or ocean as a fog or mist. Water vapor returning to its liquid form is conspicuous in any gentle rain, thunderstorm, or hurricane. It is this immense cycle of transition from water to vapor to rain/snow and back again that has sustained life on earth for millions of years.

Although this description portrays water as being the most beautiful aspect of life and human existence, many of us fail to realize its importance in our busy mundane lives. The next time that it rains do yourself a favor and do what the rest of the animal world does and stand in the rain and savor the experience.

Water has entered and left the bodies of every living creature who has ever lived since the dawn of time. So, the next time that you look out on the ocean or toss a rock into a lake, think about how a single drop of water in your body right now could have once been used to quench the thirst of Abraham Lincoln a hundred years ago, a shark a thousand years ago, or a dinosaur hatchling millions of years ago. This compound inexorably ties all living species together from the past to the present and will continue to do so in the future.

We cannot deny the importance that water has on life itself scientifically. The scientific formula for water is H_2O. A molecule of water is atomically composed of two hydrogen atoms bonded with one oxygen atom. This atomic configuration causes water to be dipolar, which means that it has one positive and one negative end like a battery or magnet.

Scientifically, dipolar means that the electrons in a molecule of water spend more time orbiting the oxygen nucleus than orbiting the two hydrogen nuclei which leaves the oxygen end more negatively charged and the hydrogen end of the molecule more positively charged. So, the entire molecule is "dipolar" that is with one end slightly positive and one end slightly negative. This allows water molecules to attract one another like tiny magnets that will align into structured states called lattices where molecules line up positive to negative and so on. This is how water droplets form and why water tends to stay together in rivers, lakes, and oceans. It is this dipolar feature of water that allows it to fit into any vase, glass, barrel, river, lake or ocean and that causes clouds to form. It is this dipolar nature of water and the lattices that the molecules form that lend itself to its most extraordinary characteristic of retaining memory.

I can recall back during my computer training days that memory (computer-wise) was nothing more than a bit being set On or Off (digitally 1 or 0). If we were to make a theoretical leap from computer memory to dipolar water molecules, we would see a striking bit type of similarity. They both have two states. An electronic memory bit is either on or off. A dipolar water molecule is aligned positive or negative and this memory feature of water has already been noticed and studied by scientists.

Around 1985, a renowned French scientist Jacques Benveniste saw strong evidence that water could retain memory. He was experimenting with human white blood cells called basophils. *Nature* published Benveniste's work in 1988 and later debunked his theory of the memory of water when a team from *Nature*, which included a magician, refuted the findings. Benveniste and his work lost funding and credibility. His experiments shut down but he never gave up, until he passed away in 2004.

Researchers are just now beginning to understand the benefits of using water molecules as memory storage. Because of its compactness, these water fragments could enable memory data storage densities of more than 100,000 trillion bits per cubic inch. To put this in prospective – you could have a music storage device the size of a deck of cards to hold enough songs to play for 300,000 years without repeating a tune. There are still monumental "nano" hurdles to get over such as the nano-sized terminals that need to be developed to be able to hook up to such tiny memory devices. Heidi and I are helping to run a neutron producing linear accelerator called the Spallation Neutron Source (http://neutrons.ornl.gov) at the Oak Ridge National Laboratory in Tennessee that one day may be able to provide scientists with the necessary tools to develop such new nano-technologies.

Now, you will learn how nature uses this dipolar feature of water. We shall see that it uses water lattices to transfer knowledge and disseminate LifeConscious memories from one generation to the next.

It was discovered through experiments by Jacques Benveniste team of scientists that water molecules will align into memory structures that emulate but mirror the electrical fields of the cells or proteins they are electrically attracted to. Some studies show that these structures can be several water molecule layers thick forming lattices.

We would like to propose that the last few layers furthest from the cells being "memorized" must have weaker electrical bonds and break away but still retain the initial formation or memory. These lattices are now loose tiny structured packets or bits of memory.

We know that a human is mostly made up of water, and now we know that water can be a carrier of memories from a pregnant mother to her fetus. The loose lattices of memories that once mirrored the mothers own brain cells journey to the mother's fetus, and this is how LifeConscious memories are transferred. Steady streams of these bits of memory find fits in the baby's ancient brain as it grows constantly downloading the mother's memories to the neutral stem cells activating them into memory storing neurons. This process will continue during the entire gestation period steadily turning neutral stem cells into job specific, memory laden neuron cells.

Other scientists have experimented and seen water as a communicator, including the Nobel Prize winner Alfred G. Gilman. He received the prize for determining how the cells of the human body communicate with one another by sending and receiving "radio" signals. Other reputable scientists, including Dr. Lorenzen, have demonstrated that this signal transduction was facilitated by the clustered or "ringed" water that is present in the cells of all living things. We will show you in the next section on *Resonant Frequency* that the initiator of these radio signals is the earth itself along with its own form of LifeConsciousness.

These radio signals, to us, is also proof that LifeConscious controls the formation of DNA strands through the use of the structured water molecules surrounding a DNA double helix in each cell. We propose that structured water molecules that surround the developing DNA strands help electrically attract and then capture the correct complimentary nucleotide – thereby guiding it into place in an empty space on a DNA strand. Once the nucleotide is in place, the electrical bond is broken with the water molecules since that section is now electrically neutral – thus causing the water molecules to move on. The structured water molecules move on to be attracted to another empty spot on the strand. To the best of our scientific knowledge, this is how LifeConscious works. We believe that scientific research will prove one day how LifeConscious communicates with DNA during its construction.

Water has indeed shown us another wonderful side to its "simple" nature. It is this simplicity that I want to delve on. When water drops from the heavens and joins a stream or river, it more or less goes with the flow. It will always take the more effortless route to its gravity-induced destination. Water simply does as nature tells it to do – it is the perfect carrier–the carrier of memories and LifeConscious. Perhaps the simplicity of water being a life-carrier is why it has been used in many cultures throughout the ages in religious ceremonies and rituals.

(Heidi) These ideas of LifeConscious may not have been called by the same name, but ancient Celtic cultures certainly seemed to understand the concept of water being the carrier of memories. speaks about this "water worship" in the Druid religious traditions in Western Europe.

> *"Presumably, the heads of the dead of the original Celtic settlement, and later the Roman occupied city, were taken through this gate to the river Thames – tamesis, the dark or sluggish river – where they used as votive offerings or simply placed for Bilé [Celtic god] to transport to the Otherworld. Hundreds of skulls from the Celtic period have been discovered in the Thames, around London, with other votive offerings (121). Professor Richard Bradley, of Reading University, in a 1990 BBC television documentary, put forward the argument that the Thames could have been a sacred river for the British Celts, occupying the same role as the Ganges (*Ellis, 122*)."*

Ellis also mentions that the Celts were not the only cultures to hold rivers and other sources of water sacred.

> *"Once again, we find this worship of rivers, springs, or wells as part of an ancient Indo-European custom. In central India, the tribes of Chota Nagpur, in what is now the Maharashtra state, offer sacrifices to the deities of wells and rivers in much the same way that their Christian Indo-European counterparts in Ireland, Wales, and Brittany still do today (Ellis, 122)."*

According to Ellis and his research, even the main deity of the Celts, the goddess Danu, is associated with water.

> *"The Dagda is Danu's son by Bilé. Therefore, Danu still takes precedence as the primary source of life. As the sacred 'waters from heaven,' Danu watered the oak, which was Bilé the male fertility symbol, and gave birth to the Dagda, 'the good god' who fathered the rest of the gods. Otherworld takes on significance. Transportation is usually via water, rivers like the Thames, or out to sea. He [Bilé] is, in fact, transporting them to the 'divine waters' – his consort Danu 'the mother goddess'* (Ellis, 122)*"*

In fact, not only were places of water named for goddesses, but places near the waters were considered sacred as well. For example, the Hill of Uisneach in Ireland is named after water as Ellis explains.

> *"It is highly significant that Uisneach, the hill, which was deemed 'the navel of Ireland,' has its root, this same word uis/esc, easily recognizable in the modern Irish word for water – uisce. Uisneach (Ráthaconradh, Co. Westmeath) is where the first Druidic fires were lit and where the great 'Stone of Divisions' (Aill na Mirenn) marked the spot at which the five provinces of Ireland met* (Ellis, 240)."

I find it very interesting that Uisneach was referred to as the "navel of Ireland" by the Druids – when the very name of the place means water. Clearly these ancient people regarded water as sacred and that the water is nearly always associated with women giving birth – especially, the goddesses.

We are merely droplets of consciousness that occasionally return to the stream of the earth's ocean of consciousness, replenishing our need to become one with not only the earth but the universe – since the earth's LifeConsciousness is part and parcel of the universe's LifeConsciousness.

There are examples of LifeConscious beliefs and practices in nearly every indigenous culture on earth. This fundamental concept of linear heritage propagating through mothers by water makes up the fundamental beliefs of cultures from Western Europe, to Native Americans, to Central Africans.

The people of the Niger-Congo region have a religious belief based on the concept of a "spirit" that is manifested in natural ways such as in the form of deities or ancestors. In southern Africa, where the Khoisan people have resided since 5000 BCE, their beliefs have recognized an impersonal condition of a force that existed outside of humans and in some animals. A shaman could tap into this "force" by going into a trance-like state through dancing. It was believed that once the shaman was overtaken by this "life-force," they could heal people of various ailments.

Uduk, a language still spoken in modern Nilo-Saharan tribes in Africa have a word called "arum." This is a force that concentrates in the liver of people that makes a person alive. They believe that arum is the source of all our strong emotions and feelings. In animals, it is believed that the arum exists after they die in the form of a disembodied spirit. This arum contains the residue of all lives of people and animals that have passed. Wandering arum is a belief held where lost souls that were never properly buried are wandering the earth and can only be put to rest by performing specific rituals and religious observances.

Another example of LifeConscious beliefs in human cultures are in the Native Americans of the United States. The Dakota people of North America believe that nature and the supernatural are one and the same. The "Wakan Tanka" as they call it, is the force that makes everything alive. It is in the rocks, trees, grass, the buffalo, and people. Everything in the world is made up of this animating force, and it could only be reached by the practice of certain rituals. Special religious men called wicasa wakan, were thought to be the only ones that could understand

the "Great Incomprehensibility." These wicasa wakan helped people of the community find their own place in the universe and aided young people through various rites of passage such as vision quests and marriages.

There is a certain Sioux story that strikingly resembles the deeply held beliefs that are so similar to LifeConscious. Storytelling, like in many indigenous cultures, is an oral tradition that has been ongoing for many generations. This story below is interesting because like many legendary stories in various cultures, the hero is born of water.

> *"Now the poor sister was nearly distracted. Day and night she wandered over hills and through woods in hopes she might find or hear of some trace of them. Her wanderings were in vain. The hawks had not seen them after they had crossed the little stream. The wolves and coyotes told her that they had seen nothing of her brothers out on the broad plains, and she had given them up for dead.*
>
> *One day, as she was sitting by the little stream that flowed past their hut, throwing pebbles into the water and wondering what she should do, she picked up a pure white pebble, smooth and round, and after looking at it for a long time, threw it into the water. No sooner had it hit the water than she saw it grow larger. She took it out and looked at it and threw it in again. This time it had assumed the form of a baby. She took it out and threw it in the third time, and the form took life and began to cry: "Ina, ina" (mother, mother). She took the baby home and fed it soup, and it being an unnatural baby, quickly grew up to a good sized boy.*
>
> *At the end of three months he was a good big, stout youth. One day he said: 'Mother, why are you living here alone? To whom do all these fine clothes and moccasins belong?' She then told him the story of her lost brothers. 'Oh, I know now where they are. You make me lots of arrows. I am going to find my uncles.' She tried to dissuade him from going, but he was determined and said: 'My father sent me to you so that I could find my uncles for you, and nothing can harm me, because I am stone and my name is 'Stone Boy'" (McLaughlin, 186-187).*

Resonant Frequency

Since Heidi and I both work at a Linear Accelerator, we are very familiar with the term *Resonant Frequency*. This just means that any object has a harmonic frequency where it naturally oscillates. It's similar to different tuning forks that can only resonate at the frequency that they were designed for. One can readily hear their tonal differences.

We all know from high school that the earth has a magnetic field thus the reason that compasses point close to the North Pole. This magnetic field is brought about by the earth's molten iron core and is responsible for preventing the sun's solar winds and cosmic radiation from frying every living thing on earth's surface. This magnetic field effectively extends several tens of thousands of kilometers into space and is called the magnetosphere.

The ionosphere is the uppermost part of the earth's atmosphere and is distinguished because it is ionized by solar radiation. A global electromagnetic resonance of Extremely Low Frequency (ELF) is caused by lightning discharges between the earth's surface and the ionosphere. This global electromagnetic resonance phenomenon is named after the physicist Winfried Otto Schumann, who predicted it mathematically in 1952. What this means is that our earth has a resonant frequency in the ELF range of 7.83 Hz.

What is even more amazing, but not quite surprising, is that mammalian brains (including humans) have a similar resonant frequency during sleep between 4 and 12 Hz. It was also found in man that the frequency during periods of relaxation is between 8 and 14 Hz. During moments of mental concentration, it was 14 to 30 Hz. What this is telling us is that since we are earth- creatures, we will naturally resonate at the same frequency as our host planet. We believe that 7.83 Hz is the tuning fork for all earthly life and the Earth's specific LifeConscious.

Dr Wolfgang Ludwig carried on Schumann's resonance research and found that because of today's modern noises that it was nearly impossible to detect these ELF readings. He had the idea of trying to measure these frequencies in deep mines. His research also caused him to make the connection with the Chinese Yin and Yang concept by concluding that the strong signal of the Schumann wave surrounding our earth was synonymous with Yang while the weaker geomagnetic waves coming from within our planet being the Yin signal. He found that Chinese philosophy teaches that to maintain one's health, both signals must be in balance.

Dr Ludwig's book *Informative Medizin* states that research carried out by E. Jacobi at the University of Duesseldorf showed that a stronger use of the Schumann (Yang) wave over the geomagnetic (Yin) signal (and vice versa) caused serious health problems on tested subjects.

Professor R. Wever from the Max Planck Institute for Behavioral Physiology built an experimental underground bunker that screened out magnetic fields, including the Schumann resonance of 7.8 Hz. Young student volunteers lived for four weeks in the bunker and experienced emotional distress and migraine headaches. Exposing the students with a brief dose of 7.8 Hz stabilized their health again.

The very first astronauts and cosmonauts suffered nausea and dizziness from their separation of the earth's Schumann resonance effect. Subsequent flights included devices to produce pulsed frequencies in the Schumann Resonance range to lessen their suffering.

These conclusions show that magnetic fields and electricity are symbiotically linked and that our bodies are a collection of bioelectrical activity. Each cell is affected by the electrical resistance and charge of its fellow cells. It is this bioelectrical communication combined with the body's carrier systems of blood, lymph and endocrine glands (that are mainly composed of water) that constitute the controlling functions of LifeConscious.

We live in a noisy modern age with wireless devices, microwaves, televisions, high power lines, telephones, and radio that we can hardly hear ourselves think much less perceive the earth's resonant frequency. We are dangerously drowning out these natural ELF signals that have been with us since the dawn of life itself. We have literally tuned out from our own environment of the earth and are suffering its consequences.

So what we have discovered so far is that LifeConscious uses the carrier of water to transfer memories. We also know that it communicates at a frequency of around 7.83 Hz to control bodily life sustaining functions. We will show in the following chapters why this is such an important function when we sleep.

Life is a linear organism

That life is a linear organism is quite obvious. You can't make life from an inanimate object. You can try like the fictional Frankenstein and put together an animal as simple as a frog from the parts of other frogs, but then to give it that spark of life is something altogether different if not impossible. In order for it to live, that frog has to come from its mother, who came from its mother, who came from its mother and so on in a linear fashion. There can't have been any breaks in that linear line of life or this last frog would never have croaked a single note.

So as we are the end result of this long unbroken line of life we should be very proud of our ancestors for having survived so long and so successfully. Imagine how many broken lines of life that there must have been – not to mention the countless numbers of species that have lived in the past and that are now extinct. It has been estimated that 99.9 % of all the species that have ever lived and enjoyed the bounties of this earth are now extinct. Species that are alive and well at this very date and time are now a part of that .1 %, including mankind.

This is why you as women are so important to the cause of life's continuation. Without your special gift of procreation, we would have never existed, which means no advent of mankind, no abstract thinking, and no possibility of writing this book. Without LifeConscious, there is no life to any species – animal, fish, plant, insect. It was a simple form of LifeConscious that helped develop life in a tepid pool of water along with the very first microbes that began to split and separate and separate repeatedly. It is this separation that began the linearity of life and LifeConscious on earth. As the complexity of life developed and grew so did its LifeConscious memories. This example is obviously the evolutionary explanation.

To be fairer then, this is the Creationist explanation. This belief says that the "spark" of life was breathed into man by a deity. His/her spirit breath (LifeConscious) initiated life and its linearity into mankind and the rest of the species. We are, then, the end result of this Divine initial breath and women are the progenitors of the continuation of this spirit.

Either way LifeConscious was initiated it has carried on a long, varied, and tenacious history with the species that it has seen, come and go. By its own tenacity, LifeConscious has been the key to the burgeoning of new species during the major catastrophes that our earth has endured over her lifetime. LifeConscious has a very single minded and egocentric agenda, and that is to keep itself alive – even after such catastrophes by constantly striving to survive by going from a newly extinct species on to help develop entirely new species. This is how we believe that new species are created and not through evolution. Yes, evolution is a valid theory, and we certainly don't deny the fact of species learning to adapt to changes in their environments over time; but the fact of the matter is that during the past few thousand years of observation by man, there has never been recorded the development of an entirely new species.

Ancient earth history constantly shows us that new species are somehow formed after the end of a historical period, a period that is always terminated by a worldwide catastrophe. One example is the boundary between the Cretaceous and Paleocene period that is marked by a devastating extinction event that caused the demise of the dinosaurs and countless marine species. This event is thought to have been caused by a collision by a comet or large meteor in the Yucatan peninsula.

The book *LifeConscious* goes into more detail about what conditions are needed to promote the advent of new species between these historical periods. We just wanted to show how tenacious LifeConscious was and still is. It is this tenacity of LifeConscious that women feel during menstruation each month. Try as you will with your own personal consciousness LifeConscious will not relinquish control over the life functions of the body – it can't because this is its job to promote procreation. It doesn't care about alleviating the pain, bleeding, headaches or nausea. This is the "price" women pay for having this gift of procreation and LifeConscious will doggedly pursue the next birthing of life. That is its purpose – to keep the linear organism going no matter what.

Is it a coincidence that the cycle of menstruation for women is 28-29 days, which is the same as the lunar cycle? Even Charles Darwin believed that menstruation was linked to the moon's influence on tidal rhythms which he believed was a legacy of our origin from the ocean. Other scientists disbelieve the reference; pointing out discrepancies in other mammalian menstrual cycles, which range from a week to 35 days. I say who cares about these differences which may have evolved from other natural influences, such as their diverse metabolisms or seasonal changes. For the most part, these animals stay within the confines of their environment anyway, whereas human females are global and populate every region of the earth. Being more global in nature causes all the women of the earth to naturally be influenced by the cycles of the moon.

The word *menstruation*'s origin is moon-oriented anyway. The word is derived from the Latin word *mensis* which means month, which in turn relates to the Greek *mene* (moon). From these roots formed the English words *month* and *moon*—reflecting the fact that the moon also takes close to 28 days to revolve around the earth.

Another interesting point about menstrual cycles is the fact that when you place several women in the same environment, say a dorm room, all the women's cycles will begin to coincide. How is this possible? It is possible because all women who live together share the same environ of air, water, body oils, and dust. These are all LifeConscious carriers, which will of course cause all the ladies' cycles to synchronize. This synchronous menstruation has been observed among mothers, sisters, and daughters who live together, and sometimes among women who simply work in the same office. There was a study of seven female lifeguards who started out one summer with widely scattered periods. Three months later they were all menstruating within four days of one another. Scientists say that this act of women's cycles synchronizing is a result of an evolutionary adaptation that developed thousands of years ago. This synchronization was necessary so that the males in a community could mate with as many females as possible in order to reproduce more quickly. This could be true, but LifeConscious explains the mechanism as to *how* this cycle synchronization is possible.

Another study of 135 residents of a women's college dorm confirmed the effect. Most of the cycle shifting occurred within the first four months and was usually complete after seven months. As often as not, the women were unaware of what had happened. Later scientific research has suggested that synchrony is caused by some sort of scent cue, or pheromone.

Scientists at the Sonoma State Hospital Brain Behavior Research Center in California identified several women who were believed to be menstrual pacesetters that apparently made other women conform to their cycles. Thinking that the effect was caused olfactory somehow the scientists placed cotton pads under the dominant women's arms for a day, and then wiped the pads on the upper lips of five female subjects three times a week. Within five months, four of the recipients were menstruating at the same time as their donors. Scientists still can't explain what causes the synchronicity but now you readers know that it is the ladies' individual LifeConscious forces that are communicating with one another and are causing their cycles to coalesce. Scientists will also tell you that it is your endocrine system that controls your menstrual cycles and this system is composed of several small organs whose job is to release a certain amount of their hormones on cue each month. Who or what do you think controls these cues? The answer, of course, is your very own LifeConsciousness.

Women's important role

Your role as a woman, if you choose to accept it, will be to help procreate the human race. This is a daunting and sometimes frightening role to undertake – especially if you seem to focus on outcomes and not on the present moment. Trying to predict the future has caused many people to spend hours on psychiatrists' couches. You can plan, you can hope, but you cannot predict the future. With that said, you will definitely be better off, psychologically speaking, by focusing on the present and just letting the future take care of itself.

You have a very precious and special gift of continuing this long line of life. Probably, the most important task once a girl becomes a woman is selecting the best male for the purpose of providing the seed for your baby. It seems like anyone can have a baby now-a-days. You see drug addicts, teenagers, prostitutes, and even same sex couples having children. This book will not delve into the social economics, addictions, sexual preferences, or make judgments to any of these issues. The purpose of this book is to show you how it all works and what you need to do as a mother to keep the lineage going in the way that nature intended.

It is important for you to realize that because you are a woman that you are definitely *not* a second class citizen and any man that thinks that this is the case is in serious denial or has lofty ambitions as a fundamentalist. Many philosophically or religious fundamentalists are notably sexist and consider women not worthy to share the same area of the church, synagogue, or mosque. In some extreme cases, like in Saudi Arabia, women are not even allowed to drive a car. They also usually require their women to wear clothing that covers as much skin as possible so as not to entice men to sin. They will furthermore require their women to speak when spoken to and are forbidden to pursue an education.

If you find yourself in such a confining relationship with a man then try to get out of that situation ASAP. On the other hand, if you find that you are quite comfortable in such a stifling association than by all means don't let us stop you, because if you are happy, then we are happy. Again – it is ultimately you who selects the male who will provide the seed for your baby, and so it is your responsibility as to who contributes to the gene pools of the future. This is an area that you, and you alone can control. So be wise, ladies, and choose carefully.

Finding the right man is, at best, a tossup since people tended to change after the first few sexual encounters or so. Afterwards, questions arise such as; will he be a good father, teacher, and provider for me and the children? These are very difficult questions to answer when your sexual desires have been heightened to the point that you don't care because you just want carnal satisfaction immediately. Racks upon racks of books have been written on this subject and are available in copious numbers in any library or book store.

So what is a woman to do? How can she make such a tough decision when there are many things to consider? How will she be able to know whom to trust and discern their honesty and sincerity from those of liars and deceivers? She needs to focus on the present and not dwell too longingly to the future, but she also needs to listen to that innate 6th sense that all women seem to have. She needs to take her time in choosing a mate and believe us, when the right person comes along, she will know it and will relish that relationship for the rest of her life.

Women also need to recognize that they are much closer to the earth's natural rhythms than men. Men used to be just as in tuned with these rhythms as the ladies, but something happened along the way to change their perspective and that something was civilization. As hunter/gatherers, men had to know as much about nature's particulars as the women or their family/clan/tribe would become extinct. This is evident when you see the paintings in Lascaux Cave, France that depicted the spirits of the animals that man was hunting at that time. It was very important to appease the spirits of the dead animals killed during hunts so that they would feel free to come back and be reborn so that they could continue to help feed their family/clan/tribes.

When agriculture and animal husbandry came along, men and their families found themselves residing in villages or city states. They no longer needed to live by hunting and gathering their food anymore. They could stay in one place and work the land instead of moving around with the herds of wild animals. Men began to forget this symbiotic relationship that they had with the hunted animals and nature. They began painting scenes of cattle, sheep and stalks of grain on earthen jars to commemorate their new found niche in life. Instead of seeing the big picture that revolves around nature, they began to get tunnel vision and see only as far as their own crops, herds and villages were concerned. As men became more and more obsessed with the martial arts, war, and empire building, they almost completely forgot their close ties with nature. To be sure, the male still has an occasional brave "hunter" streak by running down wild animals for sport.

For the most part, women are the only sex now that is still in tune with nature because of their procreative gift. Because of all the modern contrivances and distraction in everyday life, many simply can't see or relate to it any more. Women are trying to keep up with men in the job market, finances, or sports and forgetting their real role in life. Some throw away or deny their special gift of procreation. Younger women and girls are more concerned with their careers, the latest fashions, gossip, or video games that are coming out than exploring their close ties with nature. The spiritual closeness that women once had with nature in ancient times was the most important ritual in their lives. Now in many cases, it has been replaced by shopping, TV, food, alcohol, drugs, casual sex, and games.

(Heidi) Ever since I was a young girl, I always longed to be where nature was. I craved outdoor play and visiting wooded areas. I actually felt like I was meant to be in these natural settings more than I was in my own home. The forests, the beaches, the mountains, and the meadows felt much more like home to me than any home, church, or school. Although I grew up in the 1980's when video games and cable television were really taking off, I only delved a bit into this new technology. All the kids at school couldn't wait to go home and get on the Nintendo or watch the music videos on MTV. I did enjoy some of these things, but I did not prefer them over going outside to play.

I found that the more time I spent by myself outside, the more I got to know who I was. By surrounding myself with trees, grass, the soil, animals, plants, rocks, and insects, I discovered something almost magical – that I was like them. I was made up of the same stuff that they were – just put together in a way so that I was a person, and they were a flower or a tree. I am, of course, speaking in the terms, I was familiar with when I was a toddler. But, the feelings are the same whether I choose to use the language of a child, or a college professor.

The place where I have always felt the closest to nature and becoming one with the earth is when I am with horses. For reasons, I have yet to discover about myself, I have always had an insatiable attachment to these wonderful creatures for as long as I can remember. I was always reading books about horses or riding the ponies when the fair came to town. I always pointed at the horses passing by while riding in my car seat. Perhaps in a former life I was a horse handler or a farrier. Whatever the reason, the fact exists that I love to be around horses to feel a complete sense of life-fulfilling freedom.

Anyone who is familiar with horses knows that they are not the smartest creatures to live. The fact is that they have a very small "thinking" part of their brain that they prefer to ignore. However, horses are very closely tied to the earth – not unlike human females. They are extremely perceptive animals – anticipating movements, feelings, and shifts in a person's energy. In an instant, they know when you are angry with them, upset, or afraid. How many times have you been thrown from a horse simply after you thought the words, "I don't know if I can ride this horse?"

However, they can be the most loyal companions of any other animal I have ever seen. One of my best friends that I had was my horse, Quest. He was a special horse because he had been a mistake. One night about 25 years ago, a prize winning Hanoverian stallion jumped a fence and mated with a Welsh Pony mare and the result was Quest. I had saved up my money for two years to buy Quest from my trainer. I was so excited the day that I was finally able to have him for my very own. We worked very hard together and trained in the rain, snow, and Georgia's summer heat. At that time, I was going through some difficult times in my family life, and I would always want to be with Quest because he would somehow make me feel better.

One day, my father had said something really mean that upset me at the barn, and I ran to Quest's stall to cry. Quest put his nose against my stomach and breathed quietly – as if reassuring me that everything was going to be alright. Then, when Quest had the colic one day, I stayed with him in his stall as long as I could to reassure him that he was going to get better. He and I went through a lot together – everything from illness and despair, to winning a Reserve Championship in a Hunter/Jumper show.

Then, after being with Quest for only three years, my father sold Quest suddenly because he didn't have any more money to take care of him. Quest was taken away from the barn, and I never saw him again. Nevertheless, this did not stop my intense desire to be around horses and continue training. I still train horses off and on. Horses always teach me so much about myself when I train – no matter if they are a seasoned barrel racer, a Grand Prix jumper, or a 25 year old pasture gelding. The point of telling this story is to reinforce the idea of attaching yourself to nature and the earth through any means that fit you – whether it is through dogs, cats, birds, horses, reptiles, or even spiders. Finding your "natural niche" is essential for retaining happiness, in my opinion.

Hiking is also an excellent way to get back with nature. It is one of my most favorite ways to communicate silently with the intense life-force that surrounds me. The hikes do not have to be strenuous – unless I want a vigorous workout. Sometimes, I just like to walk at my own pace through the trails and drink in everything that I can. When I am walking through a forest or mountain trail, I always leave technology behind. I never take music or CD players with me when I am hiking. I will take a cell phone, but I leave it off. The only reason I take it is in case of an emergency.

Adrian and I are privileged in that we live very close to Smoky Mountain National Park in East Tennessee. We can go anytime we like and walk through the trails and visit the natural sites. I really enjoy the atmosphere and spending time with my husband. However, I have seen some people talking on their cell phones in the midst of all the beauty and majesty. I have heard people talking loudly among themselves and listening to their music as they walk along the trail.

This saddens me because these activities defeats the whole purpose of going into nature – to get *away* from these things that hold us prisoner in our everyday lives. The sad part is how many people cannot stand to be quiet and forget about their lives outside the mountains. It's as if they've forgotten how to let the everyday scramble in their life go. Some people have told me that they cannot afford to forget about these things – even for a little while because their job or their family affairs are too important. They could not be any more wrong. There is no career that is important enough that you cannot take an hour out of your time to turn off the cell phone and tune out the world. If you are a doctor on-call, wait until it is someone else's turn to be the on-call doctor and take that time to go off by yourself for a little while. Your patients and your physician staff will be grateful you did.

Sometimes when I am on hikes in the forest, I begin to let my mind fade away from all the heyday of my job and my life affairs. Eventually, I completely forget myself and allow my spirit to drift into the air and earth around me. It may sound strange, but I feel the trees speaking to the wildlife around them. I can actually hear them through my feet and throughout my whole body as I walk. I assure you I am not crazy and there are many others who see and feel the same things that I do. I have learned through experience that if you are still enough in your mind and quiet enough in your spirit, you will begin to hear the trees sending messages to everyone and everything around them – in the air and through the soil.

Dendrologists, or tree scientists, have known for quite some time that trees have an innate sense of when the seasons are going to change. Each autumn, all the deciduous (or leaf shedding) trees miraculously know when the cold weather is coming, and that they need to shed their leaves and run their sap down to their roots. Then, they will go into a hibernation stage all winter only to emerge or awaken in the spring with new growth on their branches. Although we now know that it is LifeConscious that controls when the trees react to the seasons, what other roles do trees specifically play in determining when other creatures emerge in the spring, for example?

The Druids, my ancestors, believed that trees, especially oaks, were sacred forms of life. Oaks usually live for a long time, sometimes hundreds of years, and were considered to be wise and all-knowing. The

Druids believed that oaks could help them predict the future, predict the seasons (when they were coming), and the severity of the weather conditions of the seasons so that they could adequately prepare their crops.

I believe that I have learned to do as my ancestors have done, which is communicating with trees and let them tell me when the seasons will change and how harsh the season will be. One day, many years ago, I placed my hands on the trunk of an oak tree, and I silenced my mind and focused on the pulsating rhythms of the earth beneath the tree. I could hear the gentle whispers of the wind through its branches. I felt myself becoming a part of the tree's roots – feeding from the soil and gathering nourishment from every pore. Then, after a few moments of this, I "heard" the messages being channeled through the root system and up to the very tops of the branches, and I understood them.

Trees cannot see, hear, or talk. Therefore, how can a tree communicate when spring is coming? How does it know to grow new buds on the branches? More importantly, how can I "listen" to a tree if it doesn't talk? Let me remind the reader of the last time you remember the "first" day of spring. Remember when you didn't need to wear your jacket outside or when you smelled the air, and it wasn't stifling cold? Perhaps you saw more green in your grass or felt the sun a bit warmer on your skin than it has in the past four months. You just "felt" spring coming. It is very similar with trees. They know what it feels like when spring has arrived. Therefore, when I communicate with a tree, I use only these types of feelings.

But then, how do trees know about time? They don't have clocks to tell them what time it is or an internal calendar to tell them what day it is. Or do they? Trees speak to me and other animals in terms of lunar cycles.

Farmers have known for centuries that certain crops are best planted during specific phases of the moon. Ask any vegetable farmer and he/ she will tell you that the best time to plant radishes, potatoes, carrots, and strawberries is after a full moon when it is waning to a third quarter. For those of you who are not familiar with lunar astronomy, the third quarter is the time of the month that the moon is "fading" from a full moon to about half. Then, the moon will seem to disappear for a few

days (new moon) only to emerge again as a crescent moon. All in all, it takes about 28 days for the moon to completely revolve around the earth. This is how we determine the length of a month! Each phase of the moon has a different amount of gravitational pull on the earth because the moon is shifting its position as it revolves around the earth. Plants can feel this variation in the moon's gravitational pull!

Botanists and Dendrologists alike have concluded that perhaps plants and trees have an innate sense that allows them to feel the pull of the moon's gravity – similar to how earth's tides work. Scientists think that there must be some chemical released in the plant when it "senses" a particular pull from the moon's gravity that tells them that they need to grow or go into hibernation. The scientists are correct. There *is* something that allows them to sense the pull of the moon's gravity. It's LifeConscious!

I do not think it is a coincidence that trees have always communicated information in terms of moon phases. I only recently found out in the past few years that there have been scientific studies done on trees, plants, and crops with phases of the moon. I believe that it is not just people who use phases of the moon to communicate with plants, but other creatures do, too. I believe that birds, foxes, and aquatic animals use phases of the moon to drive their instincts. There are even animals that live at the bottom of the ocean and never see the light of day. Nevertheless, even these creatures are still affected by the moon's pull on the oceans. I no longer wonder how this can be possible.

Conclusion

We have already gone over how LifeConscious is the life sustaining consciousness that is passed down from mother's to their babies using the natural carrier of water to transfer these ancient memories that have been a part of our species for thousands of years. There is only one organ in the human body that is built as a memory storage device and that is the brain, a brain in humans that has grown into a duality of minds – one brain with two consciousnesses.

We now know that one of the minds is your own personal consciousness, and the other is the consciousness that handles all of your life sustaining functions, including procreation and that is LifeConscious. These ancient memories were passed down from your mother as structured water molecules that mirrored her individual ancient memories. These "packets" of memories were transferred to the blank stem cells of your brain, stimulating the electrical polarity of the cells implanting that bit of memory while activating the neutral stem cells to form into neurons. This is just one bit in a steady stream of memories being transferred for the entire gestation period with no stopping at all. Even after you were born, this LifeConscious transference was still continuing as you suckled milk from your mother's breasts, felt her kisses, and shared her breaths. While she was stimulating your personal consciousness, she was also unknowingly still transferring not only more memories, but the antibodies and nutrients in her milk to give you a fighting chance at surviving.

Water is the carrier of these transferred ancient memories and the Extremely Low Frequencies (ELF) of 4 to 12 Hz are the communication frequencies of LifeConscious.

We have also provided examples of evidence of LifeConscious' existence. One was the organ transplants that have been occurring regularly with great success for many years but with one particular unforeseen effect of transference of an ailment or allergy of the donor to the host. How is this possible if the latent LifeConscious memory of that allergy in the kidney was not transferred to its host triggering the allergic reaction and now becoming part of that person's LifeConscious memories? This is exactly the memory transference that Dr. Jacques Benveniste experienced in his famous "Memory of Water" experiments.

A second example was the synchronous menstrual cycles caused by women living together. This is another obvious example of the transference effects of LifeConscious as the ladies breathed the same air, drank the same water and shared the same body oils in their environment. It is also an example of the communicative ELF affects that LifeConscious uses.

We discussed diseases and their spread. Allergies, for example, and other sensitivities have increased dramatically during the past generation – it is estimated that over 60 million Americans suffer from allergies and millions more from sensitivities. What could possibly be causing such an increase? We believe that it is the close proximity of people in transportation systems like planes and buses, classrooms, work places, and hospitals. It is the exact same thing that is occurring that causes synchronous menstrual cycles – LifeConscious at work when people are so compacted together sharing the air, water, food, and germs.

We've introduced you to the dipole nature of a water molecule and how this dipole nature causes the molecules to align themselves up by poles like super tiny magnets – positive pole to negative. These water molecules, when positioned against the memory cells of the mother's ancient brain, will mirror the tiny electrical charge of the cell. Water molecules will then shape themselves into a lattice behind the molecules, essentially copying the molecules' alignment in front of them. The further most lattices of water molecules will break off and enter the blood stream and eventually make it to a fetus' brain that is made up of mostly stem cells. Since the baby has not been stimulated by a LifeConscious memory, the stem cells will store that particular bit of memory from the mother. This is how LifeConscious memories are transferred through the carrier of water. Not only are memories transferred to the fetus, but chemical structural commands are sent to the fetus to "tell" what stem cells will become – liver cells, heart cells, skin cells, etc. Remember that DNA is the blueprint for building a human being. Nevertheless, it is the mother's LifeConscious that is the central force controlling the building.

Lastly, we discussed how LifeConscious controls women's menstruation. We explain how women suffer from PMS symptoms such as moodiness, cramps, headaches, and fatigue. We know that the reason for these symptoms occurring is a very ancient, natural cause of your special gift of procreation. In Chapter 7, we will talk about how ladies can reduce and possibly eliminate these symptoms – by working together with your LifeConscious instead of fighting against it.

The next chapter we will introduce you to the many faces in your very own mirror. We will explain this phenomenon and how this is caused by many generations of your own linear heritage.

Chapter 4

Many Faces in the Mirror

Women's many faces

Childhood imaginary friends

Imaginary or real

How we forget

Look in the mirror

What is ESP?

Multiple Personalities?

Reincarnation?

Are you crazy?

A child's face is his mirror. ***African Proverb***

For now we see through a (looking) glass, darkly; but then face to face: now I know in part; but then shall I know even as also I am known. **1 Corinthians 13:12**

Women's Many Faces

As a trained artist, I've drawn, painted, and photographed many subjects -especially women. The female figure is an art form in itself no matter what size, shape, age, color, clothed or not. The female form has been idolized and graces the walls in gilded Parisian galleries as well as smoky saloons in Tombstone, Arizona. We have mentioned in Chapter 1 that the very first subject to be carved from rock or scratched into cave walls by our ancestors over 20,000 years ago were depictions of the human female. No matter how enticing and titillating the female form is to me as a man, it is their faces that intrigued me the most. The myriad differences of eyes, lips, cheeks and of course the hair, is both challenging and captivating.

The face is the most expressive part of the human body. The eyes, nose, mouth and face muscles can be contorted to convey fear, loathing, hate, inquiry, love, laughter, and a smile. There are, however, other features that I've begun to perceive in the faces of some women, and that is the appearance of other faces overlapping the very face of the female I was looking at. At first, I thought that these were just my tired eyes playing tricks in my head, funny lighting, or reflections. It just never occurred to me that the multiple faces that I was indeed seeing were real but different faces until I met Heidi.

One night, I was supporting one of Heidi's divinations involving my deceased family members. I began to witness various faces overlapping Heidi's beautiful countenance. Again, I thought that my eyes were playing tricks on my brain as to what I was actually "seeing." But what I was observing was a different face every second or so superimposed over Heidi's face as she was talking to me. What was strange was that these different faces were also talking, but the voice was always Heidi's. These faces appeared to be related to her with some being older, younger, skinnier, fatter, and all with different hair styles. Except for just a few men, the majority was women's faces. Heidi's face had a whitish glow about it as the faces changed every second like a clicking slide projector. I was transfixed when she asked me what was wrong because my face must have looked confused. I told her that I was seeing multiple faces transposed on her face. She seemed very disturbed but intrigued.

Apparently, she was not very surprised at what I was seeing. She then related to me her childhood experiences with these faces. She told me how she saw these faces when she was a young child and was naturally frightened of them not knowing who they were. Because of Heidi's religious upbringing, she believed that she was being possessed or something of that nature. Heidi was very concerned about what I was seeing and walked toward a mirror in our bedroom to see for herself. What she saw is related in her own words at the end of this Chapter.

Childhood imaginary friends

First, let's touch on what happened to her as a child when she had to deal with this phenomenon of faces by herself with no help from her family, friends, or even her church. Could these people whom she saw be considered as childhood imaginary friends? According to our research, this is a likely possibility. What is described by the children and their parents as to what is actually happening to them depends on the culture, religion, and ethnic background of the child.

What is an imaginary friend anyway? They are make-believe animals, people or objects used by the child as entertainment when they are alone or want to be alone. They are used sometimes as alter egos, playing companions, heroes, voices of reason, or as instigators. Children can refer to their imaginary companions in different ways.

> *"The information from the parents gathered at the first interview also helped to clear up another source of confusion. Some children have their own idiosyncratic way of referring to an imaginary companion. At the time of the first interview, parents sometimes told us that their child used another term, such as "fake friend," "ghost sister," or "friends who live in my house." In these cases, we used the child's own term to ask about imaginary companions at the time of the second interview"* (Taylor, 28-29). [1]

---

1 Excerpt from page 28-29 from *Imaginary Companions and the Children Who Create Them* by Majorie Taylor printed By permission of Oxford University Press. (5/3/01)

The "ghost sister" and "friends who live in my house" are a very interesting and yet remarkable coincidence – or is it? Does this mean that Heidi is alone in seeing these multiple faces on her own, or in witnessing other non-living entities when she was young? I think the answer is a resounding NO.

(Heidi) I myself have had many imaginary friends growing up. The important thing is that I always knew the difference between what was going on in my own imagination and what was real – even as a small child. I still remember having fantasies about having little sisters or brothers to play with. I even dreamed about having a loving father who would spend time with me and care for me when I was upset. He was a large fellow with a red beard and was dressed like a fisherman. However, I knew this was a character that I had made up, and that he wasn't real. It was still fun for me to make-believe that he was my friend.

Then, occasionally as I was playing by myself on the playground, I would suddenly see someone walking in the background by some trees. I would look up at the person, and they would appear as a dark figure, sometimes a white figure. They would stop and look at me for a little while. Sometimes, I would sense that they were smiling at me (although I could not clearly see their faces). Then, they would move along and eventually, I would watch them disappear. I would know that the figure I had seen was real and not something that I imagined.

Before I am passed off at this point as being a crazy lunatic, I would like to point out that as I got older, I did try and pass off supernatural events as childhood phases and just a part of my normal psychological development. However, events kept happening to me despite my efforts to suppress them. In fact, I actually became an unhappy, depressed individual when I tried to deny that these gifts were a natural part of me – nothing to be disturbed or frightened about. I found out that the more I really allowed myself to experience these things that the better at it I became and the more knowledge and wisdom were given to me. With that out of the way, let's get back to my story.

As far as using "imaginary friends" as culprits for my bad behavior, I never used these dark or white figures to take blame off of myself, whenever I had done something wrong. I was a smart girl, and I knew

my mother was no idiot. I knew that there was no one else to blame but myself for my misbehavior, and I was going to be punished for it anyway because I was the only child in the house. So, what good would it have been for me to use my "friends" as a scapegoat? Besides, I never saw these figures as my "friends." I could tell that they were different from me and had no interest in childhood fantasies.

Heidi is not alone – this is an experience that apparently has been shared by many individuals when they were young, vulnerable, and confused about what was happening to them. Confused, because when they questioned the adults around them about what they were experiencing, they were given a myriad number of answers. The most common ones are: "it's your imagination", "you're dreaming", and the more frequently used, "it's the devil or Satan".

> *"The mention of Satan brings up the second type of concern that members of some fundamentalist groups have about fantasy, in general, and imaginary companions, in particular. This concern is espoused by fundamentalists who have a particular interest in or preoccupation with spiritual warfare. Parents with this belief system are very concerned about protecting their children from evil forces in the spiritual world. Imaginary companions are sometimes explicitly discussed in this context. For example, in one book on spiritual protection for children, parents are given the following advice: "Many children have imaginary 'friends' they play with. It can be harmless unless the imaginary friend is talking back. Then it is no longer imaginary.... A child's dependence on spirit 'friends' will eventually result in spiritual bondage. This must be identified as soon as possible. Satan disguises himself as an angel of light, so young children probably won't see the danger"* (Taylor, 56-57). [2]

Some parents may say that having imaginary friends are harmful to their children and try to discourage them from having any. Are having imaginary friends harmful to the child in any way? The findings and studies that were done prove just the opposite when it comes to social skills.

---

2 Excerpt from page 56-57 from Imaginary Companions and the Children Who Create Them by Majorie Taylor printed By permission of Oxford University Press.

> *"Other studies have yielded similar findings. Jerome Singer and Dorothy Singer observed 111 children playing at day cares over the course of a year and found that children who were identified as having imaginary companions were less fearful and anxious in their play with other children. They were also described as smiling and laughing more than children without imaginary companions. In another study, college students who remembered having imaginary companions in childhood were found to be less neurotic, less introverted, more dominant in face-to-face situations, more self-confident, and more sociable than college students who did not remember any childhood pretend friends"* (Taylor, 37).

Percentage of girls

What should be most intriguing to women about some of these childhood imaginary friends is that the majority of the children who experience these friends are girls and that girls interact with their companions in a character that is a more capable individual in their relationship. Boys, on the other hand, have imaginary friends who have characteristics that they would like to have or achieve.

> *"One of the most frequently made claims about the differences between children with and without imaginary companions concerns their gender. In many studies, girls are reported to be more likely to create imaginary companions than boys. Why do we find this gender difference? Is it because girls play with dolls, which are apt to be included as imaginary companions? Are boys less interested in imaginative play or more reluctant to reveal their fantasies to an experimenter?*(Taylor, 48). [3]

Why is it that women, as girls, are more apt to have childhood imaginary friends than boys? Again, it comes back to the reason that women are more attached to nature and have a closer relationship with their own and the earth's LifeConscious. Perhaps having relationships with imaginary friends nurtures this natural instinct in females to care for others.

3 Excerpt from page 37/48 from Imaginary Companions and the Children Who Create Them by Majorie Taylor printed By permission of Oxford University Press. (5/3/01)

Imaginary or real

Another social anomaly that needs to be addressed is that of families no longer living in groups within the same environmental confines as their ancestors. In the Western Hemisphere, families are usually living several states or countries away from one another. In my case, I have a brother whose family is living in Alabama, my daughter and sister's families live in South Carolina, a niece's family that calls Savannah, Georgia home, and another sister and her family living in Delaware – not to mention a niece and nephew attending colleges in Boston. This separation of families has not always been the norm until the great migrations to the "New World" from Europe and Asia in the last few centuries. With the advent of reliable transportation such as ships, trains, planes, and automobiles, whole families can be moved in a matter of hours now.

Dependable communication with family members has also increased since the dawn of mail delivery. What used to take weeks or months for information to arrive now takes mere seconds with cell phones and email. We, in the West, have become so used to instantaneous communication and fast travel that we can still sustain at least a semblance of maintaining the family unit. Even though the communication between family members is present, there is a missing element helping to maintain the cohesion of the family unit and that is cohabitation. This cohabiting or living together seems to affect interpretations of imaginary friends. In the West or so-called "modern countries" where families are more dispersed, there seems to be a predominance of imaginary friends; or at least an acceptance that these friends do exist whether it is in the mind or not. While in Asia, it's not imaginary friends, but the belief in reincarnation that takes place.

In the so-called "third world countries" where the family unit still thrives, the idea of imaginary friends is almost nonexistent or denied. There is, however, a very strong belief in reincarnation. Children are often viewed as reincarnations of deceased family members that can sometimes remember or relive a former life or even lives.

> *"Overall, children appear to be clear about the fantasy status of their imaginary friends. But a final complexity is well worth some discussion. Although some children create companions or even worlds that they never share with others, in many cases, children's fantasies are given interpretations by those around them. These interpretations are influenced by the values and beliefs of individuals in the family as well as by the culture in which the children live. It is possible that part of children's understanding of their imaginary companions as fantasy is specific to Western culture.*
>
> *My basis for this claim is a fascinating study by Antonia Mills on imaginary companions in India. She began her research in India by conducting an informal survey in which she asked psychologists as well as other adults if they knew of any children who had imaginary companions. The answer was universally "no." At first, she attributed this result to the conditions in which children in India are raised. American children who have imaginary companions tend to have periods of time in which they are alone due to the circumstances of their place in the family (the youngest child who plays alone when the older children are at school) or where they live. In contrast, Indian children are rarely alone. They do not sleep, eat, or play alone. However, Mills realized that denial might also be based on the use of the word "imaginary." She began to wonder if children who were thought to have imaginary companions in the United States would be thought to be remembering previous lives if they lived in India, and vice versa.*
>
> *Mills found that when Indian children talk to entities that adults cannot perceive, the entity is referred to as invisible rather than imaginary. The assumption is that the child is communicating with a very real being who exists on a spiritual realm or is part of the child' Past life. Mills identified cases in*

> *India of parents who claimed their children had memories for past identities. She found that the time frame that is typical for imaginary companions is similar for the phenomena of past lives and that most of the children who talked about past lives were the youngest or next to youngest in the family. At about age 7, children were taught not to remember the past life. Because adults feared the children would take on this past identity rather than pursuing their current one. Overall, memories for past lives are not as common in India as imaginary companions are in the United States (about 0.2 percent of children in northern India compared with at least 30 percent of North American children having imaginary companions). However, Mill's research suggests that the two phenomena are related and indicate that children are taught to understand and experience themselves and their perceptions in ways specific to their culture"* (Taylor, 115-116).

Marjorie Taylor made a remarkable observation concerning how some children seemed to be communicating with beings in the spiritual realm or a past life. This, in essence, is part of the focus of this book. What you are actually seeing or experiencing when you look in the mirror is past female lives who have become a part of your LifeConscious linear motherly heritage. Unfortunately, these childhood occurrences are more often than not squelched by parents or religious leaders. These imaginary friends or past lives are delegated to the dust bins of "just your imagination" or "it's the devil that you hear". It is usually a man who is making the decisions for the child to change their minds about what they are experiencing. A man who doesn't have a clue as to what exactly is happening to you and is judging you as someone who has a mental problem, seeing things, or being possessed.

Another aspect of imaginary friends whom Taylor discusses is the disturbing fact that a lot of young girls must suffer through the tremendous anguish and torment of sexual abuse from relatives. Does this abuse help these children to open the doors to imaginary friends? Yes it does, but as we shall see, these children could already have had the propensity to acquire pretend friends or see spiritual beings.

> *Another type of trauma in the lives of some of children is physical and sexual abuse at the hands of a parent, neighbor or relative. According to Dr. Frank Putnam, chief of the Unit on Dissociative Disorders at the National Institute of Health, about 89 percent of the children who are abused have imaginary companions. Thus, it appears that abused children may frequently turn to fantasy as part of their response to their difficult life situations. In cases of severe and prolonged abuse, some individuals go on to develop dissociative identity disorder (previously known as multiple personality disorder). As mentioned earlier, dissociative identity disorder is diagnosed when a person seems to have more than one distinct personality that at times take control of the person's body outside of their awareness. A person with dissociative identity disorder might suddenly realize that he or she cannot remember what has happened over the past few days or even months, a time when the alter personality was active"* (Taylor, 81-82). [4]

The faces that some women see in the mirror we feel is the real cause of some of the multiple personality disorders. Think about it – these are relatives in your past motherly LifeConscious lineage may sometimes feel compelled to whisper in your ear or even act on your behalf by taking over your own personal consciousness and replacing it with their own for brief moments. These communications are understandably troubling to some girls or women since it takes them by surprise and alarms them because of the voices that they hear in their heads – voices that are strange sounding, but somehow familiar. We also believe that this conflict of personalities could explain other phenomena such as UFO body snatching in which a person looses a big chunk of time in their lives that they can't account for. What about those feelings of Déjà Vu where a place, smell, or picture is strangely familiar to you?

So, how does a child eventually forget their imaginary friends or encounters with dead ancestors? Having heard the negative rhetoric constantly through their young life, they begin to believe "learned" individuals and the process of denial starts taking effect on their psyche. The imaginary friend is forgotten or replaced by a real person, hobby, sport, or religion. Even

4 Excerpt from page 115-116/81-82 from Imaginary Companions and the Children Who Create Them by Majorie Taylor printed By permission of Oxford University Press. (5/3/01)

though glimpses of the imaginary friend or past life occur occasionally it is automatically dismissed as unreal or improbable. As people get older, these memories are usually forgotten or at the very least denied. Many times, people may feel these entities speaking to them, experience them in a dream, or catch a glimpse of them out of the corner of the eye.

Our minds are a funny repository of past memories. How many of us can recall the names of our friends that we had in grade school? Since the mind is mostly graphical in nature, it is the "snapshot" of the last image of a face that we see that is stored in our memories. You've already read the example about the remembrance of a childhood friend that you haven't seen in many years. How the last image that you had of him in your memory was now being updated as you conversed with him and vice versa. The face that will now be stored is the one that you see before you. When and if you ever see him again in the near future, you will instantly recognize him. Not only are the faces revised, but the information of the individual that is exchanged are brought up to date.

Even this renewed knowledge can be passed on to others that question you about your encounter with the friend as they, themselves, get caught up. For example, a brother who went to the same school and knew this friend is also now relying on your recollections of him to update his own memories.

This is essentially how our minds work – by being constantly updated as we go through our routines during the day. Things that don't seem to change at all or even those things or individuals that we never want to see change like our children, homes, or workplace does, in fact, change. It fools our minds into thinking that time is not moving at all. Just go back a few years and think about or view photographs of your children from a few years back. You will see the difference and remember those faces and surroundings once again; maybe triggering a pleasant memory or two.

If we don't see or interact with individuals for a long period of time, they may be "lost" in our memories. When someone mentions their name you find it hard to place a face on them as a reference. However, we can still recall some memorable times shared together. We are all dissimilar in our memory capacities such as the differences between Heidi and I. I can't recall any of my grade school friends or teachers, whereas she can. This difference was probably due to the fact that she grew up in the same town along with attending school with the same students throughout her whole childhood.

I was constantly moving around the country and meeting new people since my father was in the military. I would never stay in the same town for more then a couple of years or so – always meeting new students with each new school I attended. However, it could be that Heidi just has a better memory than I do.

This particular memory that we have been talking about has to do, of course, with our own personal consciousness. Our personal consciousness is constantly updating itself daily as we communicate with our friends, family, and coworkers along with interacting with our environment. Remember that there is another consciousness at work here, and it is a consciousness brought about by this linear organism that has given life to all the mothers in your ancestry.

Look in the Mirror

Now that you realize that you are not possessed by the devil or verging on insanity, you can finally look into any mirror with confidence knowing that there is nothing, even remotely, daunting about it. You are experiencing a natural occurrence that happens to many women. This chapter is like getting your first sex talk from your mother when you were just a kid when she cleared up a lot of the fanciful talk that you and your other girl friends had when you were trying to figure out the sex thing. Hopefully, we will clear up any confusion you may have felt when you were young. We shall see who these people are that you saw in the mirror occasionally that looked familiar to you.

(Heidi) When do we look in the mirror? You probably look at yourself in the morning to make sure your hair, makeup, and outfit look good before you go out to your job or school. Perhaps you take an extra look as you pass by a mirror in the bathroom or in the hallway just to make sure you don't have something embarrassing on your face or in your teeth. Maybe you don't like to look in the mirror. Perhaps you don't like the way you look because you think you're ugly, old-looking and wrinkly, or overweight. Let me tell you that whatever you look like, you should always look in the mirror. To know and accept what you look like is important to recognize about yourself.

Whether you are a man or a woman, we all have to look in a mirror sometimes. Even so, have you ever looked deeper than the surface of your skin? Without sounding too narcissist, what if you looked deeply into your eyes and completely cleared your mind? You might learn some

things about yourself that you haven't seen in a long time. For example, you might remember how you used to look when you were little and that may bring back pleasant memories. On the other hand, you may see a negative person that longs to be happy again and find enjoyment in the small things. Whatever you see, I recommend that you practice looking in the mirror everyday – not to examine your appearance, but to gaze at your reflection and realize that you are the product of literally thousands of generations that made you up. Realize that their blood is your blood. Think about all your ancestors that have come before you and what they might have looked like. Who knows? Maybe you still resemble them in some ways!, When you look at yourself, think about how you can honor their memories in your life. What can you do to make a positive impact in your community and in your family?

Look in the mirror and see your past! Think about how your ancestors may have lived during their respective centuries and eras and then realize that all their hard work and all their efforts brough*t you* here! That should make you feel very important because what you are seeing in the mirror is your linear heritage. You are the end result of a long line of birthing women – women who are still there coursing through your veins and that have transferred their LifeConscious down to you. Your LifeConscious memories allow you to see and experience these women who have a long and seemingly unending relationship to you. So, look in the mirror closely, and you will see their faces; ones that you shouldn't be frightened of anymore because these face*s are* you.

We've already shown you that proof that your ancestors are still with you is evident when you ask yourself a question and an answer magically appears in your head. Where did this answer come from? Scientists will tell you that you are answering your own question. Well, if this is the case then why did you need to ask the question in the first place? We propose that these answers are coming from your own ancestors: ancestors who are still with you in mind and in spirit that is just trying to help you. Some individuals have a hard time dealing with answers that come out of nowhere, however. They feel like they are having a mental problem or that a demon is answering.

Does seeing these faces or hearing answers to your own questions mean that you've joined the ranks of individuals that have been diagnosed with some sort of mental disorder? Do you sometimes feel as if there are two personalities within you trying to gain control of your body at the same time? A lot of mental and personality disorders have been wrongly diagnosed in many women. We will attempt to ease your mind through careful and thorough research that this is not some insane dialogue that you are having with yourself.

What is ESP? Is it evil?

(Heidi) We bring up the subject of ESP (Extra Sensory Perception) because this brain phenomenon affects more people in the world than you realize. It does have a purpose, and it is real. ESP also has a lot to do with linear heritage because ESP often runs strongest within families. Some people hear the combined letters ESP and scoff at it because of all the negative connotations that come along with it. Skeptics do not even want to look at the word because they have already dismissed it as something made up. Despite these skeptics, it is estimated that 67 percent of Americans claim to have experienced an ESP event in their life, according to a study done by the University of Chicago in 1987.

The Webster's Dictionary defines ESP as "extrasensory perception (n), 1934: perception (as in telepathy, clairvoyance, and precognition) that involves awareness of information about events external to the self not gained through the senses and not deducible from previous experience."

The history of ESP starts around 1870 with a handful of university professors who would develop what is now known as parapsychology. These professors from Duke University conducted various experiments used to test the reality of telepathy. They came up with a system of cards with varying symbols on them, and the subject was to tell the cardholder what symbol was on the card without looking at it. The results of the subject were 5 out of 25 correct responses – which is precisely what probability would have calculated anyway. However, when the experiment was repeated, this time with some of the subjects

under hypnosis, the psychologists were surprised to find that these subjects got about 12 out of 25 right – a considerably higher number. It was therefore, determined that people that were in a very relaxed state of mind were more apt to be capable of psychic abilities.

This evidence sounds great, doesn't it? However, the professors could not understand why they could not reproduce these results every time they conducted an experiment. What were the conditions under which these tests would work? They found out that there were too many variables that added into the ESP equation. Subjects' personalities, belief systems, and mood at the time of the tests were just some of the many factors that could not be scientifically measured. It would be like predicting the stock market. Whenever the human factor is added to any mathematical equation, you are not going to get a very scientific answer.

This is why today's scientific community does not accept the evidence of ESP. Because the results from past experiments such as these are not enough to produce a theory out of a formed hypothesis or the lack of ingredients necessary to adequately stand alone as a physical reality. However, in recent years the study of quantum mechanics has come up with theories based on alternate universes and multiple dimensions. The possibilities of ESP are becoming more believable to many scientists – although no quantifiable scientific evidence has been accumulated. The main reason why many scientists and skeptics alike do not believe that ESP is real is because of the lack of a viable theory (scientific) behind the mechanism for ESP. On top of this lack of scientific evidence, there have been many unfortunate hoaxes over the years were fraudulent experiments were done – laughing in the face of science and reason. This only confirmed this belief in ESP to be false.

If you are a skeptic, here is your chance to read about the mechanism (LifeConscious) for ESP and all supernatural abilities that humans possess. Now that we have learned about what LifeConscious is, we can understand how LifeConscious can pass on the memory of extrasensory perception. This is how humans can have this ability and why some people do not seem to exhibit as many ESP traits. They are either passed down through generations of extra-sensory parents, or they have been possibly bred out of their particular family line for some adaptive purpose.

Then, we may beg the question, why do humans need ESP? If this is an evolutionary process that we inherit through LifeConscious in our brain, what purpose does it serve our species to keep it in our genes? This is a great question, indeed. For the answer, we must look back at the beginning of our species when we were hunter/gatherers.

Some herding animals, schooling fish, as well as insects like bees, ants and termites have been observed as having ESP. Animals and fish on the opposite side of a herd or school will react before the first sign of trouble from predators is even seen by the attacked side. They seem to sense the anxiety and fear that the attacked side is experiencing as if they were being chased and killed. Ants and termites will react to chemical messages almost immediately when their nest is attacked or damaged. Bees will begin stinging their enemies when their hive is threatened even though the stinging act itself will take their tiny little lives. In all of these cases, this sense of ESP is for the propagation of the species by helping them stay one step ahead of predators. We also think that this is how some humans attained this gift for the benefit of our own species. Perhaps we needed to sense predators that threatened groups of humans. The hunters could have used ESP to predict where the herds were located, using a technique known as "remote viewing." In this way, hunters could stay in the same location but be able to tell where a herd was located – thus reducing the amount of time to look for a herd. This skill was also useful when tracking became difficult – such as cloudy days or deep snow. There were probably many such times in human prehistory that we used ESP for our survival.

The same was most likely true for females also. We have already discussed physical LifeConscious-driven adaptations for early human survival – such as the synchronizing of women's menstrual cycles. However, there were other skills that were necessary – such as sensing their babies' needs through their cries, communicating with nature to know about the coming seasons, or knowing which herbs to take to treat illness. Even today, many of these inherited "supernatural" traits are noticeable in women. Have you noticed that some mothers seem to be able to read the minds of their own children? I know for a fact that my mother had this ability because she could sense a problem with one of her children and deduce what initiated it – even if I never told her a thing about it! But, is this ESP or just a mother's sensitivity to her own children? Whatever you believe, it seems certain that women have an innate sense to be extremely perceptive toward family, friends, and strangers alike.

So what does all this talk of ESP and evolution have to do with these faces in the mirror? Could ESP also be your ancestors helping you? Could this misunderstanding between us and our ancestors be the root cause of other misdiagnosed mental disorders? We shall see that these subjects are interwoven together and are a part of our linear heritage.

Multiple Personalities?

If you've taken a basic psychology course in college, you probably know something about Multiple Personality Disorder – a condition where there is the presence of two or more distinct personalities that will individually take control of a person's body. It's as if you were dealing with several different people with diverse personalities, but they all look the same through that person's eyes.

This disorder is felt to be a mental process of chemical imbalances in the brain and not as the result of a narcotic, medication or alcohol. This disease can cause sudden blackouts or bewildering behavior. The various characters that develop in the patient's mind are real but separate personal identities – not to be confused with an imaginary friend or some kind of fantasy enactment.

In recent years, the American Psychiatric Society has chosen to change the Multiple Personality Disorder's designation to Dissociative Identity Disorder or DID. This was done because they felt that the term Multiple Personality was somewhat misleading. The traits of a person diagnosed with DID include the following:

1 The feeling within them that there are multiple entities or independent personalities.

2 Two or more of these entities will take control of the individual's behavior for extended periods of time creating gaps of memory for the primary individual's personal consciousness.

The term "personalities" was a sticking point for the psychologists who would rather use the following expressions for these entities: alternate personalities, alters, parts, states of consciousness, ego states or identities. No matter what expression was used, it was important to these psychologists to remember that these were just manifestations of an individual person. The assumption being that there are no other "real" entities controlling the individual's body, which in our view is what is really happening.

Modern psychotherapists like to believe that while it's convenient to talk of people who suffer from this disorder as having "multiple personalities," that this is just a theoretical construct. People who suffer from this disorder actually believe that they have multiple personalities, which take on a life of their own within the individual's psyche. With the new term for this disorder, Dissociative Identity Disorder, patients feel this more accurately explains their actual condition. Their personality is the sum of these identities, which have been split off at some point in the past. They sometimes feel that the split is usually due to some single or multiple traumatic events such as abuse or death of a loved one.

Psychotherapy is the treatment of choice for individuals suffering from any type of dissociative disorder. Techniques vary, but generally involve just the individual. Group therapy is not usually recommended in these cases. The treatment usually tries to accentuate the combination of these multiple personality states into one organized, complete personality.

Even more confusing is the fact that most people tend to think of bipolar disorder, schizophrenia, and multiple personality disorders in the same vein, but this is due to the abuse of these terms in the media. These are all separate mental diseases and are handled very differently. Bipolar disorder, or manic depression, is the more commonly diagnosed of the three disorders. The most common signs are large mood swings by analyzed individuals. These swings can go from extreme multitasking when a person takes on too many projects only later to collapse into a depressive state because of the failure to complete any tasks. Bipolar treatment can involve the use of an antidepressant when the individual is dejected or depressed. Unfortunately, this may cause the patient to be in an extremely emotionless, but belligerent state. Many bipolar patients refuse to stay on their medication for this reason.

Schizophrenia is much less common than bipolar disorder and is generally diagnosed early in the patient. Curiously, more men than women receive this diagnosis. The characteristics of this disease are feelings of delusions, hallucinations, or hearing things that aren't there. These delusions can be so real that even when faced with overwhelming evidence the patient will still believe in the delusion. Treatments for schizophrenia are sometimes tricky because of the enormous difficulty in the patient accepting a rational cause for their delusions or hallucinations. The patient is often argumentative to the point of irrationality and may become violent if they feel they are cornered. Often logic is totally out of place in a person suffering from schizophrenia and will argue their point persistently. Those individuals that are diagnosed with the disorder find it difficult to interact with others in society and become confrontational when faced with resuming their treatment. This causes others to avoid interaction with schizophrenics who often can't hold down a steady job. Many eventually join the ranks of the homeless; prowling the streets for a living, or even worse, committing petty crimes to cycle through the prison system to simply have a roof over their heads.

The bottom line is that statistically speaking, women make up 90% of those diagnosed with dissociative identity disorder (split personalities), and women make up 75% of those diagnosed with borderline personality disorders. Now we know the reason – it's because women are much more in tune with nature and their ancestors than men are. Women are more responsive to the effects of changes in their environment. For instance, women are more sensitive to Electro Magnetic Forces (EMF) that are caused by high voltage lines or old electrical appliances. Heidi is very sensitive to high EMF. Her stomach gets queasy and she gets headaches. Some common sources of high EMF are found near high voltage lines, electrical power stations, and transformers.

Let's continue to explore another interesting region that I think has a lot to do with our understanding of women's natural sensitivities along with their linear heritage and that is reincarnation.

Reincarnation

The definition of Reincarnation literally means "to be **made flesh** again" a term used in the New Testament in John 1:14 "And the Word was **made flesh**, and dwelt among us." It is a dogma or metaphysical belief that some essential part of a living being survives death to be reborn in a new body. This essential part is often referred to as the spirit or soul; the "higher" or "true" self, "divine spark", or "I". According to such beliefs, a new personality is developed during each life in the physical world, but some part of the self remains constant throughout the successive lives.

A pioneer on this subject, Dr. Ian Stevenson, was the founder of scientific research into reincarnation and was best known for collecting and meticulously researching cases of children who seem to recall past lives without the need for hypnosis. He delves into the possible reasons why belief in reincarnation has disappeared in Western culture. Some southern European Christians believed in reincarnation until the Council of Nicaea banned such beliefs in 553 A.D. Nicaea marked the beginning of the end of similar concepts such as preexistence, reincarnation, and salvation through a union with God in Christian doctrine.

In *The Republic*, Plato described souls about to be reborn as choosing their future lives. Schopenhauer (a modern German philosopher) took this seriously. Another European philosopher, Voltaire, observed, "It is no more surprising to be born twice than once." Yet, most scientists nowadays do not believe in survival after death. Some have blamed Darwinism, liberalism, or atheistic ideas for contributing to the dethroning of the human soul. Reincarnation may be particularly uncongenial because it's so much identified, mistakenly I think, with the Hindu and Buddhist ideas. Perhaps many Westerners do not like their belief of the possibility of being reborn as an animal.

(Heidi) We the authors realize that the belief in reincarnation is a very hot issue for most religions – whether it is a belief for or against it. We want to offer some information that we feel compelled to share. Some of you may be able to relate the story I am about to tell below. Perhaps you have a similar situation in your family. I am not necessarily suggesting that I am a reincarnation of one or both of my grandparents. I am merely sharing my experiences in hopes that you may find comfort in knowing that you are not alone.

I never knew my grandparents on my mother's side. They both died just a few months before I was born. My mother had the unfortunate circumstance of taking care of me as a newborn baby while at the same time coping with the death of both her parents. Ironically, my first cousin was born just eight days before I was. Both my cousin and I have always exhibited remarkable physical and personality traits of our grandparents. I can't speak for my cousin, but I have always felt like I was out of place my whole life. The sort of activities I enjoyed were not typical things that young children would enjoy. For example, my favorite types of music growing up were not necessarily Debbie Gibson, Duran Duran, or Madonna like most people would be associate with children from the 80's; but on the contrary – I was listening to The Beach Boys, Tommy and the Shondells, and The Beatles. In fact, when I was seven years old, I asked my mother if we could go to a Beatles concert because I loved their records so much. To my astonishment, I did not know that the Beatles had broken up 13 years earlier – not to mention that John Lennon had been assassinated about a year before I was born.

The people whom I chose as my friends growing up were not the usual peers that I went to class with. Instead, I befriended the teachers at my school, the ladies in my mother's Garden Club, and the leaders at my church. I found that I had a lot of similar interests with them. While I overheard my mother's friends tell her how extremely mature I was for my age, I never believed that I was still perceived as a child by everyone. I certainly did not feel like a child. I could easily hold adult conversations as a small child. I was even able to read and write as far back as I can remember – mainly because I taught myself, but also

because perhaps the memories of my deceased grandparents somehow retained themselves in me. Maybe I liked old black and white movies – maybe I liked music such as Bobby Vinton and Dean Martin – maybe I enjoyed talking about stories on the evening news rather than video games on my Nintendo because my grandparents' memories were alive and well within me and were placed in my mother's womb when they passed away. I do not know exactly what could have happened. However, I do know that I have always felt very close to my grandparents – even though I have never seen or talked to them when they were alive, or after they passed away.

A famous researcher in religious studies, Antonia Mills, also noted the denial of reincarnation in the West.

> *"Western psychology has for the most part, with the exception of Jung, not considered the concept of soul or reincarnation of a soul in addressing what constitutes as a human being. Western psychology typically posits that a person's individuality is the product of the interplay of environment and heredity, an approach which creates the concept that each human being is a unique product of the chance combination of maternal and paternal genetic codes, interacting with his or her prenatal and postnatal environment"* (Mills, 212).

Here is another quote about Westerners not accepting reincarnation as a valid world-view as seen by the Native American tribes when European settlers first encountered them. Mills puts it simply here.

> *"Early colonists and, later, anthropologists were not expecting to find reincarnation belief among the Amerindians; reincarnation was not part of their world-view. Reincarnation was known to educated American colonists from its classical Greek forms; they were largely unaware of the Hindu and Buddhist reincarnation texts which were not translated and accessible to Western scholars until some 350 years after initial European colonization of the New World"* (Mills, 4)."

Another researcher in this field, Ian Stevenson, did substantial work with children and their beliefs in reincarnation. After many observations and experiments, he made some conclusions.

> *"You cannot emphasize too strongly that a child who is going to remember a previous life has only about three years in which he will talk about it. Before the age of two or three he lacks the ability. After five, too much else will be happening in his life, and he will begin to forget."* (http://reluctant-messenger.com/).

This is exactly what you would expect, since the "new eyes" of children become more focused on their new environment and the trappings that go along with it. The developing personal consciousness begins to take control over the child's young mind as their LifeConscious continues to control their life functions. As the child grows older they begin to deny or forget the connection with their ancestors when they were babes and find toys, television, religion, school and music more distracting. Young people and adults find it very difficult to remember any former lives without going through some sort of hypnosis. Unexplained artistic talents, spontaneous abilities, excellent vocabulary, and even sexual preferences are examples of mysterious skills or inclinations that some children have that certainly weren't passed down from their own families. This could explain child prodigies and homosexual tendencies

> *"Although a child might have no conscious memories (imaged memories) from a former life, his interests, aptitudes, and phobias (behavioral memories) might have been formed by experiences he or she had forgotten. Perhaps reincarnation could explain features of the human personality that other theories have failed to elucidate."* (http://reluctant-messenger.com/).

Stevenson's dissatisfaction with the scientific community's explanation of these unusual occurrences is significant.

> *"I had become dissatisfied, you see, with the methods that had been developed in psychiatry for helping people. Orthodox theory conceives human personality as the product of a person's genetic material inherited from his ancestors through his parents and the modifying influences of his prenatal and postnatal environment. But I found that some cases cannot be satisfactorily explained by genetics, environmental influences, or a combination of these. I am speaking of such things as*

> *early childhood phobias, about uncanny abilities that seem to develop spontaneously, of children convinced that they are the wrong sex, congenital deformities, differences between one-egg twins, and even such matters as irrational food preferences"(* http://reluctant-messenger.com/).

The explanation now becomes clear concerning these shortcomings that genetics can't explain when it comes to inherited memories or abilities. It comes as a consequence of LifeConscious memories passed down from mother to child. Again, these memories certainly can't come from genes or DNA as we have already found out. These discrepancies may also explain the major differences in siblings that have the same parents and general upbringing. It is amazing the amount of differences between me and my brothers and sisters. It's almost as if we all had different fathers or something and I'm absolutely sure that this is certainly not the case. To us this is proof that these differences come not through DNA but from the memories and abilities of ancestors who have passed away and are sharing these gifts with their progeny.

How the previous soul lost their lives appears to be very important for the conditions of reincarnation. It appears that if the individual suffered a violent or quick death, their memory would be more readily recollected by the host child. We think that this could be due to the dead not believing that they are actually dead and, in a panic, are desperately trying to attain a new body at any cost. Their violent death is still so fresh in their spirit, that it is transferred to the child host's memories.

We also think that this is the cause of a lot of children's bad dreams or nightmares where they dream of people trying to catch, control, attack, or get inside them. Children often experience bogey men or monsters in their bedrooms – especially if they sleep alone. Since they have a hard time communicating to their parents what they are seeing or experiencing, then they are not believed or are told that bogey men don't exist. Heidi has a very interesting experience of her own that happened to her as a child that she writes about in Chapter 5.

Stevenson's research also came to this "violent death" conclusion and the memory lapsing of older children.

> *"For example, as children grow older their memories of past lives frequently begin to fade. In addition, children who*

remember past lives often remember lives which ended in violent deaths)._ They also found that the interval between death and rebirth is shorter in the cases in which the previous personality died violently. This raises the question of how much time normally elapses between death and re-birth. Mills noted that some re-births happen in a few days or months, while in others the interval is 10 years or longer. Cases in which there is a very long interval would be less likely to be diagnosed since the child would be in a position to make fewer recognitions of people and places from a life a hundred years before. Other patterns that have been noted are that some children remembering a previous life had a phobia related to the cause of death in the past life, and some have birthmarks and birth defects related to (often) fatal wounds or other marks on the concerned deceased person." (http://reluctant-messenger.com/).

What is even more amazing is his findings of marks on the child host's bodies that emulate an occurrence of the previous life.

"Indeed, one of the striking features of Stevenson's research, featured in his three volumes of 1997(a& b), has been the correlation between birthmarks or birth defects on the bodies of young children who are said to remember a previous life with wounds or scars received in the past life. Speaking to this remarkable aspect of Stevenson's work, Mills mentioned a case she studied in India in which a person had a round birthmark on his temple (Mills 1989). The autopsy of the person that child claimed to be revealed that the fatal bullet had entered the previous personality's temple in the same location where the child had the small round birthmark. The autopsy also showed that the bullet had exited behind the right ear of the previous personality. Going back to the child, Mills found that he had a distended area in the skull behind his right ear, matching the bullet point of exit. Stevenson (1997a,b) has documented other cases of bullet entry and exit wounds in reincarnation cases, as well as a wide variety of idiosyncratic wounds corresponding to subsequent birthmarks and birth defects on children who remember a previous life and death. He notes other cases, such as those coming from the indigenous Ibo of Nigeria, in which the practice of mutilating a deceased child

> *relates to corresponding birth defects on children subsequently born (Stevenson 1985, 1997a,b). Stevenson also notes the correspondence of birthmarks on children in Burma with marks made on the deceased body of the previous personality."* (http://reluctant-messenger.com/).

Reincarnation could also explain the phenomenon of "Alien Limb Syndrome" in which the sufferer feels that an appendage doesn't belong on their body. The offending appendage is usually a leg or arm. The sufferer of this tragic disorder will often go to great lengths to rid themselves of the appendage. The limb could possibly have been lost in a previous life, and the current personality just can't cope with having it around, and so they are compelled to destroy it.

The discrepancy between western and eastern cultures concerning reincarnation is most likely the result of families in western countries being more spread out or nomadic – whereas in eastern countries, family ties are still very close and ancestor worship is still very strong. Stevenson addresses this issue as well.

> *"To begin with, these cultures remember their dead more than we do and see them as still being actively involved in life; they also have stronger family ties. To them there is no such thing as random fate. Everything happens for a reason, and that reason often has to do with someone who wishes them well or ill. They also believe, much more than we do in the West, in telepathy. The paranormal, and that dreams foretell the future. They are not clock-watchers as we are; they have time to reflect on their lives. All these factors may have some bearing on this question and perhaps put them in closer touch with their past lives."* (http://reluctant-messenger.com/).

Also intriguing, is the fact that some host children experience the feeling of not belonging to the family or feeling alienated somehow. Parents of these children will also feel the same alienation causing some to reject their own child. Some children even feel that they are not the right sex, which brings up a sticking point of a source for homosexual tendencies. The urge to be the opposite sex is so strong that it can impede the social growth of individuals. Some feel ostracized from their own environment to the point where they are rejected not only by their families, but their communities as well. They find solace and acceptance with like minded individuals and other homosexuals.

Other than these cases of ostracizing as a child grows older, they will inevitably lose their reincarnated memories if they don't learn how to tap into or deal with these past-life experiences. Stevenson feels that this forgetfulness is natural.

> *"Some persons have said it is unfair to be reborn unless you can remember details of a previous life and profitably remember your mistakes. They forget that forgetting is essential to successful living in the present. If every time we walked, we were to remember how we stumbled, we would fall again. I've also had people envy children who remember previous lives, as if these children had special wisdom. In fact, it makes more sense to look upon them as suffering from an abnormality, almost a defect. The memories they have are often more of a handicap than a blessing; and they nearly all become happier as they grow older and forget their previous lives. To paraphrase Jesus Christ, sufficient unto one life is the evil thereof."* (http://reluctant-messenger.com/).

Reincarnation in Religions

Belief in reincarnation has very ancient roots beginning with the very first of religions – ancestor worship. The family member words of father, mother, king and lord all stem from this ancient religion. The name of the head of the family or "father" denotes a stern but care taking, problem solving, decision maker, and faithful leader who achieves respect and allegiance. When we were still hunter/gatherers just a few thousand years ago, the Father was looked upon as an elder sage with the needed knowledge to carry on the fight for survival. Since humans at that time had life expectancies less than 30 years of age, anyone older than 40 was looked upon with awe and wonder. Knowledge at that time was transferred orally through poems, songs and rituals. It was important to have a fatherly figure around to carry on the traditions with the many needed abilities that age and wisdom brought.

Large families, clans, or tribes had chieftains or tribal elders who again were looked upon as fonts of knowledge and wisdom from the younger members. Later with the advent of city states and countries, came the kings, pharaohs, judges, caliphs, etc. They were the beginning of the turn from ancestor worship to king worship where they were now the "man gods." The kings were important in the agricultural and livestock communities for the many rituals to keep up with the seasons of the year. These rituals were for the purpose of appeasing the gods and providing martial law and armies. When a king died, it was as if the whole nation had fallen into chaos and, only after a successor was chosen would everyday life return to normal.

Now came a time of the prophets which challenged the current belief structures. These prophets were finding new religions with new pathways to salvation. These are the prophets of our current "modern" religions and many of them believed in reincarnation. This doctrine is a central tenet within the majority of Indian Religious Traditions such as Hinduism (including Yoga, Vaishnavism, and Shaivism), Jainism, and Sikhism. The concept was also studied by ancient Greek philosophers as well as American Indians and early Judeo/Christians. Even some of the more recent religious movements such as Neo-Paganism have embraced this concept, which has been adopted into most New Age thinking. Other indigenous groups that adopt the idea of reincarnation are the followers of Spiritism, practitioners of certain African traditions and students of esoteric philosophies such as Kabbalah and Sufism. The Buddhist concept of rebirth, although often referred to as "reincarnation," differs significantly from the Hindu-based traditions and New Age movements in that there is no unchanging "soul" (or eternal self) to reincarnate.

Passages in the Islamic Quran may also indicate beliefs in reincarnation–as by these examples:

> *"From the (earth) did We Create you, and into it Shall We return you, And from it shall We Bring you out once again. (The Quran, 20:55)"*
>
> *" 'And Allah has produced you from the earth, Growing (gradually), And in the End He will return you Into the (earth), And raise you forth (Again at the Resurrection).' (The Quran, 71:17-18)"*

Even though the references may be to a "second coming" or "resurrection," they still imply a rebirth in a new body while retaining your own personal consciousness that you died with.

The Judeo/Christian references in the old and new testaments certainly imply a belief in reincarnation such as:

> *Jeremiah 1:4 "Then the word of the LORD came unto me, saying, 5 Before I formed thee in the belly I knew thee; and before thou camest forth out of the womb I sanctified thee, and I ordained thee a prophet unto the nations."*

Job 1:20-21 "Then Job arose and tore his robe and shaved his head and he fell to the ground and worshipped. And he said, 'Naked I came from my mother's womb, and naked I shall return there. The Lord gave and the Lord has taken away. Blessed be the name of the Lord.'"

Ecclesiastes 1:4-9 "Generations come and generations go, but the earth remains forever. The sun rises and the sun sets, and hurries back to where it rises. The wind blows to the south and turns to the north; round and round it goes, ever returning on its course. All streams flow into the sea, yet the sea is never full. To the place the streams come from, there they return again...What has been will be again, what has been done will be done again; there is nothing new under the sun."

"For all the prophets and the law have prophesied until John. And if you are willing to receive it, he is Elijah who was to come." (Matthew 11:13-14)

"Behold I will send you Elijah the prophet, before the coming of the great and dreadful day of the Lord." (Malachi 4:5)

"They asked him, 'Then who are you? Are you Elijah?' He said, 'I am not.' 'Are you the Prophet?' He answered, 'No.' Finally they said, 'Who are you? Give us an answer to take back to those who sent us. What do you say about yourself?' John replied in the words of Isaiah the prophet, 'I am the voice of one calling in the desert, Make straight the way for the Lord. Now some Pharisees who had been sent questioned him, 'Why then do you baptize if you are not the Christ, nor Elijah, nor the Prophet?' 'I baptize with water,' John replied, 'but among you stands one you do not know. He is the one who comes after me, the thongs of whose sandals I am not worthy to untie.'" (John 1:21-27)

But Jesus knew better. He explained in the simplest manner to his followers.

"This is the one ... there has not risen anyone greater than John the Baptist.... And if you are willing to accept it, he is

the Elijah who was to come. He who has ears, let him hear." (Matthew 11:11-15).

"After six days Jesus took with him Peter, James and John the brother of James, and led them up a high mountain by themselves. There he was transfigured before them. His face shone like the sun, and his clothes became as white as the light. Just then there appeared before them Moses and Elijah, talking with Jesus. Peter said to Jesus, 'Lord, it is good for us to be here. If you wish, I will put up three shelters-- one for you, one for Moses and one for Elijah.' While he was still speaking, a bright cloud enveloped them, and a voice from the cloud said, 'This is my Son, whom I love; with him I am well pleased. Listen to him!' When the disciples heard this, they fell facedown to the ground, terrified. But Jesus came and touched them. 'Get up,' he said. 'Don't be afraid.' When they looked up, they saw no one except Jesus. As they were coming down the mountain, Jesus instructed them, 'Don't tell anyone what you have seen, until the Son of Man has been raised from the dead.' The disciples asked him, 'Why then do the teachers of the law say that Elijah must come first?' Jesus replied, 'To be sure, Elijah comes and will restore all things. But I tell you, Elijah has already come, and they did not recognize him, but have done to him everything they wished. In the same way the Son of Man is going to suffer at their hands.' Then the disciples understood that he was talking to them about John the Baptist." (Matthew 17:1-13)

That reincarnation was at one time very important to all 3 of the Middle Eastern major religions is a testament to its realization and belief. Reincarnation is looked upon as a form of rebirth; in which some of the memories of the former soul are somehow retained in the new living child. This is close to what we believe exactly happens to a person when they die and decide to reenter the living realm once again. This conclusion is explained in Chapter 8.

Are You Crazy?

(Heidi) Perhaps you've thought to yourself a few times, "I must be crazy. These things can never happen." While there are individuals that are mentally ill and believe irrational things, there is a difference between what is irrational and what is real, yet unexplainable. One of the things we are trying to convey in this book is all about is to try to rationalize the phenomena that many women experience every day. If you see multiple faces in the mirror, sense the presence of people that have passed on, foresee events that have not yet happened, or sense déjà vu, you are not crazy or alone. In this book, we try to explain what these gifts are and why it is mostly women who experience them. We women are often called crazy and irrational for some of the things that we can see and do. This is because others (mainly men) do not understand what we are experiencing. Most people become fearful of things they do not understand. When fear sets in, we become defensive and aggressive. I like to make it analogous to what I call the "Indian" syndrome.

When the Europeans first came to America, they met the Native Americans, who were obviously very diverse in their ways. The Native Americans had a different language, culture, religion, and skin color than the Europeans did. Many of the white men were frightened of their customs. So, in turn, they killed these "Indians" and slaughtered their land – virtually obliterating their people. It was the Europeans' ignorance and misunderstanding that made them want to rid the United States of Native Americans. In a lot of ways, women in many different cultures have been treated very similarly to the Native Americans.

Modern religions have pushed women to the wayside for centuries. Christians, Muslims, Hindus, and even Buddhists have clearly put women in a lower place of stature than men. Only recently have these major religions made efforts to embrace more women in leadership roles. As we've seen, women that challenged the teachings of their particular church were quickly accused of heresy, thereby disobeying God. Even submissive, obedient women were often ridiculed and accused of having weak minds and bodies – being ever more susceptible to the Devil's temptations.

Most of us were taught from a young age that "imaginary friends," ghosts, and other unexplainable phenomena are just in our imaginations, and that we needed to forget about them. We struggled to hold on to these images and feelings as children. However, the older we get, the more we see that no one else is experiencing or talking about these things anymore. Therefore, we reject and dismiss these phenomena as fantasies or childish dreams in order to be accepted into "normal" society. Some of us, if we were raised in a religious home, we taught to believe that anything surreal or unusual that happened to you was an act of the Devil and a sign that you were being tempted. This is a far cry from what humans used to believe centuries ago. Remember what we discussed in chapter 3 about women being worshiped in ancient times. Women were relied upon for wisdom, medicine, and divine intervention. Women were seen as advocates to the gods (oracles) as well as the vessels of life.

The important thing to remember is that women were once revered for what is now considered crazy. Perhaps if more ladies understand their own feminine history, we can be better able to cope with what we feel on a daily basis and know that we are not alone.

Faith, or what one believes, is a wonderfully abstract thing because it is so *human.* No other creature that we know of on earth can contemplate their own fates concerning the afterlife. The fact that so many of us believe in an afterlife at all is totally amazing. The difference is, of course, the individual interpretation of "heaven" and the Divine figure that they've chosen to help them get there. It, therefore, becomes

only natural to believe in the spirits, souls, angels or ghosts that inhabit this realm.

> *"The case for ghosts, creatures from outer space, and similar beings is less clear. For one thing, considerable disagreement exists about whether these beings are real or imaginary. Although there is currently no accepted scientific evidence for the paranormal, a 1990 Gallup Poll of 1,236 American adults indicated that 25 percent believe in ghosts, 17 percent report they have been in touch with someone who has died 10 percent believe they have been in the presence of a ghost, more than 50 percent believe in the devil (10 percent reported having talked with the devil), and 14 percent say they have seen an unidentified flying object"* (Taylor, 143). [5]

There are many TV shows on the air today that deal with the supernatural. Everything from horror, to sci-fi, to reality shows can be watched daily. If one were to turn their TV on right now, there's probably a program based on finding ghosts or psychic abilities. Even though shows like these are geared more towards entertainment than substance, they have helped place the afterlife in the forefront of their audience's psyche. By entertainment, I mean that these shows just don't do a very thorough job of really uncovering the sources of paranormal activity in the structures that they've explored. They just don't have the time, and their audience wouldn't stick around long enough if they did. Audiences just want the meat of the shows. They want to see the wrecks, the winners, and the punchlines.

5 Excerpt from page 143 from Imaginary Companions and the Children Who Create Them by Majorie Taylor printed By permission of Oxford University Press. (5/3/01)

Chapter 5

LifeConscious Explains the Many Faces

Empty your mind, be formless. Shapeless, like water. If you put water into a cup, it becomes the cup. You put water into a bottle and it becomes the bottle. You put it in a teapot it becomes the teapot. Now, water can flow or it can crash. Be water my friend. **Bruce Lee**

A Big Head

As noted in Chapter 2, female humans are the only animals that need some sort of assistance (midwife, doctor) during childbirth. We believe that this help is the result of humans having to birth an unusually large head (not to mention the shoulders). The average circumference of a baby's head at birth is around 35 cm or 13.7 inches. The dilation of a woman's cervix during labor is considered complete with a diameter of around 10 inches or 31.4 cm circumference. There is about a 4 cm difference here that must give when the baby is coming through the birth canal. It is therefore, not uncommon for a mother to tear her vaginal opening during birth. This ripping at birth causes a lot of bleeding and so, assistance is often needed during childbirth. Many times it is dangerous for a mother to give birth alone if she is having excessive bleeding from tearing. Without help, she could die. Just handling the excruciating pain is more than enough to ask for assistance. With experienced and capable hands, the mother can be assured that her birth will go more smoothly and safely. Her pain can be quelled through herbs or modern medications. Her anxiety can be reduced with comforting words and coaching from the birthing assistant.

By contrast, grazing animals such as wildebeests and buffalos use gravity to help during their birthing process and having four legs helps a lot. Their babies seem to pour out of the mothers' womb whereas humans are bipedal and their birth canals are limited to the size of the woman's pelvis. This limitation could be an evolutionary dead end as far as humans are concerned. How can we expect to grow our mental capacities even larger without first producing mothers with very large pelvises?

Another oddity about human childbirth is the complete dependence that babies have on their parents, especially their mothers. Many other animal young don't seem to require as much help after birth. The above-mentioned wildebeest or buffalo young will be up and walking about in a few hours and will be keeping up with the herd by the end of the day. It will have learned its mother's smell and call among all the other mothers in the herd and within a few weeks will be able to out-run a predator. A human baby couldn't outrun or out think a predator for several years much less a few weeks.

So, from this perspective, we could say that a human baby is born prematurely because the mother couldn't possibly pass such a full-term large head. The sizes of newborn babies' heads are at their limit, already resulting in more and more C-sections (Cesarean Sections). In 2006, the rate of U.S. births by C-section was 31.1%.

A baby has to be born premature and with a soft skull in order for a modern female to pass it through the birth canal, thus the deformation of a baby's head at birth. I remember seeing my daughter for the first time after birth and thought that there was something wrong with her, since she had a "cone head." My sister, who is a nurse, reassured me that it was quite normal. Still, it was a shocker!

By contrast our closest animal relative, the chimpanzee, have their babies clinging to their mother right after birth while the mother runs, swims, and climbs lofty trees. The baby chimp will be climbing and playing in no time, while a human baby is totally helpless for the first couple of years. This is due to the slow development of the personal consciousness in the human brain. There is also the heaviness of the baby's head which will grow rapidly as it learns its surroundings, faces, and communication skills. A baby's head will stop growing at around their first birthday which also coincides with the beginnings of communication, standing, and maybe walking. You will notice when you see a baby walk that the first thing that they have to do is tilt their big head forward to get their momentum going. They also have great difficulty in changing directions – often becoming disoriented easily.

Although the personal consciousness is slow to develop, LifeConscious development has been there the entire time. During the fetus' gestation and after birth, LifeConscious continues the mother's transference of memories.. As the baby suckles, shares its mother's breaths and kisses, grabs her hair and shares her body oils, transference is still occurring. Just as the mother passes on her antibodies and vitamins to her child through her milk so do the memories from her ancient brain continue to be "downloaded" through latticed water molecules to her child's new brain. This motherly closeness is essential to the child's early growth not only for protection but for the unique closeness and love bonding that naturally grows between a mother and her baby. She is the baby's main teacher, protector and guide as she stimulates all the baby's senses, which wake the neurons in its brain as it slowly develops a personal consciousness.

Emulating a Human

One of the hardest accomplishments for humans is to emulate even the most rudimentary actions of a real human being – such as walking. Not only do a robot's joints, hips, knees, and feet have to function correctly (that's the easy part), the hard part is programming and maintaining its balance. Some sort of gyroscope or balancing mechanism is needed to keep the robot upright – much like the inner ear is capable of maintaining a human's balance. The next dramatic hurdle would be to get the legs to "walk" like a human while maintaining its balance, which is a daunting task since one leg must extend forward while all the weight is carefully balanced on the other leg. Then, the weight must be evenly balanced between the legs until all the weight is on the opposite leg while its counterpart extends out into the next step. This requires quite a bit of imposing programming and a balancing system to boot and this simple accomplishment didn't even involve climbing stairs or navigating through rocks.

Although the demonstration explained above was quite wordy, we mention it to emphasize a point. Man is bent upon emulating himself as if humans were an endangered species, and we desperately need replication. Another science article came out recently about a robot head of a replica Einstein (http://www.telegraph.co.uk/technology/4861114/Robot-replica-of-Albert-Einstein.html). This robot is capable of looking at you and answering questions while providing facial expressions that are meant to emulate the real Einstein. This indeed is a dazzling feat that took thousands of man hours and over 150 people to accomplish. The goal was to try and make computers emulate just the basics of human perceptions that a real brain processes so effortlessly that you rarely have to think about it. One of the goals was to tell how sincere someone's smile is. The extreme difficulty of trying to create a living, breathing human being has been bandied about for centuries from the Frankenstein story to Robotics. The fact of the matter is that you cannot create life from inanimate objects as we have seen so far. Life is a linear organism descended from a long unending line of living and birthing mothers. It cannot be accomplished in any other way. No matter how "life like" the robot is.

My definition of *life* is that it is an organism that can replicate itself continuously (linearly) without dying out. A robot can't do this, and neither could Frankenstein's creation except for the "Young Frankenstein" version (one of my favorite movies). We have already seen that life can only come about as being the end result of a lineage of living, breathing, eating, and procreating creatures. The child with a simple and immature personal consciousness will grow into a man or a woman and begin asking questions about their purpose in life and develop their own philosophies, sets of ideals, etc.

The main focus of this section is to point out that life can't possibly come from inanimate or mechanical objects – no matter how hard you try, it can't be done. No matter how life-like an automaton is, it can't breed and procreate life thereby creating new species. Life is a linear thing in that it must come from a seemingly unending line of living organisms. A line that goes back to who knows when, but a line that was started by a deity or cellular division in some slime pool, depending on your preference of philosophy. Either way one believes that life commenced on our planet, life is continually sustained by LifeConscious.

LifeConscious Explains the Many Faces

Since we now know that life is a linear thing, wouldn't it seem plausible that the other faces that you see in the mirror are, in fact, the mothers in your very own lineage? We think that this is the case indeed. I still remember when I first looked at Heidi's face that particular night not so long ago, and I saw the faces cycling over her own lovely face, which startled me at first. I pointed it out to Heidi, who initially was shocked that I could actually see these faces. She, of course, has experienced these apparitions her entire life. She never knew what to make of them having been afraid of what she was seeing. She knew that they were dead spirits that may have wanted something from her or perhaps convey some message for them. I had pointed out to Heidi that these faces were possibly mothers in her very own lineage because a lot of them looked to be related to her. She latched on to this idea and started looking very closely to her own face in the mirror and began immediately communicating with the faces whom she was seeing. She was no longer afraid of them.

Heidi found some of these women in searches through ancestry web sites and through her own meditations. What were once frightening images to her as a child she now realized to be her very own linear line of female ancestors who are still connected to the very same LifeConscious that once controlled and sustained their lives. This singular line of LifeConsciousness is very comfortable to them all since their own bodily functions were once controlled by this same line. They are part and parcel of the same family linear organism.

So, if you look into a mirror and are experiencing such faces, do not be afraid. They are not merely ghosts, malevolent demons, or the devil but your very own ancestors. They are still very much a part of you in the flesh and in your LifeConscious memories. The difference between them and you, besides their demise, is time and space. In the later chapters, we will discuss in further detail how seeing these faces in the mirror are possible and what you can do to try and communicate with them.

Are these faces scientifically feasible? We think that there are logical scientific reasons for this phenomenon and one of them has to do with time and space.

Time and Space

(Heidi) We don't wish to go too deeply into the physics of our time and space theories here. It would deviate too much from the subject of LifeConscious and women's linear heritage. However, if you would like, in the addendum, we go into a much more in-depth look at how our ideas could be actually scientifically feasible.

The popular notion in physics about time and space is that both are thought of together as a single continuum with space being 3 dimensional and time providing a 4th dimension. According to certain Euclidean space perceptions, the universe has three dimensions of space and one dimension of time. By combining space and time into a single manifold, physicists have significantly simplified a large number of physical theories, as well as described in a more uniform way the workings of the universe at both the super galactic and subatomic levels.

(Heidi)For those of you who are not familiar with physics, let me just give you a brief description of some scientific terms so that you won't be turned away by the science jargon! First of all, when we say "theory," you must understand that we are using the scientific definition of the word. Many people use this term loosely to describe an abstract idea or philosophy. However, in science, we use the word to describe a specific step in the scientific method process. (Try saying that five times fast!)

You may remember from your middle school science class that scientists use something called the Scientific Method to come up with physical laws for the universe. The steps go in this order: hypothesizing,

researching, experimenting, analyzing, concluding, and theorizing. This last step of theorizing comes after many successful tests of a specific hypothesis that come up with the same results every time. Once the scientific community is satisfied with the success of overwhelming evidence to support a hypothesis, it is accepted as a theory. An example of this is the Theory of General Relativity. When an established theory has been around for a long time and no evidence has been shown to disprove the theory over many years, it is accepted as a Law. An example of this is Newton's Law of Gravitation.

Another precursor to a scientific discussion is to define what we mean by "proving." In science, nothing is really proven. Scientific evidence always points toward disproving through extensive experimentation and data analysis. If a theory, for example, cannot be disproven, then it is accepted as a truth of the universe. But, it is never considered to be proven.

We know all about space. When you look around your environment, and that it is indeed 3 dimensional and not flat. You can walk, run or drive a car into this space, which could allow you to travel all the way around the earth and arrive back at the very same place. You can drill down into the earth itself or fly above it in a plane or rocket to the nearest planet. The difference between your arrival points as you traveled around the earth was that 4th dimensional element called time. It took you perhaps many days or even years to traverse the globe and end up in the same spot. So what changed? Well, you got a little older and so did the earth; the difference is that you aged faster than the earth because of another factor that we call the Life Span Reference (LSR). An LSR is simply the average life span of any living creature, but we also include "non-living" items like the earth, moon, stars, planets, galaxies, and the universe. It is a reference point because of the vast differences in life spans of all the objects in the universe. For example, it is difficult to compare the vast difference in life spans between a Mayfly to that of a Red Giant star.

Man's LSR is limited by many factors such as age, health, disease, accidents, wars, murder, and suicides, etc. This brings our current LSR down to around 70 to 80 earth years. The life expectancy of man has changed drastically from 1000 years ago when it averaged between 20 to 30 years. The LSR for insects and animals varies tremendously. For instance, the afore mentioned Mayfly is just a few days, a dog 15 years, humans around 75 years, some turtles 100 years and red wood trees 2000 years. Galactic objects, like the earth, and our Solar System have an LSR of 4.6 billion years. Each living and non-living item on the earth and in our universe has an LSR and it is the vast differences in their life spans that we will focus on.

Remember that an average human's Life Span Reference (LSR) is just 75 or so odd years and that the earth's LSR is 4.6 billion years. Our belief is that our human dead don't experience time the same way that living beings do because they have rejoined and are now a part of the earth's Life Span Reference of billions of years. So, what is happening is that the dead hardly "feel" a transition of time at all as the result of the tremendous LSR difference. Perhaps many dead people think that they are still alive and that nothing has changed since their death. We believe this may help explain the faces in the mirror that Heidi and others see along with apparitions that we call ghosts.

Using my lovely wife Heidi as an example, who is much more in tuned with nature and her own LifeConscious than many people, she has the ability or gift to sense her own lineage through her line of mothers' faces. These mothers are trying to stay connected with the very same LifeConscious that controlled their own life functions during their living years. The life giving bond of this connection is still so strong that it's probably impossible not to stay attached to it somehow even after death. This is why we believe that sometimes, people that have recently passed away desperately try to take possession of living bodies – especially children.

Only gifted sensitive people can see and hear what we call ghosts, spirits, or souls. Even though these people died years ago they can still be sensed in the houses that they inhabited or on battle fields where they met horrible deaths. These locations are imprinted with their memories, and it is these memories that gifted people sense when they go to these places. They are sensing the "playback" of these memories as a kind of instant replay except these memories are now stored in the earth's own vast LifeConscious repository, a repository that may be stored in the earth's molten iron core and played back through her natural radio frequency of 7.83 Hz. Some parapsychologists call this phenomenon *psychometry* or the act of sensing spirit activity or memories through an inanimate object such as an old house or a chair. This could also explain the recordings of disembodied voices heard on digital recorders on popular ghost finding TV shows.

Can inanimate objects like furniture or an old building retain memories? We feel that certain types of memories have a unique way of keeping their longevity. You are already familiar with how LifeConscious memories are stored in the ancient parts of our brains and that these memories were passed down from our mother's to us during our gestation periods. We feel that not only people and animals can accumulate memories, but so can places and things because of their composition. For instance, an old chair made up of wood and fabric that had been passed down from one generation to another in the same family can hold certain memories. Because it is made of the living materials of wood and fabric, it too can store memories from the family members that have used and sat in it. The breaths, oils, skin, and DNA fragments of the family members slowly accumulate in the fabric and wood cells of the chair. This gradually turns the object into a repository of memories – good or bad.

So how can such stored memories in objects be restored or played back? First, you need a certain type of energy that these memories can use to "come alive" once again. We believe this energy is a living person's very own LifeConscious. Your LifeConscious is the only energy that these types of memories will recognize since they were once living humans at one time. Their own LifeConscious was the controller and source of the memory storage. It makes sense that another living human's LifeConscious would be the energy trigger to restore these deposited memories from old buildings, locations, natural objects, and furniture.

Proof of this can be found in old places that are loaded with previous living memories and will appear to be very spiritually active–especially if the building is in the process of being renovated or torn down. We feel that the increased activity is due to the memories being loosened from the building's structures as workers tear away the old memory-laden walls, floors, furniture, and framework. This makes sense to us because the worker's own LifeConscious are restoring the memories as they demolish the structure thereby exposing the workers to "residual hauntings" and causing the electronic voice phenomenon.

Traumatic memories from murders, suicides, war or accidents can become deeply embedded in the objects that witnessed the event such as a weapon, battle ground, hanging tree, or scene of a crime. Old objects such as guns, swords, hammers, saws, axes, furniture, ladders, arrows, clothes, etc. can all retain its former users' memories that can be retrieved by a living person who has the knowledge or gift of using their own LifeConscious energy to do so.

Heidi has personally experienced these awakenings of spirit activity in old buildings. She has been in museums, battlefields, and in the most ordinary of places and encountered strong memories of the people and events that have taken place there. Here is one example of something that she experienced while she was in college.

(Heidi) I had one of the strangest encounters with a stored memory, or psychometry, one day when I was a sophomore in college. I was attending Gordon College in Barnesville, GA. It is a rural town about an hour and a half drive from Atlanta. This particular day I had off from my classes and one of my professors suggested that a few of us go on a field trip to the Old Jail. This jail had been turned into a museum, but had been a working prison until the 1950's.

When I initially walked into the jail, I did not feel anything unusual. I merely found the place very interesting. I thoroughly enjoy visiting historical sites, and I came to the jail knowing absolutely nothing about it. I was intrigued that an old jail that had been used in the 1800's was still standing, and I was thrilled to have a chance to go see it.

We toured the first floor of the building, and it was quite bleak because of the harsh and cramped conditions of the cells. However, it was interesting to see how these prisoners lived. This was the floor where the minor offenders were held. I didn't start to feel anything until I moved up to the second floor of the jail. It was here on the stairwell that I started to feel uneasy and extremely uncomfortable. I felt like I should not go up there, and that I was not welcome. I was intrigued, and not afraid of this feeling, so I continued up the stairs. As I walked around the floor, it was very cramped, and I felt sick to my stomach – as if there were still evil people in these cells.

Then, as I neared the solitary confinement cells, I kept feeling a strong energy coming from one of the cells in the right corner. The closer I got, the more I got the feeling that I should leave. There was much negative energy coming from this cell. Something had happened in there. I almost did not want to go any closer, but I really wanted to know what happened in there. The concrete door to the cell was cracked open, and I gently pushed on the door to open it further so that I could

see in. Almost instantly, I saw an African-American man hanging from the top rafter in his cell. His facial expression was one of horror and disgust. He was wearing a plain navy blue jumpsuit type of clothing. He was as clear and solid to me, as if he were a real person hanging there.

I ran down the stairwell and outside the building as fast as I could. I was very frightened by what I saw. I usually was never frightened of spirits or psychometric energy. Nevertheless, this scene was so horrific! I could feel the man's pain and agony. I could feel the guilt that weighed upon his shoulders for the terrible things he had done.

Once I regained my composure, I calmly went back to the information desk where the museum worker was sitting. I asked her as calmly as I could manage if there were ever any suicide attempts by an African-American prisoner on the second floor in a solitary confinement cell. She looked surprised and told me that there was, in fact, a hanging that took place by a convicted murderer in the top right corner solitary confinement cell. She told me that he had hung himself by the rafter, and that he was an African-American. She seemed very puzzled that I knew about this and asked me how I could have known that this event occurred. She said it was not in the informative literature handed out by the museum, and none of the museum guides had ever told anyone about it. I didn't answer her questions, but I did tell her thank you and promptly left the jail. I told myself I would never go back there again.

Getting back to our Life Span Reference (LSR) idea, we believe that human dead have rejoined the earth's LifeConscious, which has an LSR of billions of years. Some of the newly dead can't handle the fact or don't believe that they have died. This is where we believe that the possession of the living may occur. We believe that in their desperation to get back into a living body and bypassing the "normal" cycle of death and rebirth that some of the dead will try to possess children or the weak minded. Children are very vulnerable to these possessive types of souls that the Buddhists call *Hungry Ghosts,* and Judeo/Christians call *Spirits or Demons.* These newly dead *hungry ghosts* have a hard time getting over the eating, breathing, drinking, partying, and sexual pleasures that they had enjoyed when they were alive and will do anything to be able to "live" again – even to the point of taking control of a child's personal consciousness. In the major religions of Judeo/Christian and Islam, this is known as *possession.* For a long time, possessions have always been blamed by religions on a demon or the Devil, but we've found that this is not the case.

A *hungry ghost* is a very determined, but lost dead soul who feels that they must live again at any cost. It's as if they were panicking. They have bypassed the natural order of the cycle of life, death, afterlife, and birth/rebirth. They are so strongly drawn to the living, that they can appear in children's dreams as nightmares of people trying to catch or eat them. These nightmares sometimes are very real attempts of possession of the child's living body.

In Islam, these ghosts are known as *Jinns* and they are often known to possess living humans. *Jinns* possess people for many reasons in Islam. Sometimes it is because the *Jinn* or its family has been hurt accidentally, or it could be because the *Jinn* fell in love with the person. However, most of the time, possession occurs because the *Jinn* is simply malicious and wicked. For this reason, Muslims have been told by the Prophet not to loiter in those places where the *Jinns* reside such as graveyards, ruins, deserts, and strangely, market places.

The oldest references to demonic possession are from the Sumerians, who believed that all diseases of the body and mind were caused by "sickness demons" called *gidim* or *gid-dim.* The priests who practiced exorcisms in these nations were called *ashipu* (sorcerer) very similar to the word *asu* meaning physician. Many cuneiform tablets contain prayers to certain gods asking for protection from demons, while other tablets ask the gods to expel the demons who have invaded their bodies.

Old children's fairy tales are loaded with the concept of possession or being eaten such as *Rapunzel, Hansel and Gretel, Cinderella,* and *Rumpelstiltskin.* These tales were purposely written to frighten children so that they could become wary of witches, strangers, dangerous animals, and even demons. The moral of these stories were all very similar – be a good little boy or girl and bad things won't happen to you. These stories seem to be based on very real occurrence and serve as warnings to parents and children.

Even the classic tale of the *Wizard of Oz* is such an example of a child's possession story. Dorothy is knocked out during a tornado hitting her house and goes into a comatose dream state when she believes that she is in another land over the rainbow. She has unknowingly gained possession of some ruby slippers that the wicked old Witch of the West wants so desperately, but all

Dorothy wants to do is find a way back home (consciousness). She gains the aid of a scarecrow, a tin man, and a lion, which all correspond to her own wisdom, heart and courage. Legions of flying monkeys and the witch constantly assail her along her way to the Emerald City. Here, she hopes she will find the wizard that she believes will help her get home. She finally kills her demon (the witch) and is told that she has always maintained the power to go back home and that was to simply wake up.

Possessions of living humans are noted in every religion or social environment you want to look at. Exorcisms of demons, Jinns or devils are a worldwide occurrence with a long history and should be regarded as real. We feel that they are real, and that you can prevent the possession of a child by educating them about how spirits can come to you in nightmares and not by pretending that such things never happen. We feel that these ghosts are not demons or devils, but newly dead individuals that want desperately to be "alive" again.

We like to think of the differences in Life Span References between the living and dying as analogous to a merry-go-round. Viewed by the dead, the merry-go-round spins quickly and contains wooden horses, lions and other pairs of animals with the living riding on their backs. The animals are emulating life by going up and down with the loud calliope blasting in the background and all the colorful lights flashing by you. Imagine that the merry-go-round emulates the LSR of an average human lifetime – spinning and flashing by at a fast rate. The dead, who are on a much longer LSR, stand around the merry-go-round watching it whiz by. The only way that they can be a part of the living timeline is to gather up enough energy to speed up along side of it. But, they can't hop on, and they can only keep up as long as their energy lasts. This is how they can be sensed or even seen by very gifted living people as shadows, clear faces, and even voices.

Hungry ghosts, on the other hand, never believed that they were dead to begin with and are determined to hop on to the merry-go-round of life and sit on one of the animals. This is a very real and dangerous occurrence that must be taught to children early in their lives – thus the advent of fairy tales. Even if you are a religious person and don't believe in *hungry ghosts* or *Jinns*, then by all means handle your child's nightmares or "monsters" as you see fit or as your religion dictates. We're just telling you that you must take some kind of action as these incidents certainly appear to be real.

So, what are our recommendations about your own or your child's experiences during sleep when these hungry ghosts tend to come? First of all, you have already come a long way in understanding what is actually happening by reading this book. We will relay stories of personal experiences that we have had to try and help you or your children about how to handle these types of situations. Secondly, remember that these dead souls can't possess you if you are mentally strong enough to prevent it. As long as you do not show fear to these hungry ghosts, they cannot harm you. Here is Heidi's experience as a child when she felt that someone tried to possess her.

(Heidi) In Chapter 4, we discussed multiple personality disorder and how we believe that some of these unfortunate individuals could be suffering from spiritual possession. We have already said that many times, children are susceptible to spiritual possession. Something happened to me many years ago as a child that proved to me that dead spirits sometimes seek live bodies to inhabit. It was something that I will never forget as long as I live.

When I was nine years old, I was already experiencing supernatural occurrences often. I had heard trees speak to me, seen people walking through forests that had passed away, seen the many faces when I looked in the mirror, and heard voices in the cemetery. I was no stranger to spirits. On the contrary, I had accepted them as part of my life. When my mother told me that I was only imagining these things, I told her that I believed her. However, secretly, I just knew that she was wrong. These things were too real and happened too often for them to be just coincidental or figments of my imagination.

This one particular night when I was nine years old, I was already in a deep sleep, and I was having a pleasant dream about a log cabin in the woods. There was a sweet lady who was making some soup and set it in front of me at a table. However, as soon as she set the bowl of soup down, she began to turn ugly in the face and was glaring at me. I didn't know why, but I knew that this lady was going to hurt me. I instantly got up from the table and started backing away. The woman was moving fast towards me, and I could not get away from her. I then realized that this was a dream, and I tried to wake up. I instantly felt like I was no longer in command of my body and that this woman was controlling me. I started to scream in my dream, hoping that I would wake up before

something bad happened. I finally did wake up, and I sat up in my bed, gasping and sweating. However, I looked in front of me at the foot of my bed, and there was the woman standing there! She was as clear to me as a solid, real person. She continued to approach me and put out her hands to grab me. I started to scream, but she continued to approach. By this time, my mother had heard me scream and came running into my bedroom. The woman did not disappear, however. It was only after I told this woman in the Name of God, that I commanded her to leave my room, and that I was not afraid of her. She then disappeared. My mother never saw her, but she told me that she had felt a presence in the room. To this day, my mother still believes that this woman was a demon sent by Satan to try and take my soul away from me. I believed that this woman was a person who had recently passed away from a horrible death and wished to re-enter the world through another body.

This event changed my life forever. Up to that point, I had only encountered "friendly ghosts." These were spirits that I saw walking around and were glad to see me. They would acknowledge my presence and then quietly go about their business. I had never seen a spirit that wanted to hurt me before. I realized afterwards that dead spirits are like they were in life. Some are kind and loving souls. Some have cruel and murderous hearts – only thinking about themselves and what they can gain for their own well being.

Why do these "attacks" by ghosts, Jinns, or demons seem to occur during sleep? We believe that when you sleep, your heart rate and metabolism slow down considerably, which brings your LSR closer to the earth's much longer LSR along with all the dead souls that are now part of the earth's LifeConscious once again. Moreover, remember that your own sleeping frequency is exactly the same as the earth's frequency of 7.83 Hz. Because of this, we know that the most vulnerable time of possession is when you sleep. When you sleep your personal consciousness has basically shut down so that your body and LifeConscious can tap into the earth's own life sustaining LifeConscious. This slowed-down sleep state may also allow dead souls to more easily "catch up" with the living's LSR. Without the guard of your personal consciousness, you are vulnerable to a possession attempt. Children are especially susceptible to this because they simply do not understand what is happening to them and don't yet have strong defensive personalities. This is where the parent needs to step in and educate and comfort them the best that they can.

Scientists and sleep experts agree that the body needs sleep to shut down brain functions and allows cells to repair damaged parts of the body. Almost everyone knows what happens if one does not get a good night's sleep. Usually, we feel tired, achy, cranky, and less alert throughout the day. Most of us that are parents are very familiar with sleep deprivations, indeed! However, lack of sleep over time can be a serious problem. Sleep deprivation affects your cognitive functions and your health. This can lead to daytime sleepiness, high blood pressure and stress. Some weight gain seems to be influenced by lack of sleep since chemicals, and hormones are released during sleep that controls appetites. It is essential that we ward off disturbances in sleep in order for us to get enough rest during the night.

"Attacks" occur mostly during the third and fourth stages of REM sleep, which is the deep sleep period. During the third stage, the brain produces delta waves with large amplitudes at ELF frequencies (7.83 Hz). The fourth stage is where we experience rhythmic breathing and little muscle movement control. This is the stage where children and some adults experience bed wetting, sleepwalking, and night visitors in their dreams. The brain is very active in this stage even though our personal consciousness is shut down. We believe that this is evidence that our LifeConscious is taking over and reconnecting with the earth's LifeConscious, again – tapping into its energy source to rejuvenate itself. The sluggish feelings that we get through sleep deprivation are a result of the lack of this energy that comes from the earth's vast LifeConscious.

Tell the child that these monsters, witches, or demons that frighten them in their sleep are harmless and can't hurt them if they believe they are in command of their bodies. Emphasize that these ghosts are in a different place and cannot take them if the child doesn't want them to. If they are confronted with any unfriendly spirits, teach them to say "no" and to "go away". Read them examples of fairy tales in which the child always wins.

(Heidi) My mother would read me stories before bedtime that were very positive and encouraging to a young child. These stories helped me fall asleep better and made me feel comfortable to be alone in my own room. After the horrific incident with the old woman that night, my mother took extra precautions to make sure that I felt safe afterwards. Since my mother is a very Christian woman, she placed a cross above my bed and told me that Jesus was always going to protect me and said that

no one would ever come to me in my dreams like that again. To this day, I've never had a person try to possess me.

If you are a faith-based family, it is a good idea to read religious passages to the children before bed. For example, my mother would read me passages from the Bible when I had a nightmare. The passages were always positively affirming scriptures such as Psalms or Jesus' words from the New Testament. It is essential for parents to help their children feel as safe as possible in their bedroom. Realize that it is very common for children to have nightmares and to have the dead occasionally visit them in their sleep. Sometimes they may even see and speak to dead relatives in their dreams. There is nothing wrong with your child, and you do not need to treat these occurrences as abnormal. This will only make the child feel insecure and helpless.

If you choose not to have a faith or religious beliefs, it is still important to reassure your child that he or she is safe in their bed. Read them happy stories such as *Goodnight Moon* or *The Little Engine that Could* that puts them in a positive mood before going to sleep. It is my opinion that children should never watch television right before bed because they could accidentally view something that could unknowingly disturb them and cause them not to sleep well. Even if you do not see the program as disturbing, remember that a child's perception of distressing images may be (and probably is) quite different from your own. For example, a simple advertisement for toothpaste may frighten a child when he or she sees a large person on the TV showing their big white teeth on the screen.

Having enough light in the child's bedroom is important also since it gives the child a sense of comfort by being able to see at night. Even if you aren't religious, you can place lucky talismans or meaningful symbols near their bed.

(Heidi) In addition to talismans or religious symbols over the bed, it is also perfectly acceptable to allow the child to sleep with a favorite toy or even their dog or cat. I know that when I was growing up, I had some stuffed animals that I slept with on different days of the week or the year. These stuffed animals helped me feel like I had a "sleeping buddy" that made me feel like I wasn't completely alone in my room while I was asleep. Sometimes, my mother would even use the stuffed

animals like a puppet and pretended like the stuffed animal was real. For example, I had a stuffed pig that my mother would use to help me fall asleep. She would use the pig like a puppet and use a distinct voice to let me know that the pig was speaking. She would make the pig say things like, "Don't be afraid, Heidi. I'll be right here with you all night. If you wake up during the night, just give me a hug, and I'll help you go back to sleep."

We've been extensively describing the bedtime habits of children. This is because we believe that if kids feel like they can be safe at night, they can more easily accept what happens to them when they dream or when/if dead spirits come to visit them. They may be more likely to accept what is happening to them if their parents have taught them that these things are acceptable and normal for them. If they learn that there is nothing to be afraid of, then they can become more confident and assured of themselves – not just in any psychic abilities they may have, but in all aspects of their life.

You're Not Crazy

So ladies guess what? You are not crazy if you've experienced these same things, even at very minor levels. The spirits you sense, and the faces you see in the mirror are real. These faces represent your very own LifeConscious lineage of your mothers who have lived and died before you. As you now know, you are the end result of these countless numbers of mothers who lived before you and that have incredibly survived to give you life.

You must learn how to embrace these faces because they are a huge part of who you really are. A bit of each of these mothers is in you right at this very moment. Their memories have helped to sustain you both mentally and physically throughout your life- time. You have garnered an important piece of memory from each of these ladies; such as your strength in dealing with people, your compassion towards children, and your insight. However, traits such as allergies and food preferences are present, too. An even more important aspect to the faces in the mirror is that you can gather answers to everyday questions that go through your mind during the day. It is the duality of mind or consciousness that is answering the questions. Remember that when your personal consciousness asks a question your LifeConscious, which also includes your ancestor's memories, is answering.

Where do you think that motherly instinct comes from, or woman's intuition? Does it come from experience and wisdom from having handled such difficulties or situations before? Yes, and these instincts and intuitions also include the accumulated knowledge that comes from your line of mothers. These are all tried and true instincts that have been used in your lineage to help it survive through the countless number of struggles that your family line has experienced such as conflicts, famine, accidents, plagues, etc.

Haven't you been somewhere entirely new or seen a picture of a place or building and thought to yourself how familiar it was to you? How is this possible if you yourself have never been to nor seen this place before? We commonly call this déjà vu. It is usually accompanied by a compelling sense of familiarity, a sense of eeriness, or strangeness. The previous experience is most often attributed to a real life event; although in some cases there is a firm sense that the experience genuinely happened, but in the past. The experience of déjà vu seems to be quite common among adults and children alike; in formal studies, 70% of people surveyed reported having experienced déjà vu at least once. This is an age-old phenomenon that the Ancient Greeks had a term for – *paramnesia.*

Déjà vu isn't just limited to the visual environ but happen also when we recognize familiar passages in a book, song, phrase, vehicle, smell, taste, feel, etc. This latent knowledge must be generated from somewhere, and now you know where. Your experience of déjà vu is from your own line of mothers and the answers to your questions come from the same source. Proof again that you are, in essence, the end result of this linear organism made up of LifeConscious memories.

Just as the same drops of water have quenched the thirst of numerous numbers of creatures on this planet, so does LifeConscious continue in the living individuals of a family line that it has helped sustain. We've learned that water and LifeConscious have a very special symbiotic relationship that has been successful since the dawn of time. Remember that water is the carrier of LifeConscious memories and life function commands. Water may evaporate before your very eyes, but only into its gaseous state, which later falls back to the earth in droplets of rain to help quench the living. Water, too goes through a cycle of life, death and rebirth just as everything else does in our universe.

Chapter 6

Heidi's Many Faces

The People That Frightened Her as a Child

Proof of Heidi's Gift

How Heidi Retained Her Gift

A Note on the Effects of Abuse

The People in the Mirror

Controlling the Situation

Objects in the mirror are closer than they appear.
An American automotive caution.

The best mirror is an old friend. ***English proverb***

I think your whole life shows in your face and you should be proud of that.
Lauren Bacall

The People That Frightened Her as a Child

(Heidi) Before I begin, let me say that I consider my abilities to see and hear spirits to be a gift, and I will therefore, refer to them as such throughout this book. I believe that a higher being – God perhaps, has given me a special gift that goes beyond normal psychological abilities such as empathy and deep perception. Each person, male or female, has the ability to empathize very well and perceive others' emotions – if given the opportunity to practice. Psychological abilities in many ways are like a muscle. If you do not use them frequently, they will atrophy and dwindle away. The gifts that I and many other people possess have been used repeatedly since ancient times.

The earliest moment that I remember in my life was very surreal. I was lying down in my crib. I do not know how old I was, but I remember I was very small and my mother was taking care of me. The crib was flat and had miniature drawings of little animals on it. Again, I do not know what the little animal prints were. I remember looking up from the crib and gazing at the ceiling. My mind was very blank, but I tried to soak in everything and learn as quickly as possible. The ceiling in my room was off-white in color. I would often look at it to see what kinds of interesting specs or lines I could see in it. This one day, however, I looked up at the ceiling and saw many faces looking down at me. I did not know who these people were, but I knew that they felt familiar to me. I was not at all frightened of them, and I actually felt comfort when they were in the room with me.

These faces continued to stay with me as I got older. I would go into the bathroom to look in the mirror, and I would see these different faces within my face. I never got scared of them until it was night-time. For some reason, I always got scared of these faces in the mirror when I would pass by it in the dark. Perhaps it was because I could see the faces more clearly in unlit places. Like most children, I was afraid of the dark – but not just because of the things that I couldn't see, but because of things the darkness enabled me to see.

At first, I did not know who these people were. I thought that perhaps they were people who had passed away that wanted something from me – perhaps to pass a message on to someone who was still alive. I thought the mirror was one way that they could communicate with me. Then, I realized many years later that these people (mostly women) I was seeing in the mirror were actually my ancestors who were still living inside of me. They're not really the actual spirits of my ancestors, but more like an echo of who they were that is now a part of me. I cannot communicate or talk with them as I would a spirit that has passed over. However, I can find out clues as to who these people were in the mirror by focusing on their image that I see. I close my eyes and keep the image of them in my mind. Then, I begin to hear words and see images from that person's life – perhaps how they died, where they lived, and in what time period.

The most predominant woman whom I usually see when I look in the mirror is a dark-haired woman with light skin wearing furs on her body. Sometimes these furs cover her head. Her face is not very clear, but her eyes are. They are a clear, dark brown. Her name was Mauve or something like that. I have seen this woman in the mirror for as long as I can remember. When I was older, I would also see her in my meditations and prayers. For many years, I speculated about who this woman could be – a goddess, a version of my Higher Self, or a Spirit Guide? I finally realized that I am this woman's descendant, and she has been helping me all my life. I am still wondering why she is so predominant in the LifeConscious part of my brain – silently giving me memories that were once hers and passing them on to me freely during glances in the mirror, meditations, and sleep.

Proof of Heidi's Gift

There are many phenomena in this world that countless individuals have experienced that are unexplainable. Much research has gone into the reasons and causes for these events, but most have come up inconclusive in the eyes of science. It is important to understand that many of these strange occurrences cannot be proven false. However, the evidence that warrants concrete proof that ghosts exist, for example, has not been backed up by enough scientific evidence. Being a scientist, I understand the necessity for scientific evidence when investigating an event or object that is not understood. However, I believe that women have the innate ability to understand these strange occurrences that seem to baffle science and skeptical individuals. This is because they use their LifeConscious energy to channel their mind in a way that detects when supernatural phenomena are occurring. Although men can have these abilities, too, women seem to be more apt to have hidden skills because of their close ties to nature and procreation.

For example, have you ever asked yourself why is it that women seem like they are always able to pick up on an emotional state of a house before they even walk through the front door? What about the way that many women seem to see and experience things that are "unnatural" or irrational, but later are realized to be true and real? How many of you have entered a place that "didn't feel right." There was no logical explanation why you didn't want to go in there. You just got a "bad feeling" about it. You may or may not have seen the consequences of your decision to go in there or not, but that is not the point. The meaning of this is that you sensed something that was wrong. There is

no scientific instrument to let others know that something is amiss, but *you know* that there is something not right about this situation. Your partner or friend who was with you probably told you that you were being silly and imagining things. I am telling you that you are not crazy or irrational! Those things that you feel are REAL! Whenever you have a small voice inside of you that holds up a red flag and tells you that this is not safe or that something isn't right with this, listen to it! We, the authors, know certain ladies who have chosen to listen to that small, still voice, and it saved their lives.

You may be asking how I know all this and why I am so convinced that these supernatural occurrences are real and not coincidental or imagined. Allow me to give you a few examples that will hopefully convince you that this is not make-believe or a hoax. This is real life.

I had a friend in college that I roomed with in the dormitory. She and I were good friends, and we shared many of the same interests. I was a Physics major, and she was an Art major. We both had experiences when we were children that we could not explain. We talked about how our parents had told us that we had overactive imaginations, and that we needed to grow up. I had no idea that my friend was so in tune with the supernatural like I was. However, she was mostly afraid of these things because she did not understand what they were. I had learned a long time ago what these experiences were all about, and I had gotten rid of my fear back when I was a child. I will explain this further in a specific experience I had later in this chapter. Nevertheless, for now let us continue with the example of my roommate and our experience together.

My friend had a dark individual that would come visit her every so often at night. This person was a girl with dark hair and dark clothing, but white skin. The girl would come into our bedroom at night and try to touch my friend on the arm. One night, I actually saw her touch my roommate's arm. She woke up frightened and told me that she had just had a nightmare about a girl trying to grab her. Then, I told her what I saw. My friend showed me her arm, and she actually had slight bruises on her arm where the girl grabbed her. It was obvious to me that this girl was in need of something from my friend – perhaps a body to inhabit, a mind to control, or some other bodily harm. I had first-

account knowledge of what angry spirits could do – like the night I had with the deceased spirit of an old woman.

One of the most recent and astonishing pieces of evidence that the abilities I have are real is my communication with Adrian's deceased family members. Let me say that when I began communicating with these loved ones, I had no idea who they were or anything about them. I had just met Adrian when I first saw them and knew nothing of their names, how they died, what they looked like, or who they were in relation to him.

The first spirit that came to me was Adrian's father. One morning as I was waking up, I saw a man approaching the bed on Adrian's side. At this time, I had only known Adrian for just a few weeks. Conversations about specific family members had not been established yet. For a moment, I thought I might be still dreaming and sat up a little in the bed. However, his form became clearer as he approached. The man seemed tall – maybe six feet. He was wearing khaki pants and a yellow, faded, and collared shirt. The most remarkable feature of this man, however, was his walk. As he approached Adrian, who was still asleep, he walked stiffly as if his knees could not bend properly. I asked this man who he was and the man only briefly glanced at me. He said that he just wanted to see "Andy," which is Adrian's nickname. The man leaned over and put his hand on Adrian's arm, then walked away and vanished. I woke Adrian up and told him what I saw. He was amazed that I had exactly described his father, who passed away in 1993. I had never seen a picture of his father, or knew anything about his personality or physical appearance. He told me his father had arthritis in both knees and could not walk very well before he died. He was also a taller man than Adrian – just less than six feet.

The second relation I contacted was Adrian's brother. I sensed his presence in the house almost from the very first time I visited Adrian's house. I only got up the courage to ask Adrian about it later. I was afraid that he would think that I was crazy. But to my surprise, Adrian asked me if I could try and contact this spirit to tell him who was in the house. He said that he had been smelling an odor of burnt cedar and sensed that someone was always watching him. I also smelled an odor of burning wood, but I did not tell Adrian about this until after he told me.

One night, I sat on the floor of Adrian's bedroom and successfully made contact with the spirit. I was able to tell Adrian his name (Eli), what kind of a person he was, and who he was in relation to Adrian – accurately. As I said, I had no prior knowledge of who he was or what he looked like. I also learned that the burning odor of cedar that we smelled daily was because Eli had been cremated. The casket that he was buried in was made of cedar. I did not probe Adrian for questions as many charlatans will do to trick people into believing that they have psychic powers. I was able to communicate with Adrian's brother so well that I began communicating with him a couple of times a week. I knew that I needed to get some concrete evidence that I was really talking to a dead person. I knew that Eli's daughter had been with him when he was in the morgue waiting to be cremated. I asked Eli to tell me about the moment in the morgue when his daughter spoke with him alone. Eli told me that she asked him if he was finally happy, and that she did not know where he was now, but she prayed that he was ok and finally at peace. When I confronted his daughter about this, she was shocked that I knew this information – as she had never shared it with anyone. I could tell her other things about her dad that only family members would have known about. She was convinced that I was, in fact, communicating with her father, who passed away in March of 2000. Again, I did not probe her with questions to see if I was "on the right track."

The third relative I was able to communicate with was Adrian's mother, who passed away in 1976. Again, like Adrian's brother, I could communicate with her well enough so that I could get her to tell me a unique story about Adrian's youngest sister. When we asked his sister about it, she knew exactly what we were talking about. However, she was very surprised that Adrian and I knew about the event because it was a private moment that she alone had with their mother. No one else was present that would have remembered this event between her and her mother.

I'm revealing these things not to sound like I'm someone special or extremely talented. I share these stories so that you might use these eyewitness testimonies as evidence to support these ideas about LifeConscious and women's innate supernatural abilities that are passed down to them from their mother. If you are a skeptic, I invite you to examine the evidence I have presented here. How could I have known

that Adrian's father was tall and had arthritis in both knees when I had no knowledge of that whatsoever? How could I have known of the very personal story about Adrian's mother and youngest sister? Adrian could not have told me about it because he was away in the Army when this event happened and had no knowledge of it either. How else can you explain these occurrences? You could say I was making it all up, but why would I do that? Why would we go to the trouble to write this book and try to inform people of the truth just to say that we were only kidding?

All we're asking is for you, the reader, to have an open mind and consider the possibility that communicating with the dead is achievable. Furthermore that communicating with the dead is not a sin or something that comes from the Devil. God also gives these gifts of mediumship for His purposes. And for the atheists, I know that many of you adamantly believe that there is no afterlife. Of course, you are entitled to your opinions, but my belief is that this is not the case.

Further proof of Heidi's gift was evident when she and I traveled to Augusta, Georgia to visit my family, and she was especially looking forward to going to my brother (Eli) and mother's (Antonina) grave sites. She wanted to try to find their grave site without my assistance, and I have to be honest in relating to you that I was still skeptical about her gifts. I perked up, however, when we first entered Hillcrest Memorial Cemetery. She immediately told me to take the first right road. This was exactly right, but then she told me to go right again, which happened to be away from their grave site, and then she asked to be let out of the car. She immediately turned around on foot and headed the other way towards their site first walking quickly, then trotting and then sprinting right toward their graves while she seemed to be listening. She was actually running so fast that she ran right over their graves crossing a road just 20 feet away, stopped in her tracks, and was looking around as if she were trying to hear something. She then crossed back over the road and was right on top of them, and she began screaming at me that they are near here, and I told her to look down at the plaques and she read the names of my mother and brother. She fell to her knees, and placed her hands on their names.

Now this is a graveyard in which there are over 500 grave sites, and she found my brother and mother's sites within 5 minutes, if that long. It was absolutely amazing and confirmed my belief in her abilities because she told me later that there were so many voices crying out to her that she had a hard time hearing my mother who she said was shouting very loudly. The other souls seemed to know that she could hear them and was trying to get her attention for one reason or another.

Another grave yard incident that also provides proof of Heidi's insight is when we went to Starkville, Mississippi to find the grave site of one of her ancestors – John McDowell.

John was born in Ireland in 1770. He immigrated to the United States around 1800 and settled with his wife and family in Lancaster, South Carolina. He lived there for a while until he heard about cheap, fertile land in Mississippi where he could establish a good-sized plantation. He lived out the rest of his days in Starkville, MS where he died in 1861. He is buried in one of Starkville's historical cemeteries.

While visiting family in the Birmingham area, we decided to take a side trip over to Starkville to see if Heidi could find her ancestor's grave. Both of us had never been to Starkville, Mississippi before.

Heidi found the location of the cemetery from her contacts on an ancestry web site. Unfortunately, no one knew where his grave site was located. When we drove into the cemetery, Heidi exited the car immediately and began using her senses as she had in Augusta, Georgia. She headed up a slight grade to a small hill but then was drawn to the right for about 100 yards and became lost and seemingly disoriented. We decided to start over from where we entered, and again she headed up the slight grade where she found a fenced block of graves with a large headstone with the surname of McDowell on it. However, none of the graves were John's. She continued to climb to the top of the hill and then yelled out to me "I found him, I found him", and fell down on her knees and began to cry.

I later asked Heidi why she went to her right after initially ascending the very hill where her ancestor was buried. She said that a very loud man was calling to her, and she was compelled to go that way. She also heard other souls that were trying to communicate with her, and she became confused. Starting over again at the cemetery entrance seemed to quiet her mind and her senses. She believes this finally enabled her to find her ancestor's grave.

How Heidi Retained Her Gift

(Heidi)You may ask how I have managed to sustain my ability to communicate with people who have passed away and be able to see my ancestors in the mirror. Why didn't I just believe my parents when they told me that these were just imaginary things that I was making up to amuse myself? Although I can't fully explain why I did not eventually lose my ability to do these things, I can tell you my thought process growing up. Here's the thing I always kept in my head – as long as I am learning something from this experience, it's ok to accept it. In other words, if speaking with a dead person is enlightening, don't stop it. If fantasizing about playing hide and seek with Daffy Duck and Bugs Bunny is rendering itself useless, then cease to do it! My mother taught me that there were always new things to learn and experience, and that I should embrace these things. Although I don't think she meant talking to the dead, specifically, I did take her quite literally.

As a child, I did not have many friends or any siblings around my age to play with. So, I found much comfort in communicating with nature around me and with people who had passed on. As I got older, I began to cultivate my abilities even more by experimenting with what I could do. By careful observations, I began communicating with trees and could predict when the seasons would change or how cold the coming winter was going to be. I found that singing to plants and playing music for them would make them grow at a highly accelerated rate. I tried this method with a Willow tree when I was five years old. I had some amazing results over a period of seven years.

A few times, I tried to approach my family members, church leaders, and friends about my abilities. I was not surprised to find out that they were either horrified or extremely concerned for my health. My mother told me that the Devil was putting these thoughts into my head, and I needed to rid my mind of them immediately. My church leaders basically said the same thing – those types of "powers" come from the Devil. Hence we go back to our argument in Chapter 2 where we discuss how many modern religious sects have practically ruined women's former esteemed reputations for their innate gifts.

I do not mean to be harsh about people's religious beliefs. Again, I do not think that belief in God, Jesus, Shiva, or Allah is unhealthy. On the contrary, I think it is very important for people to have religious beliefs that they use as a foundation for their life. However, I disagree with many of the dogmatic teachings that have been passed down from fundamental, literal interpretations of the Bible, Torah, or Koran. Some of these "literal" interpretations have been the cause of wars, executions, crusades, and witch-hunts.

For example, Heinrich Kramer, a well-known theologian in Europe during the Middle Ages, wrote a religious text called *Malleus Maleficarum*. This book was used for many years as a reference during the witch trials all over Europe and the American colonies – most famously in Salem. The *Malleus Maleficarum* contains scripture passages that actually justify killing people!

For instance, one passage used is from Deuteronomy 18:10 – 12.

> "*There shall not be found among you any one who makes his son or his daughter pass through fire, or who practices divination or black magic, or is an enhancer or a witch or a charmer or a consulter with familiar spirits or a sorcerer or a necromancer. For whoever does these things is an abomination in the sight of the Lord your God; and because of these abominations the Lord your God is destroying them before you.*" (Lamsa's Translation from Aramaic of Peshitta).

Also, Kramer uses Leviticus 19:26 and 31.

> "*You shall not eat blood; you shall not practice divination with birds, nor shall you consult an oracle. You shall not go*

after diviners neither after soothsayers, nor shall you consult them to be defiled by them; I am the Lord your God."

Then, there is the famously used passage in Exodus 22:18:

"*You shall not suffer a witch to live.*" (Lamsa's Translation from Aramaic of Peshitta)

However, one could ask the question, why did Kramer fail to leave out the passages in the Bible in which Jesus gives his apostles power to perform miracles and heal people? For example, take Acts 4:8 – 19:

"Then, Simon Peter, filled with the Holy Spirit, said to them, Leaders of the people and elders of the house of Israel, listen: If we are convicted today by you, concerning the good which has been done to a sick man, on the ground of by what means he was healed; Then let it be known to you and to all people of Israel, By the name of Jesus Christ of Nazareth whom you crucified, and whom God raised from the dead, behold this man stands before you, healed. This is the stone which you builders have rejected, which is become the corner-stone. There is no salvation by any other man; for there is no other name under heaven given among men whereby we must be saved. Now when they had heard the speech of Simon Peter and John, which they had spoken boldly, and perceived that they were unlearned and ignorant men, they marveled, and they recognized them that they had been with Jesus. And because they saw the lame man who was healed standing with them they could say nothing against them. But when they had commanded them to be taken aside out of the council, they conferred among themselves, Saying, What shall we do to these men? For behold a miracle has openly been performed by them and it is known to all that dwell in Jerusalem; and we cannot deny it. But, so that this news should not spread further among the people, let us threaten them that they speak henceforth to no man in this name. And they called them, and commanded them not to speak at all nor teach in the name of Jesus." (Lamsa's Translation from Aramaic of Peshitta)

Is this a sin because they are dealing in occult practices? To the majority of Christians, the answer would be a resounding *no*. Of course,

Jesus can give power to anyone he wants as long as they use it in *His* name. When the Church elders saw the miraculous deeds that Simon Peter and John were doing, they became afraid because they had never seen anyone do these things before. They immediately saw their deeds as something evil because they did not understand it. Just like many people today, their abilities were shunned because people thought that psychics and mediums had to be bad people who should be ostracized. What if those people really were not trying to do anything wrong? What if they were just using God-given abilities to help others and gain nothing for themselves? Were they still sinful?

I had to hide my abilities for most of my life for the fear of my family, friends, and peers ostracizing me. I started to accept what society said about women who claimed to be able to do these things. I began to convince myself that perhaps I was just imaging everything – or that I was a raving mad woman. Studying physics for five years in college did not help this opinion, either. By the time I was a freshman in college, I thought that all this childish nonsense about believing that I talked to the dead and trees was ancient history. However, I was wrong. No matter what I did, I kept seeing these dead spirits. I kept hearing the trees whispering. I felt the change in the seasons and knew when they would occur. I began seeing situations and events in my dreams before they occurred. Then, I realized that I could not deny myself any longer. I had to accept that this was who I was and that there was nothing wrong with me. So, I decided to keep my abilities to myself and practice them in private.

Then, I met Adrian. He spoke with me about LifeConscious, and I read his book about it. I was stunned that a man actually came up with this LifeConscious concept and how it helped to explain my abilities. I finally was able to put some meaning behind what I could do and why it was happening to me. Adrian was not at all surprised at what I could do. In fact, he wanted to know more about it. He asked me all sorts of questions that I had never been asked before. He showed me that I didn't need to be ashamed at all of my gifts. That is why he encouraged me to help him write this book – in the hopes that some women and men may find comfort in reading about my experiences and realize they are not alone.

A Note on the Effects of Abuse

While I initially did not want to write a section about abuse in this book, I eventually decided that it was an important issue that needs to be addressed. While this subject may seem unrelated to the topics that we are talking about in this chapter, I will explain how abuse factors into the abilities that I have been able to cultivate and cherish throughout my life.

It is important for everyone to understand how abuse affects people long-term. Being a past victim of abuse myself, I felt it was significant to bring up how my experiences have affected the way I live my life and how I perceive the world and myself. I can say with great certainty that if it had not been for my abusive childhood, I would not be the woman whom I am today. My personality and the way I look at my own relationships would be very different. If you, the reader, has been abused, it is very important to understand this and accept that this did happen to you. Embrace it as a part of your own experiences and file it away into your personal library of life lessons that are special to you.

I have always found it difficult to talk to others about my abusive past – mainly because I was afraid of being misunderstood or treated differently than everyone else. I used to feel like the abuse was my fault and that somehow others would look down on me like I was dirty or a bad person. Nothing could be further from the truth. I now know that discussing my abuse with others that have been abused cannot only help others, but also aid in my own recovery. In my experience, I have found that most people do not like to admit that they have been abused

– especially if the abuse was sexual in nature. In fact, I would estimate (even though there are no statistics to prove this) that about a third of the people in the United States have suffered some kind of sexual abuse at some point in their lives. These men and women are to be commended for overcoming such overwhelming and stressful circumstances.

The abuse that I went through as a child encompassed all levels of abuse from sexual, to emotional, to verbal, to physical. My innocence was taken from me when I was just a toddler. The abuse lasted until I was about 14 years old. I suffered tremendously at the hands of someone whom I was supposed to trust and give my life to. Although I hold no malice toward him now, I was angry and depressed for most of my teenage and early adult years. I struggled with severe anxiety, suicidal thoughts, and delusions for years. It was only after I spent time alone with myself in prayer and meditation that I finally realized what I needed to do to get over this pain.

While all of the abuse was going on in my childhood, I clung to my abilities that I had. I rejoiced each time I heard a spirit in the woods or listened to an oak tree tell me when the seasons would come. Every small and simple joy that I could find in my life, I held on to that. I felt like someone was telling me that I had to find happiness in these places, or I was never going to find it at all. Since I didn't have the privilege of having all the wonderful things in a child's life like many of my peers at school did, I had to find my own things to excel in that would make up for the hurt that was going on in my life. I found solace in my room where I would write, draw, and meditate on my own self-purpose. I found solace in spending time with animals or playing in the woods. There, I would communicate with spirits of people, trees, and animals. I felt that these abilities made me special and that when I was engaging in these activities, I did not need to be fearful.

But unfortunately, as I got older, I was forced to become more involved with the family church and accept more of my family's strict religious principles. I was taught that my abilities came from the Devil, and that I would go to hell if I practiced any of these "abominations" that my father referred to as "witchcraft." I was so frightened of going to hell (and perhaps more of my father becoming angry with me) that I tried stopping all my communications with spirits or my quiet moments of meditation with myself. I only prayed to what I thought was God and participated in many church activities in hopes that my father would approve. It took me a long time to realize that there was nothing that I could do in the church or anywhere else that make my father love me or approve of me. One day, when I was 18 years old, I told him I did not want to believe in his strict doctrines anymore. He told me that I had become a child of Satan, and he no longer wanted me in his house. I was essentially dead to him.

After this, I became quite depressed. I had spent the last five years trying to reconcile with my father to see if there was anything I could do to repair the damage that had been done in my childhood. I tried everything to get him to approve of me and become close to him so that I could have the father whom I always wanted. Unfortunately, this could never happen. Once I realized this in my late teens, I fell into a sorrowful despair. I didn't know who or what I was. I attached myself to any male figure that would have me. Again, this continued the cycle of abuse as I would involve myself with men who were unhealthy for me.

But, in 2005, I began meditating on myself again as well as reconnecting with the earth and the people in the mirror. I could hear them again! My inner strength started to return, and I realized that I did not need a male figure in my life to be happy. I began to seek the good in life and in myself again. I was optimistic about the future and actually looked forward to getting up every morning. My depression had gone away! Each day since that time, I have remembered who I am and what I have accomplished. I engage in only positive, healthy activities that benefit me in a spiritual, physical, and emotional way.

Now, I am helping to write this book so that others may know that they are not alone in their abilities and experiences. I want everyone to know that even with overwhelming odds; a life can be turned around – if one is willing to change it. I am also helping fellow abuse sufferers by co-teaching domestic violence and self-defense classes for women in my community. I feel like I can give these women the confidence to fight off an assailant and get away from an abuser. On our LifeConscious blog, I have even written a post regarding how to overcome abuse. Here is an excerpt from it.

You may ask yourself, "Will I ever get over the pain of abuse?" The short answer is no. The pain will always be there. But, the fact is that getting over the pains of abuse are much more complicated than meets the eye. Over the years, I have dealt with every conceivable emotion regarding my abusive past–everything from hate to depression to confusion. Then, one day I realized that these emotions will always be there. There's nothing I can do to take away the pain from those memories. So, I learned that the best things to do are these:

1.) Cut off anyone or anything connected to your abusive past–especially the person that did the abusing.

2.) Whenever you get a flashback or nightmare, stop thinking about it and realize that this was in the past and you are ok now. Those memories cannot hurt you anymore. Also, hugs are nice when these things happen!

3.) Take self-defense classes or violence/abuse prevention classes to learn more about how you can avoid this type of treatment in the future (most victims of abuse unfortunately flock toward abusive people without realizing it). Taking these classes will empower you and give you the confidence you need to fight off anyone that would hurt you.

4.) Find a faith that works for you and that you sincerely believe in. Praying to God has always been an essential part of my life and my recovery. There were times I know that I would not be here if I had not relied on my faith and trusted in the mercy that I would be given.

5.) Don't think of yourself as a victim anymore. This pitiful behavior does not support recovery and continues to give your abuser power over your life. Instead, realize that your experiences made you the person that you are today. It shaped you into a strong and powerful woman–capable of doing anything!!

6.) Move forward. Moving forward and not dwelling on the past promotes a healthy attitude toward the abuse. Don't worry about latent memories that could come back to haunt you. Believe me, they will anyway without you wanting them to. But, the less you think about it and dwell on it, the less often they will happen.

7.) If certain situations or events make you uncomfortable, don't do it!! If something that your partner or friends want you to participate in, but you know it's going to trigger a flashback, don't do it! For me, watching horror movies or certain things on television will trigger these. So, I don't do it. I don't care if my friends think that I'm being irrational or silly. It's not silly to me, and that's all that matters.

8.) Remember: There's nothing wrong with you and none of this was your fault! Sometimes, people are just victims of circumstances that they cannot control. This is usually the case with abuse sufferers. In my case for example, I was a child that had no control of my situation. But, I still felt like that what happened was my fault. Guilt is a normal emotion for abusees to feel. But, you must accept that whoever this person was that abused you was just wrong! YOU were the one that was right!

9.) Recovery is a lifelong process. But, if you keep your head high and have faith, things will get better! Change is inevitable in a person's life. If you are in a situation now where you are being abused, there are so many ways out! There are many options that are available to you such as shelters and churches that will take you in at no charge. Once you realize that you are being abused, that is a huge step. The next one will be what you plan to do about it. You have to decide when you need a change in your life. Will you have the courage to take that step?

The People in the Mirror

Now that you know a little more about my background, let's get back to the people whom I see in the mirror. How can you look in the mirror and see what I see? How will you know what to expect? The most important thing to remember is to not be afraid. Your first reaction might be to look away or cower. But, you must force yourself to stare your fears in the face – literally. This is the only way you will get through to your ancestors.

In their book, *Druid Magic: The Practice of Celtic Wisdom*, the authors Sutton and Mann explain the way ancestry reveals itself in the mirror according to ancient Celtic beliefs.

> *"In the miracle of life, DNA passes life from parent and child, parent to child, over thousands of years. Therefore particles and living traces of the actual bodies and minds of your ancestors are within you now. If you look at the inner side of your forearm through the thin skin, you will see veins that carry the blood of your ancestors. If you imagine looking inside every cell, you will see the chromosomes that came from your parents. If you look at the DNA inside the chromosomes, you will see the living genetic messages, half from your mother and half from your father, that make you who you are. If you look in the mirror, you will see the presence of your ancestors (*Sutton,167*). If you were a Celt, you would pray to your mythic ancestors whose spirits dwell within the universe. You would know they live in the earth, the waters, and the*

*sky, where their presence makes those places sacred (*Sutton, 155*). The Druids honored the ancestors and tradition, usually expressed as honor for a clan or tribe, as it makes each person what they are now (*Sutton, 162*)."*

Try looking in your mirror with the lights dimmed in the room. What you will begin to see is your face slowly beginning to transform into a person who looks a lot like you, but has some differences. Sometimes, you will see huge differences – for example, a mole or scars begin to appear that you do not have on your face. You may even see someone of the opposite sex as they appear in your face. But, do not be frightened. These people, although strange to see, are really a part of you! There's nothing to be afraid of because you are in control of them.

Controlling the Situation

The most important thing is not to let the faces overwhelm you. Sometimes, the faces will appear and disappear very quickly, and it may be difficult to focus on just one. Nevertheless, if you want to get through to these ancestors, you must call them forth one at a time.

While looking at yourself in the mirror, close your eyes for just a moment and say to yourself in your mind that you are going to allow these faces to surface, but only one at a time. Open your eyes and look in the mirror again until you see your face begin to change into someone else. Try focusing on this new person and concentrate on the details of their facial features. Get a good picture of this person in the mirror and then, while keeping this image of them in your mind, close your eyes again. Continue to look at the person in your "mind's eye" and ask them questions. For example, try and find out where they are from and what time period they may have lived in. Once you become good at this, you can try to ask for their name and how they died.

Do this for each person that you see. The point of this is to try and get to know as much about these people as possible. The more you learn about the ancestors you see in your mirror, the more you will learn about yourself. You will learn to appreciate yourself for everything that you are – and realize that if it were not for these important ancestors, you would not be alive today. You will learn that even though these ancestors may have lived in a time many years before you were born, that they had the same feelings, hopes, and dreams that you do. They may have had different struggles to deal with (e.g. harvesting the crops so that the

family could eat vs. finding the money to put gasoline in the car), but ultimately they were a lot like you are!

Again, because of LifeConscious, these hopes, feelings, and desires are passed down from mother to child. These are where your creative thoughts come from – or your brilliant ideas. Each of their precious memories and creativity as human beings are locked away inside your brain right now! Their wisdom is your wisdom. You can use their life experiences and memories to help you become wiser as you age. Think of how incredible it is that you have inherited such precious traits from your parents who teach you how to reason, think, feel, and form new ideas!

Chapter 7

What Can I Learn from Heidi's Experiences?

Confront the People in the Mirror

Find Them in Your Ancestry

Continue to Communicate with Them

Behind every mirror there is a reflection of another face. **Unknown author**

Confront the People in the Mirror

(Heidi) Earlier, we discussed how we look in the mirror for various reasons – most of which have to do with our outward appearance. But, what if we look in the mirror to confront the people that we are inside?

When those different faces appear to you when you stare at yourself in the mirror, you may be frightened at first. I know that when I was little, I ran away from those faces because I didn't understand what they were. I thought maybe they were monsters trying to get me or some demon trying to take over my body. Even so, one day, I said to myself that I was not going to be afraid of the faces anymore. I wanted to know who they were! I wanted to know if I was crazy or not. So, I decided to sit with myself in my bedroom and finally meet the faces who had been in the mirror with me my whole life.

I was shocked to see that the faces that I saw would change, and I would see many different faces – one after the other. Some of the faces would repeat themselves as they were shown to me, but I could not believe how many there were. The most surprising thing was they all looked a bit like me! Some of them were older, some of them were younger. Some of them were men, but most of the faces were women. I saw they had different hair styles and markings on their face. But, each of them looked a little like me. I could see traits in their eyes, ears, noses, and chins that were very similar to my own. They all looked so familiar to me, even though I had never seen them before. Then, it occurred to me that these people must be my ancestors who have come before me.

I began to meditate on these people whom I saw in myself in the mirror. I wanted to know exactly who they were and where they came from. I sat in front of the mirror until I saw one face appear. When I saw her, I closed my eyes and focused on the face that I had seen. I would clear my mind and ask questions about her – who are you? Where did you come from? When I cleared my mind, the answers came to me in visions. It was like I was experiencing memories that were my own, but yet they were obviously from this other person. One of the women told me her name was Elizabeth Crofton. She was wearing her hair up, and it was curly. She was dressed in British colonial-type clothing. I looked her up on my ancestry.com web page and found out that she was one of my direct descendants from Ireland. She was born in 1660 in County Mayo.

I saw another woman who did not speak English. She was a woman with long hair and a dirty looking face. She felt like she had lived a long time ago. Her name sounded like Althred or something similar. She also could very likely be my ancestor, since my relatives originated in the British Isles and this name sounds Saxon-like.

Then, I saw a woman that I have been seeing my whole life. She was a woman who wore furs and had long, dark brown hair and eyes. She was not a particularly beautiful woman. Her hair was unkempt and her eyebrows were thick, and her teeth were a shade of yellow. She looked to be an older woman – perhaps in her fifties. I have seen this woman in my dreams, in my meditations, and in the mirror for as long as I can remember. When I finally confronted her that night in the mirror and asked her who she was. She told me her name was Mauve or some derivation of that. I don't know exactly where she was from or when she died, but she is certainly my ancestor, and she has been with me and helping me all these years.

Once I got to understand that these women were my ancestors, it occurred to me that these women must be a part of me. After all, was I not born from the same genes as they were? Did not the same blood that flowed through their veins in the same way it flows through mine? It just makes sense that their memories – their life would be innately a part of my life experiences and in my subconscious also.

Find Them in Your Ancestry

If you have not done so already, try asking relatives about your ancestry and ask them to tell you about their experiences. We have found that the older relations have very interesting stories about their upbringing and may have family stories that were passed down to them from generations ago. Be sure to write these stories down and place them in a safe place or a scrapbook. When these relatives die, their stories will die with them, unless we preserve them in a special way so that they may always be remembered.

Researching your ancestors is a much easier process than it was even ten years ago. What used to be long years of searching through library records and microfilm has become available with a few clicks of a mouse. There are several ancestry websites that are designed to help people find who they are related to – even if you thought that records in the family were lost, you may be surprised at how technology has saved them. Many libraries, churches, and census data have been uploaded into ancestry databases and are searchable through ancestry search engines. It is a fascinating experience, and we recommend that everyone try to do as much research as possible. You may be surprised to find out who you are related to. For example, we found that Adrian is related to Sir Richard Wydeville, a prominent figure from the War of the Roses. He was beheaded by the King of England on August 12, 1469.

I also found out that I have relations to President Thomas Jefferson. My direct descendant is Martha Jefferson, my mother's great x 5 grandmother. She was Thomas Jefferson's aunt.

We do caution that there are some web pages that claim to have found a famous ancestor in your family. What you find (after giving them your credit card number) is that if you carefully trace the ancestry forward, it is a mistake. It is best to go over individual records carefully and not assume that they must be correct for your family.

Continue to Communicate with Them

While it is a fascinating prospect that we may see our long deceased ancestors in the mirror when we look at ourselves hard enough, you may ask why it is so important that we speak with them at all. Furthermore, how can I communicate with them if they are dead? The answer is that your ancestors are not dead at all. They are alive in you. You carry their memories and their LifeConscious through your blood. When you talk to them in the mirror, you are calling up deeply latent memories that belonged to them. Embrace them as your family because they are you!

The purpose of talking to these faces in the mirror is to better understand who *you* are. If we understand where we came from and who we are, we can live better, more fulfilled lives! By knowing my ancestors from Ireland, Scotland, England, France, and Germany are here with me in my body and spirit, I feel happier about who I am. It is nice to know where I came from and where the origins of my culture are. I can really cultivate the knowledge my ancestors had in their past by practicing the ways of their culture and then passing these things on to my own children. This way, I am keeping who we are in the family – keeping our ancestors' spirits alive and remembering where we came from and who we are. By doing this, I am fulfilling a valuable purpose that is just as important as LifeConscious. I am passing along knowledge of our ancestors – just as LifeConscious passes on past memories and adaptations from mother to child.

Whether you choose to believe in a religion, or if you choose to believe in the absence of religion, you can still see the evidence of LifeConscious

memories being passed down from generation to generation. You can see the importance and purpose of communicating with ancestors from your past in the mirror. This is the main reason why Adrian and I decided to write this book. We saw evidence of what we call LifeConscious in our everyday lives everywhere around us – regardless of what religion people believed in or not. In this way, we knew its importance for this message to be spread so that *everyone* could see the evidence for LifeConscious and judge for themselves.

My husband and I are firm believers in the powers that women naturally have. Whether the reader believes that this is a gift from a God, a natural occurrence of evolution, or that the LifeConscious Entity wills it in us, the evidence still remains that females have definite abilities that make them very special. I am hopeful that there are many readers out there that are very skeptical about what I am about to tell you. Indeed, I am a skeptic myself and as a scientist, I also demand the need for concrete evidence to support ideas. My intention is not to convert the reader to adopt my philosophies or reject their own sacred beliefs. I only wish to present my findings that I managed to acquire from many years of study and research – although many of the findings are quite subjective. The reader must decide if he or she accepts this evidence as proof that there is something supernatural that we as human beings have been trained to ignore and suppress from ourselves for many generations.

We began earlier talking about children and imaginary friends – explaining how sometimes (not each case) that children have close connections with LifeConscious. We spoke about why children seem to be so in tune with LifeConscious but gradually become more and more out of touch as they grow closer to adulthood. Most children grow out of this "childish" phase of thinking that they can talk to trees, having imaginary friends, and so forth. However, my experience was quite different. I never really "grew out" of this phase in my life. It is true that I grew older, I matured, and I gained valuable life experiences that have shaped me into the person that I am today. I function normally in society, have a good paying job, do not receive psychological treatment or medication for any mental condition, and I am of sound mind and judgment.

However, I cannot begin to describe how many supernatural experiences I have had, since I was quite small. As far back as I can

remember, I have been able to do and see things that few people could do or understand. I come from a very traditional Christian upbringing where my parents were very much against any supernatural occurrences. My family and friends were convinced, that whenever I spoke about supernatural events happening to me, that those things must have come from the Devil. I was not allowed to talk about seeing spirits, talking to trees, or traveling out of my body.

I began to realize that my abilities were something special that I did not have to be ashamed of. So, I continued to communicate with the spirits that I saw instead of running away from them. Most spirits that I have spoken with and seen are happy and friendly. In fact, many are eager to speak to me. Sometimes, they want me to pass messages on to other family members that are still living. Many times, they feel like they need to pass on these messages because perhaps their death was unexpected, and they left things unfinished here.

If you have any type of mediumship or divinatory abilities, I encourage you to not be afraid of what you are seeing and sensing. You will learn many things if you open your mind and heart up to listen to what these spirits have to say. I regard these passed away individuals as heroes – mainly because they are adventurers. They have gone where we, the living, have not yet experienced. These wonderful people whom I have spoken with have taught me that death is nothing to be afraid of. They have given me hope, once and for all, that perhaps there is an afterlife, and we definitely do not just fade into non-existence when we pass away.

Chapter 8

Conclusions

The importance of Water

Support one another in groups

A Few Words on PMS, Pregnancy, and Alternative Medicine

You are definitely not alone

The LifeConscious web site

Physicists and mystics have looked at the universe and observed the same things, but the mystics spoke in poetry, images and parable, and the scientists spoke in numbers, equations and formulas. ***Abby Willowroot***

Death is no more than passing from one room into another. But there's a difference for me, you know. Because in that other room I shall be able to see.
Helen Keller

The Importance of Water

We can't emphasize enough how important water is to our lives. The next time that you take a drink of water after you've read this paragraph, look deeply into the glass and ponder about the number of times that this glass of water has passed through the guts of countless numbers of animals, insects, fish, and plants. It could have been used by a giant shark a hundred million years ago, a duckbill dinosaur 75 million years ago, then to be expelled by a giant sloth 30 million years ago, and then to be frozen during the last ice age just 100,000 years ago. This same drop ice that was frozen in a glacier thawed out 12,000 years ago to be drunk by a modern human and then to be lapped up as milk by a kitten a few months prior to the very same drop entering your mouth. This is a cycle that has major implications because water is the key ingredient to life and the carrier of LifeConscious memories.

Water is so essential to us that the above thought must be reemphasized, but in another point of view. If you take any plant in your home and deny it any water it will begin to wilt and sag in a few days. The plant needs water to keep itself pumped up and standing erect facing the sun but the water will eventually evaporate from its leaves as it gives off the gas oxygen as a byproduct. It also needs water to transfer the nutrients in the soil gathered by its roots to the upper parts of the plant needed for photosynthesis. A plant lives to do one thing, and that is to procreate and extend its living linear organism, just as we humans.

(Heidi) If you think about it, all the water that you drink is pretty old – just like the rocks outside your house. True, many urban rocks

that you see may be man-made, but a lot of those are rocks that were created by the earth millions of years ago. It may be disgusting to think about how many animals may have lived and died in this water that you drink. Just remember as you gaze through the clear liquid in your glass that without this, you would not be alive and neither would any of your children.

It is this transference of LifeConscious memories from mother's to their young that is the whole key to the successful continuation of our species. You are the end result of a long line of very flourishing and tenacious ancestors who have endured countless famines, plagues, wars, conflicts and migrations to go on to build villages, city states, countries and empires. Yours is a linear heritage to be very proud of.

(Heidi) We have come quite a long way as a human species. We have had many chances over the eras to eliminate ourselves into extinction. We have survived so much suffering and hardship. However, if we are to remember who we are and where we have come from, we must pass down our history and our heritage to our children. It is essential that they understand the struggles we have overcome and how they can learn from our experiences so that they may know how to continue this cycle. As mothers, we have already done a lot by carrying our child in our womb for nine months and nursing them with our milk that they not only take for nourishment, but for the passing on of innate memories. In addition to these motherly duties, we must teach them through oral tradition, written documentation, or by whatever means are available, the experiences of the ones that have passed on so that they may pass them on to their children.

We cannot forget who we are; otherwise, we become like an empty shell – useless and vulnerable to deterioration. I once had a friend tell me that he did not believe it was at all important to know his family roots and that for adopted people, there was not even a point in trying. He told me that people should only embrace the Here and Now and forget what happened in their ancestor's past. I totally disagree. So, we should forget our history? How can we learn from our mistakes and move forward if we refuse to learn from the elders and the ones that have passed on? Why is it that older people in some societies are looked down upon as if they are waiting for them to die? The elders are the ones that should be most respected in societies because they are our *living*

history. By speaking with them, we are learning essential oral traditions that can be passed on. Their legacy will continue to live – even long after they are dead.

This has been the way of life for many generations and will be the way for many more to come. If we are to survive for as long as the earth is alive, we must carry on in this fashion.

A Few Words on PMS, Pregnancy, and Alternative Medicine

(Heidi) I want other women to feel empowered by what has been written here. As a woman, I feel led strongly to share with you my coping abilities and skills that have taken me years of research, trial and error, and experimenting on myself. I am not a doctor, but I have found that some basic, alternative methods for women's issues are most beneficial and work better than any drug that is out on the market today.

I know that many general practitioners and OB-Gyns advise their women patients that they should never take any herbal supplements to treat your ailments – especially during pregnancy. It is because of my experiences with myself and other ladies whom I have talked to that lead me to believe that this advice is incorrect. The reason why doctors tell you not to take herbs during pregnancy or any other ladies' ailments are because the American Medical Association (AMA) has not approved the use of herbs for treatment of disease. Therefore, doctors can be held liable for prescribing herbal supplements to their patients. If the doctor or their practice were to be taken to court for malpractice, the AMA would not back them up and therefore, those physicians would lose their license to practice medicine.

Another reason that many physicians do not want their patients to take herbal supplements is because they are afraid of the drug interactions that could take place if you are taking other prescription

medications. It is true that many anti-depressants, Beta-blockers, and heart medications (to name a few) should not be supplemented with some herbal treatments. The combination of the right ones in your bloodstream could be deadly. Therefore, I recommend that you consult your physician before trying any of these methods I'm about to tell you. Always tell your doctor if you are taking any herbs for your health.

I have been studying herbology for over 10 years. I have talked to herb specialists as well as doctors and read many scholarly texts on the subject. One of my favorite books to consult is *Culpeper's Complete Herbal.* This book was written by Nicolas Culpepper back in 1653! In his day, he was considered to be a knowledgeable apothecary and pharmacist. Some of his methods that he wrote about are still in use today.

> *"[Culpeper] suffered much criticism for his scathing comments in the translated work, but went on to publish* The English Physician, *which was an enormous success in England. It still endures as an archival text, and is considered representative of the strong English tradition of domestic herbal medicine of that time…*
>
> *At present, it is estimated that 40% of prescription drugs sold in the United States contain at least one ingredient derived from a natural source. Up to 25% of prescription drugs contain an ingredient derived from a flowering plant. Common examples include the use of the periwinkle (Catharantbus roseus) for chemotherapy, and foxglove (Digitalis purpurea) for production of cardiac glycosides"* (Kligler, 108). [6]

Unfortunately, many of Nicolas's contemporaries disliked his philosophy of medicine and called him a heretic. He believed that his lengthy experience with herbs, his astrological methods, and his belief that no authority was above questioning, made him a devoted physician. However, the Society of Apothecaries in England tried to shut down his practice around 1643 and called him a witch. Ironically, he ended up dying nine years later of tuberculosis – a disease he adamantly tried finding an herbal cure for.

---

6 Kligler, Benjamin and Lee, Roberta, A. (2004) *Integrative Medicine: Principles for Practice.* McGraw Hill (2004).

Culpeper and many other herbologists over the centuries have come to know what many medicine women in ancient societies already knew – that herbs were the key to women's overall health. They knew that when women ate healthy, slept adequately, exercised, and drank plenty of water, that herbal supplements would only enhance and improve their overall health. Herbs are not a cure-all. When women are practicing healthy habits in their life, herbs are a nice solution to any ailments (female related or otherwise) that may come up. I find that during the few days before my period and while pregnant or just having a tired/headachy day, that there are some herbal supplements I can take that really improve my ailments.

First, I will address tired/headachy ailments that we all get sometimes during menstruation, during ovulation, and even at random. For these times, I sit in a quiet room and close the door to be by myself. This is important when trying to deal with fatigue and headaches because if you are stressed or have too many things going on at once, it will only worsen your symptoms. I realize that with our busy lives and children, it can be difficult to go somewhere and be alone for a while. Try and see if you can have a family member or a friend come over and stay with the children for an hour so that you can be quiet. While sitting in this tranquil room, I like to drink a tea that is made of chamomile (a natural relaxant) and rose-hips (a natural pain-reliever). I also find that for some persistent headaches, an ice-pack placed over the painful area and held there for about 20 seconds seems to help me. Try and keep your mind as quiet as possible. Don't think about all the things that you have to take care of or what you need to be getting done right now. Trust me; these thoughts will all be there in an hour. They're not going anywhere. You can choose to put them away for a little while and regenerate your mind and body.

The next ailment I have is for the dreaded monthly visitor. I always drink a great tea made by Yogi Tea called Women's Dong Quai. I find that it does wonders for my mood swings and fatigue. You can find this tea in most grocery stores. I also like to drink rose-hip, red raspberry leaf, and chamomile tea for the other PMS symptoms I have such as cramping, headaches, and anxiousness. Again, try to find your quiet place and meditate/pray about letting your body do what it needs to do and there is no need to try and control what is going on inside of you. The LifeConscious forces in your body know what to do. Fighting the

feelings that you are having at this time of the month just worsen your symptoms. Realize that there is nothing wrong with the way you feel and that your body is taking control. The sooner you realize this, the better you are going to feel. Don't let anyone tell you that your PMS symptoms are in your head and that you have the power to stop them anytime you want. They are wrong.

The next ailment is not an ailment at all. In fact, in my opinion, it is the most wonderful thing that can ever happen to a woman – and that is pregnancy. Although some women have a unforgettable time being pregnant, a lot of women have many problems. Even though these problems are normal, they are still quite uncomfortable (and sometimes unbearable) to expectant mothers. Although I have never had a baby myself, I have helped some of my friends and family members that have been plagued by severe nausea, fatigue, and moodiness (just to name a few) during their pregnancy. For the nausea, I recommend a combination of peppermint and spearmint tea. This feels very soothing going down the throat and settles the stomach quite well. Also, the tea helps during the last trimester when many expectant mothers are getting heartburn. I have found for myself that spearmint and peppermint have relieved my most severe heartburn – even better than Tums or Milk of Magnesia.

For the Braxton-Hicks contractions, uterus expansion, belly bulging, and other muscle pains associated with pregnancy, I recommend red raspberry leaf. This herb has been known for quite some time as a uterus muscle relaxant and helps tone the muscles in the pelvic region in general. This herb helped my friend during her first trimester when the uterus has spasms because the womb is growing at a rapid pace. It relieves pain in the pelvic region when consumed in a tea.

Most of these herbs can be purchased in grocery stores. Fortunately, most tea brands (YogiTea, Bigelow, and Celestial Seasonings, especially) that are sold in stores have warning labels on the back if they are not safe for pregnant or nursing mothers. Again, you should consult with your doctor if you are with child and want to take these herbal supplements. The ones that I have named above are perfectly safe for most pregnant women. However, there are some herbs you must avoid while you are expectant – which is why I recommend reading the label on the back of the tea before purchasing in the store. Never buy herbal supplements from the internet, unless you know the manufacturer.

Some herbal suppliers on the internet buy their products from India, which sometimes use lead or arsenic in their products.

You are Definitely Not Alone

(Heidi) Although what we offer here in this book is what we feel is the truth, we understand that many readers will see this work as fiction or a joke. There are many individuals that choose to believe that there is nothing else beyond everyday living – those supernatural events or occurrences that cannot be explained by science are not real. For those of you that have seen and experienced things that are real, but no one will believe you, there are support groups available for you online and locally in your hometown. You may not believe that there are groups in your community that share these beliefs. But, believe us – they are everywhere, even in the smallest towns.

If you have had similar experiences to the examples that we have given in this book, we encourage you to share those experiences with others. Do not do what many others have done, which is ignore the experiences and pass them off to imagination or coincidence. People that have continuously ignored these special experiences eventually lose their abilities to see or divinate. These abilities such as mediumship and divination are like muscles – if you do not use them for a while, they become atrophied and useless. It is important that you keep your skills active and use them often. Practicing with your gifts will only make you stronger and better able to help yourself and others.

There is one more thought we would like to leave you with. As women, we are privileged by birth to have these abilities that have been passed down to us for hundreds of generations. We have a great responsibility to our families, communities, and our race. After all,

people used to look to us for guidance regarding the things that religious leaders, government officials, and doctors failed to reconcile. It is for this reason that I never charge money for any divination, séance, or any other supernatural knowledge that I may give another. I believe that it is my duty as a woman blessed with this gift that I give my abilities freely with no strings attached. I do not ask for anything in return for the help that I give others. This is only the opinion of the author. I know there are others with my abilities that feel differently and have made careers out of their mediumship skills. I believe that it is a mistake to seek fame and fortune for what is a special gift that is given to you by your mother at birth. I encourage all of you to ask yourself what you would do if you, in fact, have some of these abilities. Why would you feel the need to be on TV or make a lot of money from this? What and whose purpose would you be fulfilling than? Contact us on the website and tell us how you feel about it.

Support One Another in Groups

It is our hope that this book has helped shed some light on the women's legacy and how this has been passed down through hundreds of generations. You have seen, through this work, how women have very special abilities that allow them to bring a deeper sense of who we are as a people. We have shown how some women are still able to communicate and interact with people who have passed on. In our ancient history, we have discussed how these skills of divination, herbal medicine, and mediumship are passed down from mother to child through LifeConscious.

Since now you know the truth behind the faces in the mirror, this new understanding will probably start some novel types of support groups pushing the ideas prevalent in this book. Our website at LifeConscious.com will shed light on these new groups as they begin to develop.

The LifeConscious Website

You can always go to www.lifeconscious.com, our website devoted to the study of LifeConscious and how it is passed down from mothers to their children. You can blog and chat on the site, or you can send us a personal email with questions, comments, or testimonies. We will be more than happy to answer your questions and give you any help or support that you need. If you send us a testimony, we may ask if we can post it on our website so that others may see that they are not alone with their experiences.

We will also post the latest news and findings that we think is pertinent to supporting the LifeConscious theory along with help groups that will be forming as a consequence of the publishing of this book.

Addendum

Is not the South the source of life, and does not the flowering stick truly come from there? And does not man advance from there toward the setting sun of his life? Then does he not approach the colder North where the white hairs are? And does he not then arrive, if he lives, at the source of light and understanding, which is the East? Then does he not return to where he began, to his second childhood, there to give back his life to all life, and his flesh to the earth whence it came?

Black Elk – a holy man of the Oglala Sioux

Why an Addendum

This addendum is actually a precursor to our next book that will deal with the religious aspects of LifeConscious. The book will also provide many examples and evidence of LifeConscious' existence in ancient and modern scriptural texts and documents. Our ancient ancestors called LifeConscious by many different names, but it is essentially the same concept and the point of the book. You may ask us, aren't you just giving these old themes yet another new name? The answer is yes, but these names were essentially all the same concept in the beginning, and we are just returning to the original shamanistic beliefs of our ancestors. Let's not forget that shamanism was the very first of man's religions. We will attempt to trace back to these ancient ideas that have been skewed, chastised, and even condemned by the current modern status quo religions and give it the universal appeal that it still deserves.

So with this in mind, please note that this Addendum can't help but be religious in its content and may cause those of you who are extremely pious and hold close to your chosen faith's principles to have them shaken a bit if you read any further. **Please do not continue reading if you don't want your faith questioned.** Like we've both stated before, if you believe in a positive, compassionate religion then you are more than OK by us, and we would like to think that we would be the last people in the world to try and change your beliefs by ramming our beliefs down your throat.

Is it a wonder that modern religious buildings are often built upon older, similar structures – even the so-called pagan religious sites? For instance, the French Notre Dame Cathedral in Paris is built upon an older catholic church, which is built over a Roman temple dedicated to Isis, which is probably resting upon a site that was spiritually significant to the predominant local tribes. New religions, like these buildings, just don't appear out of thin air. Much like humans, they are the result of a linear heritage of religious knowledge from pagan to modern beliefs.

First of all, to start a new religion you must have two elements – a prophet and a traditional, older religion to branch off from. For example, Buddhism broke off from Hinduism with the prophet Siddhartha Gautama, the original Buddha. The Jewish religion broke away from a Sumerian faith when its prophet, Abraham, left one of its city states of Ur of the Chaldeans. Both Islam and Christianity were off-shoots of the Jewish religion with the prophets Mohammed and Jesus.

Successful religions know how to build one on top of another. Take Christianity's use of the gods from local tribes by simply replacing their names with that of saints but keeping the qualities and personas of the former pagan gods. This was of course done to make it more palatable for the local tribes to embrace the new religion. All the modern religions, in order to survive, had to absorb the characteristics of native pagan deities and retain many of their qualities to this day.

So, modern religions have had to be flexible to continue to survive and grow when new people and cultures were encountered during the empire building years from 6th century to today. Sometimes this persuasiveness was accomplished by the sword and at times through the drummed- in fear of the everlasting damnation of hell. Either way, the new cultures lost their uniqueness and innocence as their civilizations were torn apart by the old world's greed, ignorance, superstition and diseases. Countless tribes, clans and families have been swept into the dust bins of history to be forever lost and forgotten as their linear heritage ended in oblivion.

We've already seen how women suffered the most during these religious revelations. Not only was Eve to blame for all of mankind's ills and sins in the Judeo/Christian dogma but even in the belief of the new Trinity, women are completely left out. A Trinity made up of the Father, Son and Holy Spirit is an obvious attempt to bar women out of this holy triangle. We're positive that the original trinity included *mother* in place of Holy Spirit. Nevertheless, because of the church's changes toward women 2000 years ago, this latest Trinity has become the traditional norm.

What is funny though, is that the old church founders in their quest to rid themselves of female involvement in Christianity had inadvertently put it all in the correct perspective. Remember that the Holy Spirit meant the *breath of god* or the initial spark of life to the lineage of mankind (LifeConscious). We now know that women are the carriers of this lineage and LifeConsciousness, therefore, are indeed included as part of the current trinity as the Holy Spirit. We are quite sure that the old trinity probably referenced Sophia (mother goddess of wisdom) as the mother member of the trinity, who was eventually replaced by the Christian Virgin Mary, who was relegated to just be the Mother of God. Our next book will probe more deeply into this subject as we humans try our best to find ways to live forever – either spiritually or scientifically.

This addendum will also go into the physics side of some concepts such as time, black holes, etc. to help show that we delve into the scientific side as well. We are not only writers and artists, but scientists by trade. I have worked for the Department of Energy in many of the National Labs for 30 years, and Heidi has a degree in physics, also working at a National Lab. We do not believe that science, and religion are part and parcel separate from one another. Unfortunately, this is a common viewpoint that our modern, technical society holds concerning these two fields. We feel that this is unjustified, and that they actually have a symbiotic relationship. Science and religion can ultimately work together to find common ground no matter what the subject may be. Hopefully, we can provide evidence of this to you as you continue reading.

Is it Possible to Beat Death?

So, is it possible to fight death through modern science or is there some miracle anti-aging process in our future? Some scientists believe that this is a possibility through genetic experiments and the fact that modern man's life expectancy is continually climbing.

(Heidi) In a sense, the anti-aging revolution is already here. Many celebrities such as Oprah are endorsing hormone replacement therapies. There are ads on television and the radio about drugs that can help you feel young again and give you increased sexual endurance. Moreover, there are countless products that promise reverse-aging wrinkle creams. I don't even need to talk about how popular Botox, lipo-suction, and facial lifts have become in the past decade – even among younger people.

While I feel that these procedures are not natural, I realize that many people disagree with me and have had great happiness and success with their anti-aging products and surgeries. I only hope that by giving themselves the illusion that they look and feel younger, they realize it's how they feel on the inside that makes them young or old – not their outward appearance.

Scientists are looking at single celled creatures like yeast cells that seem to age slowly and generate themselves as long as the environment and food diet is favorable, or in the case of longevity, a restrictive diet. Researchers have discovered that these yeast cells that were maintained on a glycerol diet lived as much as five times longer than normal cells and were more resistant to cell damage. This glycerol diet yielded a similar result as placing the cells on a restricted diet. In other words, the cells lived longer on a restrictive diet rather than the usual sugary fare. Restrictive diets are known to aid in the anti-aging process – even in humans. By the way, have we ever seen that many obese centegenarians?

Research has found that restricting the caloric intake of animals of between 25 to 30% can show extension to their life spans. One particular five year study of healthy volunteers below middle age took part in an experiment that either placed them on a restricted diet of 75% of their caloric intake. The rest was placed in a control group for comparison. The resulting data indicated that a restricted caloric intake can reduce the levels of insulin, body temperatures, energy, and DNA damage. In other words, they would take longer to age.

There are actually two strategies to longevity that are happening here. One is the anti-aging effect of the restrictive or glycerol diets. The second is what we have found to be the abundance of procreation. In the above described experiment, the yeast cells lived longer and divided into more cells. The cells seemed to be fighting death because of the large amount of procreation, but they did die eventually while their progeny lived on continuing their lineage. We now know that this is another example of a linear organism – just like man and all other living organisms. The difference is in the packaging where the yeast cells are single-celled living organisms with no form of transportation and must fend for themselves when it comes to finding food and protection. The cells that make up a human being is also single-celled creatures, but they help make up a somewhat intelligent body that not only provides transportation but finds and supplies food for all the different cells. The human cells also provide protection in a pliable case of skin and bones. It doesn't matter what type of job, sex, or region that the body resides in because the cells only care that they can continue to procreate and divide. We are essentially sophisticated taxi cabs for these single-celled organisms that make up our bodies. However, there is no magic formula to their longevity, since we are a linear organism bent on the continuation of our species.

There is yet another strategy used by our bodies to help us live longer, and it has to do with your body's continued ability to procreate, which induces menopause in women. Menopause occurs when a woman's body can no longer produce eggs that could be fertilized. The eggs trigger a secretion of estrogen to the woman's system. Around the age of 50 (give or take 10 years) a drop of this estrogen level occurs and that induces menopause and stops menstrual cycles. Surgery such as hysterectomy along with some forms of radiography and/or chemotherapy can also induce immediate menopause.

Even though some women show no symptoms of menopause other than the ending of their cycles, 80% do experience menopausal indicators such as:

- hot flashes
- night sweats
- palpitations of the heart
- mood changes such as irritability, depression or anxiety; although it's possible that these are due to life changes rather than the menopause itself
- difficulty sleeping (insomnia), due to night sweats or mood changes
- thinner, drier skin and hair, and brittle nails
- aches and pains in the joints
- loss of interest in sex (libido)
- weight gain
- headaches
- vaginal changes–dryness, pain during sexual intercourse, and increased risk of vaginal infections
- urinary changes–inability to control urination (incontinence) and increased risk of urinary infections

All of these symptoms can lead to debilitating long term effects such as:

- osteoporosis (loss of bone density)–the bones may become brittle and break more easily
- heart disease, increasing the risk of having a heart attack
- stroke
- weight gain, which increases the risk of heart problems
- weakness of the pelvic floor and vaginal muscles

The female body seems to shift gears when the child-bearing years are at an end. It shuts down the sexual urges while aging the body more quickly as if it's own LifeConscious were giving up on it. Remember that the primary focus of your LifeConscious is to aid in the procreative process so that the linear organism can continue unabated. When menopause sets in, it will naturally give up on maintaining your reproductive functions because your LifeConscious knows that you can no longer have babies. A whole new medical business has flourished over the past few decades to help menopausal women cope and resist this natural process by artificially inducing hormones. We believe this "tricks" your LifeConscious into thinking that you are still able to bear children.

(Heidi) Although this may seem quite discouraging to the ladies out there, do not fear menopause. If a woman takes care of herself and remains healthy as she begins to go through menopause, then it is unlikely that you will experience menopausal symptoms severely. You may go through some bouts of decreased libido, hot flashes, and vaginal dryness, but these symptoms are usually mild and temporary. If you are concerned about weight gain, osteoporosis, or heart disease, talk with your doctor about some things you can do at home that can help you deal with these potential problems. There are also alternative and herbal treatments to help you cope with these life changes better.

Men will undergo a similar fate when their bodies can no longer produce sperm and testosterone and will gradually suffer the condition known as andropause. After middle age, men will experience a 10% drop in testosterone every decade or so and when it gets low enough the symptoms of andropause set in.

- lethargy or loss of energy
- decreased or loss of sexual interest
- erectile dysfunction or loss of erections
- muscle weakness
- insomnia
- hot flashes
- night sweats
- infertility
- thinning of bones

Testosterone replacement therapy can slow the debilitating affects down, but eventually the body will succumb to the inevitable. Andropause is known to cause health hazards such as heart disease, osteoporosis, and gaining weight, which can lead to diabetes. The main point is that even a man's LifeConscious will slowly abandon its host body when it knows that this body can no longer make additions to the linear gene pool.

So is there any hope sometime in the near future that humans will be able to lengthen their living years? I think this is probably so and that scientists will eventually come to the same realization we have; and that is that as long as your body can maintain its procreative processes, the lengthier the longevity of life because your own LifeConscious will take care of the rest. As long as your own LifeConscious is convinced that you are still able to contribute to the procreative process then it will provide the needed life giving controls and conditions to do so. There are many examples in nature that support this procreative longevity concept.

Posidonia oceanica is a species of sea grass that is prevalent to the Mediterranean Sea. This marine plant form large underwater meadow-like colonies, some of which are estimated to be 100,000 years old and are considered to be of high importance to the environmental conservation of the sea. It is still procreating as its fruit is free floating. It is known in Italy as 'the olive of the sea'. Balls of fibrous material from the foliage of the plant, known as *egagropili*, are washed up to nearby shore-lines.

Pando is a colony of a single male Quaking Aspen tree located in the state of Utah, all determined to be part of a single living organism by identical genetic markers. These share one massive underground root system that weighs over 6,000 tons and estimated to be over 80,000 years old, making it one of the oldest known living organisms on the earth. The colony has around 47,000 stems (those are the trees that you see), which continually die and are new saplings sprout up by through its roots.

King's Lomatia is a Tasmanian plant that has shiny green leaves and bears pink flowers, yet it yields neither fruit nor seeds. It is unusual because all the remaining plants are genetically identical and yet are sterile. Procreation occurs when a branch falls and grows new roots, establishing a new plant that is genetically identical or a clone to its parent. Although each plant is separate and has its own root system, it is collectively considered to be one of the oldest living plant clones. Each plant's life span is approximately 300 years, but the plant has been cloning itself for at least 43,600 years (possibly up to 135,000 years). This estimate is based on the radiocarbon dating of fossilized leaf fragments that were found over 5 miles away.

There are many more plant examples of longevity – such as a *huckleberry bush* in Pennsylvania thought to be as old as 13,000 years of age, *Eucalyptus recurva* clones in Australia are claimed to be 13,000 years old and Creosote bushe*s* in the Mojave Desert are estimated at 11,700 years old (http://forests.org/archive/spacific/oldshrub.htm).

What about animals, though? Some animal species that scientists have called "living fossils" seem to defy the theory of evolution, such as the horseshoe crab or the coelacanth fish. These species never found it necessary to evolve during their 445 million year existences. How is it that these animals could survive the catastrophic events that killed off the dinosaurs or the chilling ice ages without having to adapt to the changing environment? This is a question that has puzzled scientists to this day.

Today, some animals are capable of attaining ages of a century or more while still retaining the ability to procreate. A tortoise named Jonathan was photographed during the Boer War around 1900, and his life has spanned eight British monarchs from George IV to Elizabeth II, and 50 prime ministers. He is believed to be 176 years old today and despite his old age, locals say he still has the energy to regularly mate with the three younger females.

A scientific team from Wales was dredging the waters north of Iceland as part of routine research when they found a specimen belonging to the clam species *Arctica islandica.* It was hauled up from waters 250 feet deep. Only after researchers cut through the clam's shell and counted its growth rings did they realize that it was between 405 and 410 years old and still healthy enough to procreate.

Some deep sea corals like the (*Leiopathes*) black corals and (*Gerardia*) gold corals that thrive at 1,000 feet depths in Hawaii are quite old and still procreating. The gold coral colonies have been found to be as old as 2,700 years, and deep black corals can be older at 4,000 years.

How about human longevity examples? Well, an environmental example exists on the Greek island of Ikaria – one of many, so called, "blue zones" and home to a group of healthy residences of elderly citizens who are 90 years old or older that encompasses over 30% of the population. Their excellent health is partly due to a diet of olive oil, fish, greens, and herbal tea. However, they are also very sexually active – again pointing to procreation as a requirement for longevity.

"Blue zones" are small geographic pockets inhabited by the world's longest-lived populations, according to Dan Buettner who launched the blue zones quest in 2005 to study these unique regions. He wanted to share what these rare individuals can tell the rest of us about how to live longer and better lives.

So far, Buettner and his team have explored two Blue Zones regions: Okinawa, Japan and the Nicoya Peninsula in Costa Rica. Buettner has also written about two other blue zones: the Barbagia region of Sardinia, Italy and Loma Linda, California. In each of these regions, people reach 100 years at rates significantly higher than the rest of us, and on average live longer, healthier lives. They also suffer about one fifth the rate of heart disease and cancer found in America.

Analyses show that lifestyle habits play a greater role in increasing your chances of longevity than genetics. Diet, exercise, spiritual values, even mental attitude are important determining factors.

Based on the blue zones research, nine key factors can help produce the same positive results for many of us. They are:

- Stop eating when you're 80 percent full
- Eat more veggies, less protein, and fewer processed foods
- Drink red wine, in moderation
- Have a sense of purpose in life
- Maintain a spiritual or religious belief system
- Work less, slow down, take vacations
- Make physical movement a vital part of each day
- Create a healthy social network
- Make family a priority

We would, of course, like to add another key factor and that is the continued ability to try to procreate. The key word here is "try" since the elderly women would not be able to birth babies. It is important enough for your LifeConscious to know that you are still trying to continue the species of the human kind.

Additionally, you also have to take into account the quality of life. Diseases due to aging will affect all older men and women with over half past the age of 65 showing signs of osteoarthritis. Half of the adults over 50 have osteoporosis or loss of bone mass. Other common diseases are cardiovascular disease, cancer and diabetes and over 4 million Americans suffer from Alzheimer's. There are so many debilitating effects by the environment that it is tough to fight the inevitable. Things like the food and drinks that you consume with preservatives, alcohol, drugs, diseases, allergies, and stress all add up to make it extremely hard to live long lives. Remember that it is only recently that the average age of humans has increased from 70 to 80 years old. A few centuries ago, it was down to around 40. Two thousand years ago, the average age of a human being was just around 25 to 30.

While humans have succeeded in lengthening our average life spans we have to rely on medicine, organ transplants, joint replacements, and family care to do so. We may live to be 70 years old, but our joints just aren't going to make it because they were designed to last 30-40 years just like our teeth. It wasn't that long ago that dentistry finally became a medical specialty along with neurology, orthopedics, OB-Gyn, cardiology, etc. to add pain free longevity to our lives.

I've so often stated that if I get so old that I'm not capable of maintaining my own hygiene, feeding myself, thinking straight, seeing, hearing, etc., then I've already given my wife permission to go ahead and just shoot me! I know that she would never do that, but my point is that if I were in such tremendous pain all the time and wasn't aware of my surroundings, then the quality of life is near zero. If the quality is so low, then why would we want to live so long to begin with? Through death, you can be reborn and enjoy life the way it was meant to be once again.

It is amusing to me when I see religious men and women who espouse desperately to be with their chosen prophet at death their whole clerical lives, instead fight to stay alive through transplants, mechanical additions and surgery. Wouldn't a religious person want to join and worship the prophet whom they've been praying to their entire life rather than suffer through the afflictions that constantly need medical attention? It's just something to think about when you hear of a bishop getting a pace maker, an imam receiving a kidney transplant, or a prominent Baptist minister on life support. These learned and enlightened clerics are still under the delusion of the "one shot at life" perception and don't really understand the cycle of life, death, afterlife and birth.

The Cycle of Life, Death, Afterlife and Birth

So what really happens to us when we talk about the afterlife? Do we just fade away into the dust bins of history as atheists believe or do we continue, somehow, in some spiritual guise? In our way of thinking, we do indeed continue, but not as souls awaiting the second coming nor martyrs yearning for 72 black eyed virgins or even nirvana. You only need to look at Nature herself to see what really happens after you die.

Everything is in some kind of cycle from all the ecological systems on our earth all the way to the universe itself. The moon circles the earth, and the earth circles the Sun, the Sun circles around a huge black hole in our galaxy, and our galaxy obviously circles around who knows what at the center of the universe.

There is also a cycle that involves the phases from life, to death, to the afterlife, and then to birth again. We like to call this the LifeConscious cycle since LifeConscious is inexorably linked with each of these phases as it is the driving force for the cycle. You already know about and are currently living in the life phase. The death phase is merely the end of the life phase where your LifeConscious has left the body. A body that now decays and becomes part of the earth once again helping to replenish its resources while promoting the life phases of those insects, animals, and plants who are feeding off of decaying tissues and fluids. This is how life phases are able to sustain themselves by feeding on the dead phase bodies of those animals and plants that we hunt, kill, or harvest to maintain our energy and LifeConsciousness. By consuming these plants and animals, our bodies use the food as energy to sustain and build new cells that are needed to continue functioning in our own life Phase. Everything that dies is consumed by one of the earth's inhabitants to be reused to promote the continuation of life.

All you have to do is watch what happens to a dead creature that was recently killed by a vehicle on the side of the road on your way to and from work each day – let's say a deer. The next day after it was hit you'll find that the deer is still posed in its last mangled seconds of life. The birds, animals, insects, and bacteria will slowly consume the decaying body as if it were melting back into the earth. Yes, the creature is dead but its DNA and fluids are still alive and well. It sustains the bodies of the living creatures who consumed it; just like the dead animals and vegetation that we consume sustains our own bodies. In other words, these dead animals and vegetables are not really dead but are still alive – being used by the bodies of the plants, insects, animals and humans that consumed them. They are now a part of these living bodies – helping to grow new cells, repair damaged cells, and to help with their continued procreation.

It is a timeless symbiotic relationship that we have with the plants and animals that give up their lives for us to consume. We sustain the lineage of these domesticated crops and animals by enhancing their breeding and growing abilities. This domesticated bond is beneficial to all concerned and there are many other examples of these types of symbiotic relationships.

Some of the more obvious relationships that don't rely on feeding off of the dead are bees and pollen. The flowers offer bees nectar to feed on while they transfer pollen to other flowers to help with their sexual reproduction. Humming Birds do the same thing. Milk cows and goats are cared for by their human owners so that they may continue to provide them with milk, butter and cheese for many years. Chickens lay unfertilized eggs to be consumed as they in turn are cared for by their owners.

Examples of relationships that feed off of the dead are apples or berries that are eaten by animals and birds. The animals will pass the tough fruit seeds through their digestive system to be dropped incased in natural fertilizer to help spread the growth of the plant as the animals move and fly about. For instance, a bear may consume several pounds of blue berries in one corner of a small valley and roam to the other end where it releases the seeds in its dung. In a few years, the bear will have another area to forage for tasty berries. Again, both species linear heritage gains from the relationship as the bear's family grows and procreates while the berries prosper as they are spread to other areas of the valley.

Herding animals like the North American Bison (buffalo) that once roamed North America in gargantuan herds had literally eaten and drunk themselves as they migrated from one lush grassland to the next. The grass and waters that passed through their guts were dropped in mounds of dung and were filled with grass seeds that provided nourishment for the herds the following season. In this way, the grass and the Bison share the same DNA fragments in a symbiotic relationship that lasted for thousands of generations. Buffalo once inhabited the grasslands of North America and Asia in massive migrating herds, ranging from the Great Slave Lake in Canada's far north all the way to Mexico in the south, and from eastern Oregon almost to the Atlantic Ocean. North American Indians planned their own migrations with that of the buffalo and they used every bit of the animals for food, clothing, shelter and even weapons in a deeply spiritual symbiotic relationship with these animals.

We clearly know about life and death, but it is the afterlife and rebirth phases that have everyone mystified which we would like to clear up. All the diverse religions and denominations of these religions have varying opinions about the Afterlife phase. Some are very complicated with different levels that look like Dante's *Divine Comedy* with nine circles of hell and nine circles of heaven, which probably led to the miraculous inclusions of Limbo and Purgatory as middle grounds between Heaven and Hell in the Catholic Church. Judeo/Christians believe that a Messiah will either rise from the dead or as a newborn warrior to rule over them in a new world where those that don't believe are cast into a fiery hell. Those that do believe are destined to perpetually worship the Messiah or God forever.

Then there is the complicated dogma of Buddhism and the attainment of Nirvana, a place where there is no clinging or suffering. To get there the student must dedicate countless hours of meditation, chanting, studying and reading.

An example of this complicated dogma from Wikipedia follows:

> *"The realizing of nirvana is compared to the ending of avidyā (ignorance) which perpetuates the will (cetana) into effecting the incarnation of mind into biological or other form passing on forever through life after life (samsara). Samsara*

> *is caused principally by craving and ignorance. A person can attain nirvana without dying. When a person who has realized nirvana dies, his death is referred as parinirvana, his fully passing away, as his life was his last link to the cycle of death and rebirth (samsara) and he will not be reborn again. Buddhism holds that the ultimate goal and end of samsaric existence (of ever "becoming" and "dying" and never truly being) is realization of nirvana; what happens to a person after his parinirvana cannot be explained, as it is outside of all conceivable experience"* (http://en.wikipedia.org/wiki/).

Islam's afterlife was definitely designed for and by men. Islam believes that your reward in Heaven will be 80,000 servants and 72 black haired wives or maidens (virgins) all standing under a dome of pearls, aquamarine, and rubies. It is believed that this is the least of the rewards in Heaven for those souls that are not quite *Muttaqun* or righteous. For the truly righteous, there awaits a paradise of gardens, grapevines with young full-breasted maidens, and a never-ending full cup of wine. A Muslim woman may also go to heaven but each is said to have just one husband, usually her earthly husband.

Muslims believe that God will hold every human, Muslim, and non-Muslim accountable for his or her deeds at a preordained time unknown to man. An Archangel will sound a horn sending out a "blast of truth". Bodily resurrections of the dead will begin and is followed by the judgment of all souls. According to the Koran, sins that can consign someone to hell include lying, dishonesty, corruption, ignoring God or God's revelations, denying the resurrection, refusing to feed the poor, indulgence in opulence and ostentation, the economic exploitation of others, and social oppression.

All three of the major Middle Eastern religions promote the "one shot at life" concept. To us, this seems limiting and unnatural, because they feel that they have just this one life to prove themselves worthy of going to heaven. The faithful to these religions tend to hoard possessions, waste resources and energy, start conflicts, promote mistrust, promiscuity, and bias against the other religions. This conflict between the religions is a direct result of this "one shot at life" notion since its only natural to promote your belief above any of the others for your own peace of mind even to the point of killing those that don't believe as you do. Not only that, but these "religious" folks denies the earth's use of their decaying dead bodies by locking their bodies up in airtight coffins and crypts in the false impression of awaiting the second coming or a messiah. We believe that this wasteful burial practice of modern civilization over the past several hundred years has been detrimental to the replenishing of the earth's resources. Air tight coffins and crypts prevent bodies from rejoining the earth's decomposition cycle for a very long time. The embalming practice of pumping a preservative solution of formaldehyde (or similar concoction) into dead bodies is actually poisoning these bodies enough to be unusable to living creatures as it decomposes. We also believe that your own LifeConscious memories can't return to the earth's LifeConscious because the body simply isn't decaying fast enough to completely release its connection to the body.

Heidi has always remarked to me how she can sense the sleeping presence of the dead which are still with their bodies buried in air tight coffins and crypts. Now we know why. Since their bodies can't decompose and cycle back into the earth's environment, neither can their LifeConscious *memories* be released back into the earth's own LifeConscious. They have to continue to sleep while enduring the excruciatingly long process of decay. This could take hundreds of years to accomplish before finally releasing the body's hold on its LifeConscious memories.

So, what needs to be done to keep you from sleeping so long after death? Firstly, we need to get the idea of preserving dead bodies out of our heads. We need to re-consider natural burials in which no embalming takes place. The dead should be buried in decomposable coffins of common wood or have our bodies cremated.

Many other burial practices throughout the world show this concern about the bodies returning to the earth's environmental food cycle. The Tibetans have a ritual called a "sky burial" in which the body is cut up, then broken, and fed to the birds on top of mountains. A carefully planned Mongolian ceremony practice culminates in the body being consumed by local dogs. The northwestern American Indian Haida tribe cast their dead bodies into a large pit to decay naturally and be consumed by animals and insects. The African Maasai believes dead bodies are harmful to the earth and simply leave them out in the fields for the predators to take care of. Many oceanic and pacific island cultures practice water burials at sea or cremations on burning boats.

So, to recap, the major religions, except for Buddhism and Hinduism, believe that there is an end to the cycle of life, death, afterlife, and birth. We have explained how various observations that are prevalent all around us in the universe and on our earth seem to disagree with this "end." To make an analogy, every grain of sand cycles through becoming sediment on the ocean floors and land through a continual erosion process. We believe that everything in the universe is like this grain of sand – going through constant phases of erosion, change, and cycling. Cycles like the ones that the grain of sand goes through, or a drop of water.

We've already gone over a cycle of a drop of water, but what about the carbon dioxide/oxygen cycle that plants go through? Carbon dioxide will be absorbed by a plant, tree, fresh water or oceanic plants, and algae to help them produce organic compounds of sugars to grow and reproduce. With a little help from the sun and water through a process called photosynthesis, these plants will produce the waste byproduct of oxygen. This released oxygen will filter into the air and eventually be breathed by an animal or insect. Then, with the aid of red blood cells, the oxygen is transported to the cells within tissues of the body which transports the waste byproduct of carbon dioxide in the opposite direction to be exhaled back into the atmosphere.

This mutually beneficial relationship between plants and animals is analogous with carbon dioxide and oxygen as a collective cycle that has a long linear history as well. We believe this was created to benefit everyone concerned to help sustain the heritage of these linear organisms. The carbon dioxide-breathing plants are consumed by animals and insects that excrete dung and urine that are broken down by bacteria which the plants will use as food for their own survival. The bodies of the dead animals will also decay and become consumed by other earthly creatures. We have already gone over how herding animals like buffalo, wildebeest, and reindeer that have migrated on the same paths for thousands of years – eating plant life that are byproducts of their own excrement and decaying dead bodies. This again is evidence that they are eating themselves in yet another way that LifeConscious memories are transferred from one generation to another.

In the seas, the same thing is happening. Salmon migrate back to the very stream beds that they were conceived in years ago only to milt and lay their eggs and then die shortly afterwards. The water is the carrier of their own LifeConscious memories to their fertilized embryos. Sea snakes, eels, lobsters, and turtles do the same type of thing all in an effort to sustain their unique species and their LifeConscious lineages.

The earth is teeming with countless examples of cycles of life, death and rebirth – here are some more examples: A drop of water is ejected as waste from a deer, and it evaporates to become a gas. Then, it rises to help form a cloud with billions of other droplets. The cloud becomes heavy with moisture and the droplets fall from the sky, replenishing a thirsty earth and its inhabitants once again. How many countless times has this one drop of water been consumed and used by a living creature?

The great oceans of the world traverse the globe in immense currents that act as giant lungs for our Mother Earth gobbling up huge volumes of oxygen and minerals like some kind of gigantic aquarium pump that provides life giving nutrients to billions of fish, crustaceans and mammals. Some of these animals ply these currents into ancient highways in order to procreate and/or to feed. For example, the larvae of European eels are carried with the Gulf Stream across the Atlantic and after one to three years they'll reach the coasts of England and Europe. They begin a brutal migration up rivers and streams, overcoming all sorts of natural challenges – sometimes by piling up their bodies by the tens of thousands to climb over obstacles as they reach even the smallest of creeks. They then make the arduous 4,000 mile journey back to their spawning grounds north of the Antilles, Haiti, and Puerto Rico.

From these examples, we can see how our earth is an obvious living embodiment that has somehow come into existence and has a consciousness – its own LifeConscious that we are all a part of whether we are alive or dead. When we are living we are using the earth's resources of food, water, and air to survive. When you die, your body helps to replenish the earth's resources when your body itself becomes a source of food for insects, birds, animals and plants in yet another cycle that has been in existence since the dawn of time. It doesn't matter whether or not you believe that the earth started this cycle from the actions of a deity or from a scientific phenomenon. All you need to understand is that the cycle has started, and that you are the current end result of a long linear heritage of recycled human beings.

As a final example, the universe itself is teeming with yet more evidence of this cycling of life, death and rebirth only on unimaginable time scales. Stars will be born from star nurseries or clusters that will take billions of years to move to their positions in their galaxy and forming their own solar systems of planets, moons, comets and meteors. Hundreds of millions of years later, they will lose their core supply of hydrogen that they used for their fuel. The star will most likely grow very large in size near the end of its life, they will be trapped in the gravitational embrace of a black hole and slowly lose their energy to be pulverized into subatomic particles. It is hard for the both of us to believe that these black holes are endless compressible repositories. What we believe happens at an event horizon (the edge of a black hole) is that particles are jetted back in time into a distant part of the universe to be reborn again in another star nursery. In other words – time itself is recycled.

This is how we think that the universe really works. Once the matter around a black hole is completely consumed, the black hole will begin to invert swallowing itself up and will jet itself back in time into a much smaller version of itself in the star nursery that it had already formed. Thus, the birth of a new galaxy occurs but billions of years back in time. This is how we believe the universe replenishes itself – by using time and black holes as tools to regenerate and it has been doing so eternally. This may also account for the tremendous lack of matter in our universe that scientists have been scratching their heads over. The missing matter is simply jetting back in time.

The Concept of Time

Black holes exist in every nook and cranny of the known universe and at one time were considered indestructible or non-ending. Today, some scientists believe that this is no longer true. Evidence has been found that super massive black holes have a limit. Scientists at Yale and Stanford University have revealed that even the largest of these gravitational monsters can't continue to wolf down matter forever. They appear to restrict their own growth when they gather about 10 billion times the mass of our Sun.

Monstrous, ultra-massive black holes are found at the centers of giant elliptical galaxies in huge galaxy clusters. Even the black hole at the center of our Milky Way galaxy is thousands of times less massive than these giants. These gigantic black holes seem unable to grow beyond this limit – regardless of where and when they appear in the universe and no matter what epoch.

These findings suggest that black holes have a limit to how large they may get. Could we assume that this value of 10 billion times the mass of our Sun is the trigger that sets off this time reversal process? Perhaps we will find in the future that the mass of the black hole determines how far back in time the matter inside of it regresses. How can this ever be done? We have no idea. However, we believe that perhaps someday, scientists will have methods to determine this information – just like we did not know about the speed of light 150 years ago.

When we talk about the subject of time, we are entering a gray area between science and spirituality, which proves that it is still one of the most misunderstood concepts for mankind to comprehend. What is most intriguing is that only man is capable of trying. Here is a popular story circulating among scientists and philosophers that seems to hit the nail on the head:

> *An immigrant to America has lost his watch. He walks up to a man on a New York street and asks, "Please, Sir, what is time?" The scientist replies, "I'm sorry, you'll have to ask a philosopher. I'm just a physicist."*

Let's talk about the concept of infinity. When you talk about time you have to start not at the atomic seconds or microseconds level but on its opposite – infinity. Infinity means that there is no beginning or end of time – no alpha or omega. We can easily believe that the universe is infinite because we have yet to find an end to it. Nevertheless, how is infinity possible when we take into account the Big Bang Theory, the predominant theory of the beginning of the universe in scientific circles? It's impossible because supposedly the Big Bang Theory *is* the beginning of time as we now know it. If the Big Bang Theory is, in fact, the way that time began then the concept of infinity would be a mute issue, wouldn't it?

(Heidi) Infinity must exist. If so many of our mathematical equations are solved using infinity, if there is an infinite amount of numbers (both positive and negative), then how can a finite universe with a beginning and an end be possible? In a macro-world of large, non-relativistic objects, we understand the concept of finite time. However, it is difficult for our complex minds to even fathom infinity, which is why it's hard for us to accept it.

For example, I can say that I want to begin walking toward the park starting at a time t. Let's call this beginning t, zero. If I start now, at t = 0, then I will arrive at the park at a later time, say t = 5; as in 5 minutes from now. This would be an end. I would have reached my destination. What about the concept of time for things that we don't fully understand such as dark matter, black holes, and the universe? How can I say that the universe started at time t = 0 with the Big Bang? I cannot say that there was not a time before t = 0 where something could have existed that caused the Big Bang. Now, time does not seem so linear and finite. Now, all our perceptions and understanding of how time works is confused. Perhaps time was moving backwards or operated in a non-linear fashion before the galaxies that we know of existed. According

to Big Bang theorists, we have relativistic particles moving in a way that we still don't fully understand. There were energies present that we cannot even begin to understand their magnitudes. What can we say was actually happening then? The truth is we really don't know, and I believe that we should consider all possibilities that sound reasonable – even concluding that the Big Bang could never have happened.

We, earthbound creatures are standing on this planet that is rotating at 1,040 miles per hour while cruising around the sun at 66,600 mph, while our solar system is rocketing at 558,000 mph around a black hole, and our galaxy is spiraling at 666,000 mph around what, I have no idea. Just note that nothing in space is static as far as velocity and time are concerned. Everything is moving and time starts to take on a different connotation when you take into account distances in space and a subject's LSR (Life Span Reference–average life span). Here's an example to show you what I mean.

My brother Nathan Eli died in March of 2000, and this is September of 2010 as I write this sentence down, some ten light years from here (if there were a powerful enough telescope to view the earth) he would still be shown to be living, playing golf or cutting the grass in his yard. This is due to the difference of reference points in space time. If you looked at another reference point in space time compared to earth of about 1,500 light years, Mohammed would be seen walking in Mecca; 2,000 light years and Jesus would be a toddler; 2,600 light years and Gautama Buddha would be seeking his enlightenment; 4,000 light years ago Abraham would have departed from the city of Ur. What this means is that any star or galaxy you are looking at in space is showing the way it looked like a thousand light years or even a billion light years ago.

An observable anomaly of a black hole is that when light gets near its event horizon, the light itself can't escape. This is because of the tremendous gravitational pull causing matter of any kind that is near it to be swallowed up by the hole. Our feeling is that time also stops at the event horizon – hence the name black hole. In other words, if time stops at the entrance of a black hole, then nothing moves outward or escapes from it – only inwards.

Our intimate knowledge of particle accelerators allows us to make the following leap in thinking. All the hardware in an accelerator must be under a high vacuum. A tremendous amount of energy is needed to supply the acceleration force needed to transport a beam of hydrogen ions (or electrically charged atoms). Harmonic resonant frequencies are needed to gradually speed up or accelerate the beam. We use cryogenic (or super cooled) tanks as acceleration tanks because of the low resistance or friction due to the extreme cold. Electromagnetic fields are needed to guide the beam of ions to a target.

Similar to an accelerator, space has very low density and pressure – very close to a perfect vacuum. It has effectively no friction – allowing stars, planets, and moons to move freely along ideal gravitational trajectories. The coldness of space also aids in this frictionless effect. The pulverized stars and star matter are mainly made up of the elements hydrogen and helium. A tremendous amount of electromagnetic energy is churned up due to the spinning of star matter within the black hole. Similarly, galaxies, black holes, and anything else in the universe have tremendous energies that vibrate at certain frequencies. Like an accelerator, black holes must have a resonant frequency.

We believe that when matter enters an event horizon and hurdles into a black hole, time starts to do the unthinkable. It starts to go backward at an accelerated rate as the tremendous gravitational force takes its deadly hold. Anything that gets swallowed up by a black hole will get pulverized into subatomic particles and accelerate backwards in time faster and faster. It becomes a perfect *Inverted Accelerator* in the vacuum and cold of space. Whatever is at the other end of a black hole is jetted out into space as subatomic particles. It is possible that particles may travel back many thousands or even billions of years backward in time. An inverted, accelerated, and massive beam of particles, we believe, is the process which constantly replenishes the known universe with fresh new subatomic particles. These particles will eventually form into gases and then star matter. I believe that the star nurseries that we can observe thousands of light years from earth are the ends of black holes in the center of our universe. Hence, this causes a never ending cycle of star-making, pulverizing black holes with time and the universe essentially recycling themselves in yet another example of the life, death, afterlife, and birth cycle.

We think this also explains the red shift that astrophysicists see when they calculate the velocity of galaxies and other distant heavenly bodies. In physics and astronomy, red shift occurs when electromagnetic radiation of visible light is emitted or reflected by an object shifts towards the less energetic red end of the electromagnetic spectrum due to the Doppler Effect.

(Heidi) What Adrian is referring to here is the Hubble Effect (named after the famous astronomer), where all the objects in the universe have been observed to be moving through something called the Doppler Effect. Think about how the sound of a fire truck's siren changes pitch as it travels past you. This is similar to what heavenly bodies are doing when they are moving through their space in the universe. Hubble used this concept to explain the Expanding Universe Theory. However, the past 30 years of research on the Expanding Universe have shown that the universe is probably not expanding in the way that we think.

Here is another common example used to show the Doppler Effect. Imagine a person standing on a platform of a train station while an oncoming train is coming toward them blowing its whistle. The person's point of view on the platform is the point of reference. As the train is moving towards them at about 50 mph, its train whistle is higher pitched because the velocity of the train is added to the whistle's sound waves velocity. As it passes their reference point the sound of the whistle will drop in tone significantly because the velocity of the train is now subtracting from the velocity of the whistle's sound waves.

The same Doppler Effect can be seen also in light waves. When astrophysicists use light spectral analysis to determine the velocities of stellar objects, they all seem to be moving away from our reference point of the earth or red shifted. This red shift has given them the mistaken notion that everything is hurtling away from us – thus the advent of the Big Bang Theory. The Big Bang Theory speculates that at one point in time all matter in the universe was compacted together somehow, and it exploded. Scientists believe that we are billions of years from that explosion, and that is why everything that we see in space appears red shifted and moving away from us – just like the train whistle getting lower as it moves away from us!

The Big Bang Theory has been under a lot of criticism lately because it can't explain why there is a lack of matter in space. The amount of matter that should be calculated in space and the amount that is actually there is very different! How then can the Big Bang explain why some of that matter is "missing?" Theoretical physicists have come up with some exorbitant mathematical gems that were developed to help support the Big

Bang Theory. Big Bang also can't explain why we are seeing galaxies that are over 13 billion light years away when the universe is estimated to be just 14 billion years old. How can a galaxy be formed in just a billion years? I suspect that with improved technology, we will be able to see galaxies further than 13 billion light years. Then, Big Bang scientists will see that their theory cannot possibly be held valid anymore.

We believe that Einstein was correct when he proposed the theory of a Static Universe. This means that space is neither expanding nor contracting but, dynamically stable. The major proponent to the Static Universe theory was how to explain all the red shifting that is going on? We think that these red shift observations from galaxies aren't considering the influence of time loss in black holes. Here's what we mean. Man will someday show that every galaxy and other stellar anomalies will have gigantic black holes at their centers. Since we already know what happens to light as it gets near a black hole's event horizon, then it's going to give the effect of red shifting. This is because matter is increasing in velocity as it enters the hole thereby giving us the mistaken observation that these galaxies are moving away from us at tremendous speeds. Scientists haven't considered that time is going backward in the black hole, and this is what is causing the red shift reading. Essentially, what they are seeing is a time shift and not a red shift. A galaxy that is measured to be red shifted ten million light years away is actually maybe only one million light years distant. These time shifts could explain much of the phenomena in black holes and other mysterious objects in space that seems to baffle science.

In conclusion, we've already gone over how time itself is cycled through black holes along with the jets of subatomic particles hurtling backwards in time. At other ends of the black holes, the sequence of galaxy building starts all over again. Time itself is recycled along with every particle caught in an endless cycle of life, death and rebirth. We propose this different philosophical hypothesis that at the center of our universe are the limitless numbers of opposite ends of black holes jetting pulverized subatomic particles into space that in time will generate new stars. These new stars will generate new galaxies with new black holes and the cycle continues ad infinitum. The universe has and always will constantly keep rebuilding itself while recycling time in new galaxies. Since the universe rebuilds itself (and time along with it), it has its own slow time frame of when an atom is recycled. Once matter enters a Black Hole and then spewed back in time out the other side, it could possibly go back billions of years into the past!

Afterlife

There is no doubt in our minds that an afterlife exists. Many people feel connected to it as if they had been there many times before. As a new born child and then as a toddler, a person has a fresh connection with their own LifeConscious that is controlling all of their bodily functions. At the same time, the child starts slowly developing their unique personal consciousness. This freshness may include memories from previous lives or at least those that are part of the child's linear heritage. Most people were just too young to realize this and even if you did experience these memories you were probably told that it was your imagination or even the devil and to pay no attention to it. By constantly denying these memories and the afterlife's existence, we grew to be skeptical and withdrew from life's true meanings. Nature and the earth became toys to explore, tear up and use up as we grew older since we were constantly told that this life was a one shot deal. The more that we cheated death or at least tempted fate by doing things like extreme skiing, sky diving, racing, or fighting, we felt more alive as the adrenaline kicked it – giving us a false sense of what life was really about. These activities are poor modern substitutes to when we were hunter/gatherers and when we were much closer to the truth and nature.

As hunter/gatherers, the continuation of the family/clan/tribe was the most important thing of all. To live with and respect nature and its creatures was a close second. We knew that if you did not respect the animals and plants whom you subsisted on that they would vanish and so would the possibility of a future for the family. When a family member died, they rejoined something of the earth. What that something was they didn't know but their gut feeling told them that their spirit remained with the family. This gut feeling is real and continues to sustain us to this day.

So here is the bottom line about we have come to believe about the afterlife. When your own LifeConsciousness leaves your body, you begin the dead phase of the cycle. Your body returns back to the earth's environment as food for insects, animals and microbes and the same thing happens to your own LifeConsciousness. It returns to the earth's own vast LifeConsciousness to be regenerated; eventually to be used as part of the continuation of your family's heritage helping another new baby to be born. Your memories are part and parcel of your LifeConsciousness and because you are dead it is at first a great shock. It may take a good while to deal with this mortal fact. Some may not be able to deal with it at all and will do anything to get back to the living and may do so by possessing a young child or a feeble minded person causing split personalities.

As you get more comfortable within the earth's LifeConsciousness, you begin to realize that you have been here many times before and it is home and a resting place for your LifeConscious. You may even want to become what we call a "traveler" and visit other parts of the earth's LifeConsciousness around the world. Some may even want to explore the LifeConsciousness of our galaxy or venture to the center of our universe itself – never to return.

Whenever the time comes that you decide to return to the living, it will be done so knowing that the memories of your last lifetime will be mostly forgotten as your LifeConsciousness enters the embryo of a new born baby with no personal consciousness at all. The pull back to life is so strong that losing your previous lifetime's memories would be of no importance to you. This is because the continuation of life and LifeConscious overrides the loss. The earth's LifeConscious is not totally lost to you as a child or as an adult because it will always be with you when you search for an answer to a question, meditate, or regenerate your body when you sleep.

Sleep and Sexual Orgasms

Why do humans and animals need to sleep in the first place?

(Heidi) The bottom line of why we need to sleep is this. The better quality sleep we get, the better our orgasms will be. Many studies have shown that people that get a good night's sleep most nights have higher libidos and tend to have more pleasurable orgasms. People who do not get good quality or quantity of sleep have fewer orgasms and do not have much of a sex drive. Naturally, when one does not get proper amounts of sleep, our bodies do not get recharged. We actually do not get the cues we need to get out there and make babies! LifeConscious taps into our brains during sleep and not only recharges us, but reconnects us with the earth's LifeConscious – kind of like plugging a rechargeable battery into the wall socket. When we become unplugged, our life forces that we feel so strongly on a day to day basis become dull and unimportant in our lives. Our drive to reproduce goes down and our purpose in life becomes confused.

Scientists say that we spend as much as a third of our lives in blissful unconscious sleep. We still have no idea why and how sleep is regulated or even what causes it. Why do we need to sleep when we can just sit down and relax our bodies? There seems to be something about our brains that needs them to be shut down for several hours each day because, even if you sit down and relax our brains are still very much active.

Animals and even insects need to sleep so the consensus is that they must be something special about brain cells called neurons. These cells have the highest energy requirements of all the cells in the human body. The brain contains only 2% of our total body weight but uses up to 20% of our energy, which makes it the most energy consuming organ in our bodies.

This unusual consumption of energy has led scientists to believe that neurons need the loss of consciousness to replenish themselves for future workloads. Sleep may also be necessary for the body to repair muscle tissues since growth hormones are known to be secreted during sleep. These hormones are not only needed for growing young bodies but for repair work too.

It's obvious to Heidi and I, that sleep is a regenerative process but where does this regeneration come from. We propose that this also comes from the earth's own vast LifeConscious. When we sleep, we are reconnecting our own LifeConscious with the earth's and this can only be done when our own personal consciousness is "shut down" for sleeping purposes. Have you ever noticed that when you can't sleep that it is your own personal consciousness preventing it when you are excessively thinking too much about the day's activities, the kids, work, the future, etc.? It's very clear that the personal consciousness must be at sleep while your other consciousness (LifeConscious) takes over to replenish and heal your body and mind.

Remember also that the human body's resonant frequency at sleep is exactly the same as the earth's resonant frequency of 7.83 Hz. This is proof that our LifeConscious controls and replenishes our bodies as we sleep and reconnect with the earth's LifeConscious energy.

We also propose that sleep, and sexual orgasms are connected as well through our own LifeConscious. These two things may seem unrelated, but our reasoning stems from a natural occurrence during sleep that many of us have experienced. The nocturnal emissions commonly known as "wet dreams" can be again explained through LifeConscious. These emissions are inherent in both males and females as men and women ejaculate sexual fluids during sleep. We believe that this is caused by the close connection with the earth's LifeConscious that one has as they sleep. Not only is our energy replenished during sleep, but our brains are constantly being reminded what our purpose is in life – to continue to procreate.

Remember that the purpose of LifeConscious is to make sure that it can survive, and it can only do so if our lineage continues as well as the lineage of all other living organisms on the earth. It is therefore, very selfish in this regard and will do anything in its power to help life to continue. We can look in the past through earth's history for plenty of examples as she has gone through numerous conflagrations, impacts, climate, and polarity changes that life has had to endure. Life and LifeConscious have survived all of these hurdles and will do so in the future, with or without man-kind's help.

Heidi and Adrian would like to take this opportunity to thank each and every one of you for purchasing and reading our book. Thank you!

Bibliography

Arvin, Adrian H. (2004). *LifeConscious: An Alternate Theory to Evolution and Creationism.* Lincoln, NE: iUniverse, Inc.

Bowman, Carol & Bowman, Steve. (1997). *Scientific Proof of Reincarnation, Dr. Ian Stevenson's Life Work.* Retrieved from http://reluctant-messenger.com/reincarnation-proof.htm#about

Cole, Ellen and Rothblum, Esther D and Mahoney, Donald B. and Mahoney, Martha. (1995). *Racism in the Lives of Women: Testimony, Theory, and Guides to Antiracist Practice:* Binghamton, NY: Haworth Press Inc.

Culpeper, Nicholas (1980). *Culpeper's Complete Herbal: Comprehensive Descriptions of Most Herbs, Their Medicinal Properties, and Instructions for Making Herbal Remedies.* Toronto, Canada: Coles Publishing Company Limited.

Ellis, Peter Berresford. (1994). *The Druids.* Grand Rapids, Michigan. William B. Eerdmans Publishing Company.

Freud, Sigmund. (trans.) Brill, A.A. (1920). *Three Essays on the Theory of Sex.* Washington and New York: Nervous and Mental Disease Publishing Company.

Heffner, Christopher. *Psychology 101, Chapter 3: Personality Development.* Retrieved from www.allpsych.com/psychology101.

Howard, Beth. Depression During Pregnancy. *Parenting.* Retrieved from www.parenting.com

Kligler, Benjamin and Lee, Roberta, A. (2004) *Integrative Medicine: Principles for Practice.* United States: McGraw-Hill.

Levak, Brian P. (Ed.). (2004). *The Witchcraft Sourcebook.* New York: Routledge, Taylor & Francis Group.

McLaughlin, Marie, L. (Ed.). (1995). *Myths and Legends of the Sioux.* Lincoln, NE: University of Nebraska Press.

Mills, Antonia and Slobodin, Richard. (1994). *Amerindian Rebirth: Reincarnation Belief among North American Indians and Inuit.* Toronto, Canada: University of Toronto Press.

Sharp, Jane (1999). *The Midwives Book or The Whole Art of Midwifry Discovered: Women Writer in English 1350 – 1850* (Elaine Hobby, Ed.). New York: Oxford University Press.

Summers, Montague. (1929). *Demonolatry.* (Nicholas Remy, Trans.). (Original work published 1595).

Summers Montague. (1928). *The Malleeus Maleficarum of Heinrich Kramer and James Spenger.* (Heinrich Kramer , Trans.) (Original work published 1486).

Sutton, Maya Magee and Mann, Nicholas R. (2000). *Druid Magic: The Practice of Celtic Wisdom.* St. Paul, Minnesota: Llewellyn Publications.

Taylor, Marjorie (1999). *Imaginary Companions and the Children Who Create Them.* New York: Oxford University Press.

http://wordnet.princeton.edu/perl/webwn?s=consciousness

www.pbs.org

www.sutterhealth.org

McCracken, Leila. (1999). A Declaration of Rights for Childbearing Women. *Midwifery Today.* Retrieved from www.midwiferytoday.com

www.Shamanportal.org

http://en.wikipedia.org/wiki/

http://www.momknowsbestonline.com/Depression_And_Pregnancy.html)

http://www.telegraph.co.uk/technology/4861114/Robot-replica-of-Albert-Einstein.html